ROSALYNN CARTER

MODERN FIRST LADIES

Lewis L. Gould, Founding Editor

TITLES IN THE SERIES

Edith Kermit Roosevelt: Creating the Modern First Lady, Lewis L. Gould

Helen Taft: Our Musical First Lady, Lewis L. Gould

Ellen and Edith: Woodrow Wilson's First Ladies, Kristie Miller

First Lady Florence Harding: Behind the Tragedy and Controversy, Katherine A. S. Sibley

Grace Coolidge: The People's Lady in Silent Cal's White House, Robert H. Ferrell

Lou Henry Hoover: Activist First Lady, Nancy Beck Young

Eleanor Roosevelt: Transformative First Lady, Maurine Beasley

Bess Wallace Truman: Traditional First Lady, Sara L. Sale

Mamie Doud Eisenhower: The General's First Lady, Marilyn Irvin Holt

Jacqueline Kennedy: First Lady of the New Frontier, Barbara A. Perry

Lady Bird Johnson: Our Environmental First Lady, Lewis L. Gould

Pat Nixon: Embattled First Lady, Mary C. Brennan

Betty Ford: Candor and Courage in the White House, John Robert Greene

Rosalynn Carter: Equal Partner in the White House, Scott Kaufman

Nancy Reagan: On the White House Stage, James G. Benze, Jr.

Barbara Bush: Presidential Matriarch, Myra G. Gutin

Hillary Rodham Clinton: Polarizing First Lady, Gil Troy

ROSALYNN CARTER

EQUAL PARTNER IN THE

WHITE HOUSE

SCOTT KAUFMAN

UNIVERSITY PRESS OF KANSAS

© 2007 by the University Press of Kansas
All rights reserved
Published by the University Press of Kansas (Lawrence, Kansas 66045), which was organized by the Kansas Board of Regents and is operated and funded by Emporia State University, Fort Hays State University, Kansas State University, Pittsburg State University, the University of Kansas, and Wichita State University

Library of Congress Cataloging-in-Publication Data
Kaufman, Scott, 1969–
Rosalynn Carter : equal partner in the White House / Scott Kaufman.
p.   cm. — (Modern first ladies)
Includes bibliographical references and index.
ISBN 978-0-7006-1544-5 (cloth)
ISBN 978-0-7006-3951-9 (paperback)
ISBN 978-0-7006-3957-1 (ebook)
1. Carter, Rosalynn.
2. Presidents' spouses—United States—Biography.
I. Title.
E874.K38   2007
973.926092—DC22   2007028881

British Library Cataloguing-in-Publication Data is available

CONTENTS

Editor's Foreword

vii

Preface

ix

CHAPTER 1: The Making of a First Lady

1

CHAPTER 2: Creating a "Caring Society"

34

CHAPTER 3: The First Lady Goes Abroad

61

CHAPTER 4: Hostess and Home Life

91

CHAPTER 5: The First Lady and the Media

117

CHAPTER 6: The Unfinished Agenda

133

Conclusion: Ambivalence Surrounding the Office

168

Notes

175

Bibliographic Essay

191

Index

199

EDITOR'S FOREWORD

In the late 1970s, Rosalynn Carter's activism in the White House drew scorn from the media. She was a "steel magnolia" who dared to attend cabinet meetings and even traveled abroad without presidential supervision on her own diplomatic missions. The press at the time, already more inclined to sneer than to analyze, paid scant attention to the substance of what Mrs. Carter was doing. When her husband's presidency encountered difficulties, the first lady's energetic style seemed to be part of an administration that had lost its way. That judgment became a fixed element in the negative historical assessment of the Carter record in the years that followed.

Scott Kaufman's fresh analysis of Rosalynn Carter challenges the stereotypes about her performance as first lady. His research into the extensive primary sources at the Carter Library and his interviews with those who participated in Mrs. Carter's work reveal a talented, purposeful woman who pursued an ambitious agenda as the president's equal partner. Mrs. Carter's role as an informal envoy in Latin America and her personal commitment to the issue of mental health are among the strong aspects of Kaufman's engaging narrative. He also shows that the Carters had more of an impact in the area of culture and White House entertaining than had previously been realized. Thanks to Kaufman's work, a searching appraisal of where Rosalynn Carter stands among activist first ladies is now possible. She is another of the important Democratic innovators, beginning with Eleanor Roosevelt and including Lady Bird Johnson and Hillary Rodham Clinton, who did so much to shape the institution of the first lady into its modern form.

Lewis L. Gould

PREFACE

Her contemporaries questioned just how much influence she had in Washington, with some suggesting that she was in fact the copresident of the United States. Commented one journalist, "Never before has a First Lady shared so fully in her husband's Administration."[1] These comments might seem to apply to Eleanor Roosevelt or Edith Bolling Wilson, both of whom were known for being powerful first ladies. Yet they refer instead to Rosalynn Smith Carter. In retrospect, it seems unlikely that Rosalynn Carter, who, by her own admission, was shy and insecure as a child, would join the ranks of America's most influential first ladies. In fact, she would play an important, if not central, role in the administration of her husband, Jimmy Carter. She took part in cabinet meetings and acted as the president's sounding board, adviser, and surrogate. She is the only first lady who traveled abroad as her husband's representative to discuss substantive issues with foreign officials and became only the second to testify before Congress. Indeed, at the same time that her husband's approval rating was at a record low, a Gallup poll found that Rosalynn Carter was tied with Mother Teresa as the most admired woman in the world.[2]

Such praise masked a long-held ambivalence about what the role of the first lady should be, however. Eleanor Roosevelt had been very much an activist, engendering strong reactions from both supporters and detractors. Her successors had been far more passive, but a renewed activism started to appear with Lady Bird Johnson. In addition, the postwar feminist movement was a catalyst that gave women greater opportunities outside the home. Although Rosalynn Carter was determined to be an active and involved first lady, her activism was not based on a conscious intention to follow in the footsteps of her immediate predecessors or to promote a feminist agenda. Rather, it was an outgrowth of the partnership she had developed with her husband. Mrs. Carter had her defenders, who saw nothing wrong with a first lady who had influence in the Oval Office. But she had many detractors as well, who accused her of overstepping the proper bounds of her position. Even feminists, who seemingly would have been supportive of an active, influential first lady, never felt that she was truly one of them.

Although the criticism hurt, Rosalynn Carter never allowed it to stop her from pursuing her own agenda of projects or from advising or representing her husband. To this day, she remains an outspoken advocate of causes ranging from insurance coverage for mental health care to curtailing the spread of disease at home and abroad. It is safe to say that she sees her present activities as a continuation of the initiatives she began (or continued) when she lived in the White House.

What is most intriguing about Rosalynn Carter is the lack of attention she has received from scholars. Not counting her own 1984 memoirs, *First Lady from Plains,* there has not been a single biography written about her since 1980.[3] More recent works on the first ladies have rarely devoted more than a single chapter to her. In light of the important roles she played both as a wife and as a first lady, a biography of Rosalynn Carter is long overdue.

Completing this work would not have been possible without the support of numerous individuals. The staff of the Carter Library was exceptionally kind and always ready to help me find documents and answer my questions. My appreciation is also extended to those members of the Carter administration who were willing to take the time to be interviewed: President and Mrs. Carter, Mary Hoyt, Joseph Califano, Robert Pastor, Terence Todman, Greg Schneiders, Dr. Thomas Bornemann, and Faith Collins. I would like to acknowledge as well Deanna Congileo, director of public information for the Carter Center, for arranging my interview with the former first couple.

In addition, this book could not have been completed without the assistance of those who read the manuscript. Lewis Gould, the editor of this series, was amazingly fast in conveying his suggestions for improving the work. Susan Hartmann of Ohio State University and my father, Burton I. Kaufman, also made helpful comments.

Furthermore, I am grateful to the Francis Marion University History Department and the Francis Marion University Foundation, which provided research funds and other financial assistance for this project. My colleagues in the History Department were wonderfully supportive of my work.

I cannot express how enjoyable it has been to work with the staff of the University Press of Kansas. I would particularly like to thank director Fred Woodward for his encouragement.

Finally, I would like to thank my family—my father; my mother, Diane; and my sister, Heather—for their love and support.

ROSALYNN CARTER

CHAPTER 1

THE MAKING OF A FIRST LADY

Those who knew Rosalynn Smith as a child could see that she was bright and likely to succeed at whatever she did. Yet, even if they believed that she might one day become first lady of the United States, it is unlikely that they would have guessed that the shy and insecure girl would become such an active and influential national figure. But as she grew, Rosalynn developed qualities that made her increasingly strong, independent, and sure of herself. Those qualities became even more pronounced after her marriage to Jimmy Carter, to whom she became an equal partner emotionally, intellectually, and politically. By the time of the 1976 election, it was clear that Rosalynn was going to be an outgoing and powerful first lady.

Eleanor Rosalynn Smith was born on 18 August 1927 in her grandparents' house in Botsford, Georgia. She was the oldest of the four children of William Edgar Smith and Frances Allethea ("Allie") Murray. Edgar, as he was called, was a descendant of a cousin of John Smith, one of the founders of Jamestown in what became the Virginia colony. He worked as a school bus driver and ran an auto repair business in Plains, a town of about 600 people located just over five miles from Botsford; he also tended to a farm he owned near Plains. Allie, nine years Edgar's junior, met her future husband when she was in high school and he drove the school bus. They waited to wed, however, until after Allie had graduated from Georgia State College for Women, where she received a teaching certificate. Rosalynn, whom they named after Allie's mother, Rosa, weighed six and a half pounds at birth. Allie laughingly recalled that her daughter's "forehead was right flat . . . and I thought she was ruined. But [in the] next day or two it was all right."[1] The Smiths eventually had two sons and another daughter: Jerry, Murray, and Allethea.

Rosalynn's family was by no means wealthy. Edgar had lost his life savings when the bank in Plains failed in 1926, and not long after Jerry's birth, the stock market collapsed, followed by the Great Depression. The Smiths lived in a white house that had no indoor plumbing or central heating. The family grew its own food on the farm, and all the cooking was done on a wood-burning stove. Allie, who was a seamstress, made nice clothing for her children. The family even had a car, and although it was old, Edgar's mechanical know-how kept it running. Because the Smiths' house was situated on a dirt road, dust would often blow inside, especially whenever a car drove by, making it difficult to keep the home clean. Yet Rosalynn never felt like she lived a life of poverty. "Although we didn't have a lot of money," she recalled, "I was never concerned about it."[2]

The future first lady had a happy childhood. With the exception of her best friend, Ruth Carter, there were no girls in Plains near Rosalynn's age (Ruth was two years younger), so she spent time with her brothers, with the other boys who lived in the neighborhood, or sometimes with the children of the African Americans who worked as laborers on her father's farm. They played kick the can, swam at a nearby spring, hung out at the railroad depot, looked for hens' eggs, or danced. Rosalynn also spent time alone, playing with her dolls, sewing, or reading.

Her parents were loving but strict. Edgar enjoyed playing horse with Rosalynn, getting down on all fours and letting her ride on his back. He would perform tricks for his children, tell them stories, and even baked them a cake one time. But Edgar and Allie also expected their children to do chores and would punish them if they got out of line. For instance, they did not permit Rosalynn to "run away," which meant crossing the street in town so that she could play with her friends. For that, Edgar would spank her. Allie did not like seeing the children punished, but she was prepared to paddle them if necessary.

(In fact, one journalist reported that Rosalynn's mother spanked her when she and her brother Jerry tarred and feathered each other, although Mrs. Carter denies that the event ever took place.)[3]

Religion was an important component of the Smiths' family life. In part, this was because most of the social activities in Plains revolved around the town's churches. But more important was Allie's influence on her children. The daughter of a devout Baptist father and an equally pious Lutheran mother, Allie had chosen to join the Methodist church to which Edgar belonged. Although Edgar could not attend services every week, Allie did, and she expected her children to do so as well. "We always knew we had to go to church and Sunday school," recalled the younger Allethea. "There was no question about it. She [Allie] got up on Sunday mornings and got us all dressed and sat us down on the sofa and told us that's where we stayed until she got dressed." Because the Smith children had Lutheran and Baptist grandparents and Methodist parents, they attended functions at each of those churches.[4]

If Allie emphasized religion, Edgar stressed education. Rosalynn's father had not been able to get an education, and he regretted that fact. He did not want his children to follow in his footsteps and once commented that he would be willing to sell his farm so his children could complete their schooling. Rosalynn pushed herself hard to do well in her classes—sometimes too hard. In primary school, she later wrote, "the burden I put on myself of always having to do well began to be heavy." But she believed that not getting good grades would disappoint her parents and even her fellow classmates, who considered her very bright. And doing well brought its own rewards, which she discovered at age twelve, when she won $5 for having the highest grade point average in school. "I . . . began to see," she remarked, "that the satisfaction of accomplishment sometimes compensates for the hard work."[5]

Of her teachers, two in particular influenced the future first lady. One was her seventh-grade teacher, Thelma MacArthur. MacArthur was interested in current events and urged her pupils to read newspapers and listen to the radio to keep up with what was happening in the world. That suggestion came during 1939, as World War II was beginning. Through MacArthur's prodding and her assignments, Rosalynn began "to discover a world of interesting people and faraway places," although she learned that it could also be "a menacing and ominous world." The other mentor was her eighth-grade teacher, Julia Coleman, who influenced Rosalynn's future husband as well. Coleman wanted her students to be well rounded, and so she made sure that they learned not just the basics of reading, writing, and arithmetic but also about music and art.[6] The desire to learn more about the world and to enjoy its cultural diversity would have an impact on the future first lady throughout her life.

During Rosalynn's eighth-grade year, tragedy struck. In the summer of 1940, she had received permission from her parents—after months of pleading—to go to summer camp. Before leaving, she noticed that her father had not been feeling well, but her parents told her not to worry. When she came home, however, her father was very sick. Although she did not know it, he had leukemia. As Edgar grew worse, Rosalynn blamed herself, believing that she had somehow caused his illness. In October, with the end near, he spoke to his children, telling them that he wanted them all to get the good education he had never had. "I was devastated," Rosalynn remembered after that talk. "My childhood really ended at that moment." From that point on, people were always at the house helping out. Not long after, Edgar passed away at the age of forty-four. "When I went to bed that night," Rosalynn said years later, "I never wanted to wake up."[7]

With Edgar's death, Allie and her children had to take on additional responsibilities. Rosalynn recounted that her mother "had never even written a check."[8] The family had the help of Allie's parents, but a year after Edgar died, Allie's mother passed away. Her father moved in with the family, meaning that Allie now had to worry about him as well as her four children. (Allie's father would stay in his daughter's home until he died in 1966.)

The Smiths' situation was not as bad as it might have been, however. The family home was paid for, they had income from renting out the farm, and they received $18.75 a month from Edgar's insurance. But there were still bills to be paid, so to make additional money, Allie took several jobs, first as a seamstress, then as a school lunchroom worker, and finally as a postmistress. As the oldest child, Rosalynn became a source of support for her mother. Allie not only relied on her daughter for advice about finances and employment opportunities but also expected her to take care of her younger siblings. In short, at age thirteen, Rosalynn became cohead of the family, acting as a role model for her brothers and sister and making decisions for them. Rosalynn understood that she had to assume these responsibilities, and she admired how her mother had done the same following Edgar's death. Allie became an example of what a strong, independent woman could accomplish, but Rosalynn did not feel strong. "Underneath I felt very weak and vulnerable," she wrote. "I had lost much of my childhood enthusiasm and confidence." She doubted her ability to meet her mother's expectations and whether she was doing enough to help the family survive, and she had begun to question her faith in God. So whenever she felt unsure of something, she asked herself what her father might say. For instance, she did not smoke because he had thought it made women look unattractive. Nor had he approved of drinking, so she avoided alcohol.[9]

As Rosalynn later explained, "In my family, the women always have worked, and worked hard." That meant more than simply helping around the house. It also meant adhering to her father's wish that she finish her education. Rosalynn continued to indulge her love of reading. Assured by her mother that God would watch over them, she read the Bible and regained her faith. She also kept up with her studies at school, and her high grades helped boost her self-confidence. By the time Rosalynn reached high school, her siblings were old enough to care for themselves, so she got a job as a hairdresser. Having a job—and wages that her mother let her keep—only added to her self-assurance and inner strength. Her hard work paid off, and Rosalynn graduated as her high school class's valedictorian.

Influenced by MacArthur, Rosalynn had hoped to leave Plains and travel after graduation. But with World War II under way and her mother anxious about the eventual education of Rosalynn's three siblings, the future first lady realized that she "had no choice but to attend Georgia Southwestern," a community college located in Americus, about ten miles from Plains. So she lived at home and caught a ride with a neighbor to Georgia Southwestern, using her $4.50 a week allowance to pay for bus fare home. She continued to spend time with her friend Ruth, who was still in high school. It was during Rosalynn's sophomore year that she saw a photograph of Ruth's older brother, Jimmy, and fell for him.[10]

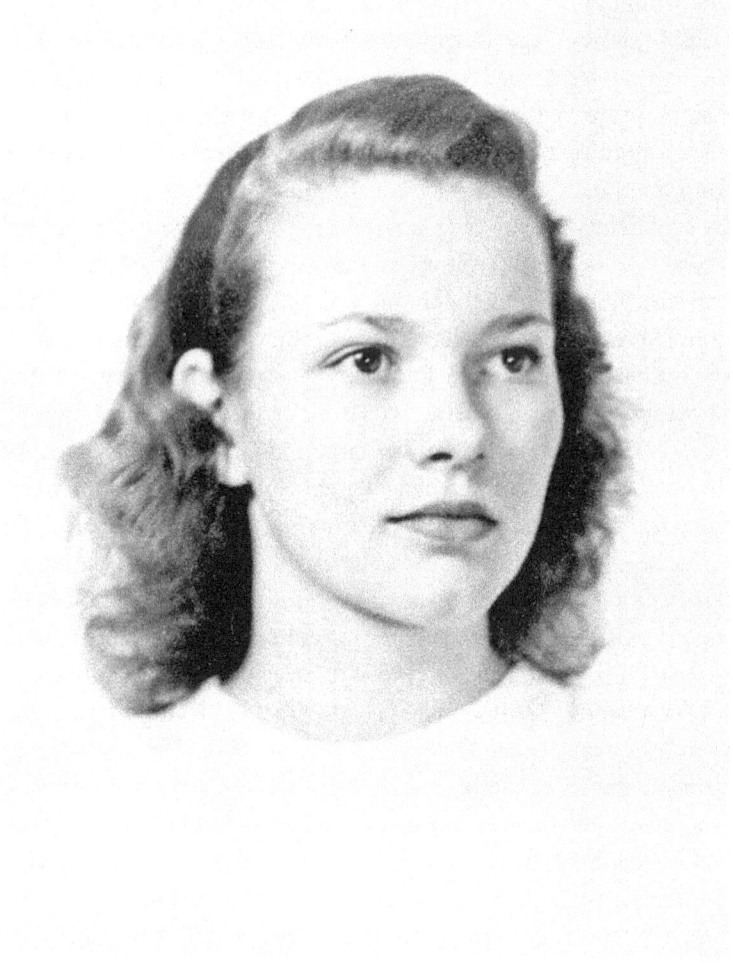

Rosalynn Smith, around age seventeen. Courtesy of the Jimmy Carter Library.

Born 1 October 1924 in Plains, James Earl Carter Jr. was, like Rosalynn, the eldest of four children. Not surprisingly, given the size of Plains, there were a number of ties between the Carters and the Smiths, aside from the friendship between Ruth and Rosalynn. Jimmy's mother, Lillian, a registered nurse, had tended to Edgar during his last weeks. Jimmy's father, James Earl Sr., had been one of Edgar's customers and served as a pallbearer at Edgar's funeral. Although Jimmy knew Rosalynn, he had taken little interest in her, believing that she was too young for him. After Jimmy left Plains to attend the U.S. Naval Academy, he came home only periodically. Each time, Ruth would invite Rosalynn to visit, in the hope that Jimmy would notice her. Sometimes, Rosalynn would get dressed up and go over to the Carters, but to no avail; other times, she panicked and refused to go. Finally, in 1946, fate—with Ruth's help—stepped in.

That summer, Jimmy was home on leave, and he and Ruth had plans to go to Pond House, a place their father had built outside Plains that the Carters used for social events. Jimmy and Ruth intended to do some cleaning there, and Ruth invited Rosalynn to join them. Rosalynn agreed and had a wonderful time. She and Jimmy talked, but she was disappointed that he did not ask her to go out with him. Rosalynn went to church that evening for a youth group meeting, and she was thrilled when Jimmy drove up in his car and asked her to double-date with Ruth and her boyfriend. "After dreaming about him for so long, I was actually with him, and it couldn't have been more wonderful," she remembered. Jimmy felt the same way. He had been dating a girl named Annelle, but he found Rosalynn very attractive, both physically and intellectually. "There was a, you might say, instant transformation in my life." He was so taken with her that, on the way home, he kissed her. Rosalynn had never allowed anyone to do that on a first date. "But," she wrote, "I was completely swept off my feet."[11]

Jimmy Carter has written in several books that after that first date with Rosalynn, he told his mother, "She's the one I'm going to marry." There is more to the story, however. "I had a fetish against ever telling a girl I loved her," he explained. After he took Rosalynn home, he spent the rest of the night gathering his thoughts. Not until the next morning, when his mother asked him about his date, did he tell Lillian his intentions. "It maybe was at that moment," he stated, "that I decided that I was going to invest my whole love interest in Rosalynn."[12] Thus began a whirlwind romance. The couple spent as much time together as they could that summer. Apparently, the only thing that made Jimmy feel a little awkward was having dinner at Rosalynn's house. He was taken aback by the relaxed atmosphere at the dinner table, with the Smiths "talking about relatively insignificant events within their family, among their friends, at the schoolhouse, or in the Plains community." In contrast, at the Carter home, family members often read while eating, and any discussions were generally "brief, narrowly focus[ed], and often involv[ing] controversial subjects."[13]

After the summer, Rosalynn and Jimmy would not see each other again until Christmas. During that time, the two wrote back and forth regularly and signed their letters "I.L.Y.T.G.," for "I Love You the Goodest."[14] When he came home for the holiday break, Jimmy asked Rosalynn to marry him, but she rejected his proposal. She thought that she was too young, and she had promised her father that she would finish her education. Though disappointed, Jimmy did not regard that rejection as her final answer. He was right. The couple continued to keep in touch after Christmas, and Rosalynn gradually changed her mind. When she went to Annapolis during a long weekend in February, he proposed again, and this time, she accepted.

The two of them broke the news to their respective families. At the time, Rosalynn had been preparing to attend Georgia State College for Women, with the intention of becoming an interior designer, but that was now abandoned. Allie was not surprised to hear of her daughter's change in plans, and although she had concerns, Allie consented to the marriage. She liked Jimmy and thought that Edgar would have approved, since Jimmy was Lillian Carter's son. It also occurred to Allie that by the time Rosalynn wed, she would have completed two years of college, which would have pleased Edgar. Lillian and Earl did not share Allie's feelings. Neither believed that Rosalynn was good enough for their son, but Jimmy ignored them. Lillian's reaction to Rosalynn represented the awkward beginning of a long and often tense relationship. In fact, at Jimmy's graduation from Annapolis, both Lillian and Rosalynn pinned his insignia on his uniform. Hugh Carter, a cousin of Jimmy's, noted that generally "only one loving female has this honor."[15] The struggle between Rosalynn and her mother-in-law for Jimmy's attention would last until Lillian's death.

Jimmy and Rosalynn wed on 7 July 1946, but they almost missed the ceremony. As they arrived at the Methodist church, they could hear the organist playing the last notes of "Here Comes the Bride." The couple sprinted inside, the organist started the song from the beginning, and the bride and groom walked down the aisle together. It was a simple wedding, with no attendants or other fancy trappings. Afterward, the couple borrowed Jimmy's father's 1946

{ *The Making of a First Lady* }

Lillian Carter. The relationship between Rosalynn and her mother-in-law was often tense. Courtesy of the Jimmy Carter Library.

Plymouth and drove to Atlanta, where they honeymooned for a night at the Biltmore Hotel. They then drove to the Appalachian Mountains to spend some time at the summer home of one of Jimmy's friends. On the way, Jimmy crashed into another car and totaled it but caused virtually no damage to the Plymouth.

After their honeymoon, the two moved to Norfolk, Virginia, where they rented an apartment and Jimmy began his service on the battleship *Wyoming*. To help Rosalynn adjust, Jimmy got her a copy of the book *The Navy Wife,* but she found that reading about her new life and actually living it were two different things. With the exception of weekends and some Fridays, Jimmy was at sea, and Rosalynn was left to take care of the responsibilities at home. She had to pay the bills, fix anything in their home that broke, and cook. The last task was especially difficult, because Allie had done most of the cooking for the Smith family. But with Jimmy's help—Rosalynn was not sure where he had acquired the art—she learned to prepare meals. Having developed an interest in cabinetmaking while in high school, Jimmy also made some furniture for their home.

Rosalynn's responsibilities grew with the birth of the Carters' first child, John ("Jack") William, in July 1947. (Told that the baby would not arrive until the following day, Jimmy Carter was at a movie theater when his son was born.) Sometimes Rosalynn broke down and cried from all the work she had to do on her own, but she persevered. As a child, she had had to assume new duties to help take care of her family, and she did the same now. Because "there were no collapsible strollers then," Rosalynn had to carry Jack in her arms when she went grocery shopping. She took a streetcar to and from the store, carrying both her shopping bags and the baby on the return trip. She would leave the groceries at the streetcar terminal, take Jack home and put him in his crib, run back to the terminal, and hope that her bags would still be there. Rosalynn also took up knitting and crocheting, cut recipes from magazines, and got a sewing machine, which she used to make clothes for herself and the baby. It was a life that forced Rosalynn to be strong and independent, and she came to love it. "[I] was more content than I had been in years," she later wrote.[16]

In 1948 the Carters moved to New London, Connecticut, following Jimmy's acceptance into submarine school. "For the first time in our two years of marriage," she recalled, "Jimmy kept regular hours and was home at night." The family lived in a house on the base, so Rosalynn could socialize during the day with the other submariners' wives. They ate together, spent time at the officers' club, went to the movies, and babysat for one another. "It was wonderful. I felt free for the first time since Jack was born, and no longer lonely."[17]

From New London, the family was transferred to Hawaii, where Jimmy served on the submarine *Pomfret*. They spent about eighteen months there, enjoying their new Studebaker, the climate, and Jimmy's work schedule, which allowed him to join Rosalynn and Jack for lunch each day. Rosalynn took hula lessons, and Jimmy learned to play the ukulele. During their time in Hawaii, the Carters welcomed another child, James Earl III ("Chip"), in April 1950.

Two months later, the Korean War began. The *Pomfret* had received orders to head to New London for overhaul, but with tensions high in Asia, the submarine's crew was sent to San Diego instead.

Rosalynn hated leaving Hawaii, but even more, she hated her new living conditions. Their house was in a run-down section of town; there were no necessities, such as pots or pans, and the sofa was damaged; the landlady was nasty; and Jimmy was home only on weekends. After five months of living in Southern California, Rosalynn was elated to learn that the family would be returning to New London. The move came as a result of Jimmy's request to serve on the submarine *K-1,* the first ship to be built by the U.S. Navy since World War II. When the family arrived in New London, the *K-1* was still under construction, which allowed Jimmy to spend evenings with the family. It was during this time in Connecticut that the Carters had their third son, Donnel Jeffrey, in August 1952.

Not long afterward, Jimmy applied for a job with the nuclear submarine program, the brainchild of the highly intelligent and highly demanding Admiral Hyman Rickover. Rickover interviewed all the applicants himself, and after questioning Carter for more than two hours, the admiral offered him a position with the program, where he was assigned to the *Sea Wolf.* The Carters headed to Schenectady, New York, where the submarine's nuclear reactor was being built.

The Carters may have envisioned Jimmy's making a career of the navy, but they were wrong. Shortly after moving to New York, Jimmy learned that his father was dying of cancer. Although he and his father had once been close, they had drifted apart since Jimmy left Plains, and Jimmy felt that he had abandoned his family to pursue his own career. After his father's funeral, he decided to return to Plains; his brother Billy was still in high school, he reasoned, and there was no one else to run the family's peanut warehouse business. He also wanted to emulate what he considered his father's more rewarding lifestyle. That decision led to one of the two biggest quarrels the Carters ever had (the other took place in the 1980s, while they were writing a book together). Rosalynn enjoyed living away from Plains. Although she sometimes complained about her husband's being gone for days at a time, she had come to cherish the independence she had gained from taking care of the house and family on her own. Returning to Plains, she thought, would mean giving all that up. Back in her small hometown, she would be living close to both her mother and her mother-in-law, who would likely try to run her life. But Jimmy refused to budge, and in 1953 the family returned to Georgia. A furious Rosalynn hardly spoke to him during the entire car trip. If she needed to use the restroom, she would tell Jack, who would tell his father that they had to stop.[18]

Lillian was pleased that her son had come home, but she was not happy about living in the same town as Rosalynn and having to compete with her for Jimmy's affection. So, shortly after her son and daughter-in-law returned to Plains, Lillian left town to work for a college fraternity; she eventually returned to Plains in 1961. Rosalynn demonstrated her unhappiness about being in Plains by cutting herself off from the community, focusing her attention on taking care of her home and her family. After seven months, with some prodding by her mother, she began to take part in Plains society. The Carters started attending church—something they had failed to do while Jimmy was in the navy—and spending more time with the extended family.

Money was a problem, however. Having no income, the Carters qualified to live in a government housing project in town. They paid $21 a month for their apartment, but they would have trouble keeping it if the family business failed to make any money. At first, the signs looked ominous. A drought left the Carters with a mere $200 profit and a $90,000 debt at the end of their first year in Plains. Moreover, because of their precarious financial situation, none of the banks would give them a loan.

Possibly the greatest threat to the Carters' monetary well-being was their response to the civil rights movement. In May 1954, in its famous *Brown v. Board of Education* decision, the U.S. Supreme Court declared school segregation unconstitutional. That decision aroused anger throughout the South, where segregation was commonplace. Numerous Southern lawmakers, including the governor of Georgia, Herman Talmadge, denounced the Court's position, declaring that it would undermine education in the South. White citizens councils sprang up throughout the region and joined the anti-*Brown* chorus. The Carters were urged to join the movement to overturn *Brown*, but both Jimmy and Rosalynn refused. Neither had taken much note of the unequal treatment of blacks and whites in the South until their teens. In high school, Jimmy realized that his African American friends were unable to continue their schooling. Rosalynn became aware of the situation when Annie Floyd, a black woman who had grown up on the Smith farm and was attending an African American college in Forsyth, came to the Smiths' back door and asked Rosalynn to type her thesis, which she needed to graduate. Rosalynn was shocked by Annie's poor spelling and grammar. Disturbed by the terrible conditions confronting blacks in the South, both of the Carters supported integration. Rosalynn commented years later, "There were only five people in the whole county—and no one in Plains—that we could talk to about [integration]."[19] Both she and her husband understood that by taking the position they did, they risked repercussions, including a boycott of the family and business and destruction of their financial well-being.

Nothing of the kind happened. In fact, the Carters' financial fortunes began to look up. Although they were unable to get a bank loan, the firm that supplied fertilizer to the warehouse permitted Jimmy to "keep a small inventory if I paid them after I collected for the sales we made."[20] Better weather in 1955 meant a larger crop, and the business began to make a decent profit. That same year, Jimmy asked for his wife's assistance in running the company. He could not afford to hire help and found himself overwhelmed trying to oversee the crops, work with the farmers who rented land from the family, and deal with government officials. Rosalynn borrowed some books on accounting from a friend who taught the subject at a technical school in Plains, and she began to keep the firm's ledgers. At first she worked just one day a week, but she soon found herself spending as much as sixteen hours a day weighing peanut shipments and tracking the business's finances. The Carters' sons joined her at the warehouse, where they helped by pulling up weeds and labeling bags of peanuts, under their mother's watchful eye. When she found time for a break, she would go home and make them dinner. Her work for the family business made Rosalynn feel both involved and indispensable, and it led her husband to see her as his partner. "As the business developed," she recalled, "Jimmy would come to me and say, 'Does this work; should we continue to do this in the business. . . . Are we making any money on that?' And I could advise him."[21] Jimmy's confidence in Rosalynn gave her confidence in herself and in her ability to grow.

Now financially secure, in 1956 the Carters moved into a 100-year-old, reportedly haunted house in Plains. (Although there was no evidence of a ghost, the Carter boys did find a hidden room.) Four years later, they moved again, this time to a house they built in town. Jimmy also found time for other pursuits, such as serving as a deacon of the Plains Baptist Church and as a member of both the Sumter County Hospital Authority and the school board.

Not all the Carters' time was spent on business. Jimmy's father had been a hard worker, but he had also believed in taking time off for fun. With the business generating a profit, the future president could follow his father's lead. He took the family to sporting events; they also played tennis and golf and took dancing lessons. On Saturday evenings, Jimmy and Rosalynn would often leave the children with a babysitter and spend time with friends. They loved jazz, and they and another couple traveled to New Orleans, Miami, and Baltimore to attend jazz concerts. Strong believers in learning and self-improvement, the Carters took a speed-reading course and learned square dancing. Once a year, they attended a Georgia state square dancing convention, where they made new friends.

The Carters also spent time with their children. Rosalynn and Jimmy were loving but strict parents. Jimmy helped his sons with their homework and read poetry to them. Each Saturday, Jimmy and Rosalynn closed the business and took the boys fishing. The children also had responsibilities: they to keep up with their schoolwork and do their chores, including keeping their rooms neat. If Jack, Chip, or Jeff refused, they would be punished. Rosalynn, like her mother, opposed the idea of paddling her children; she preferred to send them to their rooms. Earl, however, had been known to use a switch when Jimmy and his siblings got out of line, and Jimmy sometimes spanked his own children.

It was during this time that Jimmy got his first taste of politics. As a school board member, Carter proposed the consolidation of three existing schools. He argued that doing so would offer the students a greater variety of classes and a better education. But voters in the county, believing that the change would promote integration, shot it down. Carter had shown himself to be a fighter, however, and his friends suggested that he run for public office in 1962. Jimmy agreed. His father had served in the state legislature for a year prior to his death, and Jimmy's competitiveness drove him to prove that he could succeed in politics just as he had succeeded with the family business. In addition, a seat in the senate would give him the opportunity to pass legislation that he believed would be beneficial to the state. Having long supported the Democratic Party, he would run on that party's ticket.

Rosalynn had no inkling of her husband's intentions beforehand. On his birthday in 1962, she saw him set aside his work clothes and put on a suit. Because it was a Monday, she asked him, "Is there a funeral or something today?" "No," he replied. "I'm going to the county courthouse and qualify to run for state senate." Though taken aback, Rosalynn supported his decision and believed that her spouse could bring about positive change in Georgia. And, like Jimmy, she had a competitive streak. The one difference between them was that whereas he thought that trying and failing was better than not trying at all, she considered failure unacceptable.[22]

While Jimmy campaigned, Rosalynn ran the warehouse, took care of the family, and, in her free time, contacted voters. She called people throughout the county and, with the help of Jimmy's sister Gloria and family friends, mailed thousands of letters. Always protective of her husband, she cried when she heard his opponents say bad things about him. One of those opponents, Joe Hurst, did more than that: on the day of the primary, Jimmy learned that Hurst, the boss of Quitman County, had stuffed the ballot boxes. With the help of Charles Kirbo, an Atlanta attorney who would become a close friend of the Carters, Jimmy took his case to court and won. Following a recount, Carter was declared the winner of the primary, and he went on to win the election. Hurst, however, was not finished; he sent threatening letters to Rosalynn while Jimmy was in Atlanta during his first session as a state lawmaker. Fearful, Mrs. Carter kept a close eye on her sons, checked the house each night to make sure no one had broken in, locked all the windows, put chains on the doors, and left lights on over "the porches and in the halls." Fortunately, the threats were never acted on, and when Jimmy returned home, Rosalynn felt more comfortable.[23]

That comfort, however, was severely shaken by an event unrelated to Hurst. One day, while her husband was in Atlanta, Rosalynn received a call from her friend Beth, who asked her to come over to her home immediately. "Something has happened to Jack," she told Mrs. Carter. "But don't worry about him. Everything is going to be all right." When Rosalynn arrived, she found Jack "lying on a bed with a bloody towel around his neck" and laughing. Jack and his friend had been studying at Beth's when the friend took a gun from a closet, pointed it at Jack, and, assuming that it was not loaded, pulled the trigger. Beth thought that the bullet had only grazed Jack, but it turned out that it had passed through his neck. Rosalynn took her son to the hospital in Americus, where the doctor told her that Jack had missed being killed "by a few millimeters."[24]

The Carters' partnership continued to blossom. Because Jimmy's new job required him to be in Atlanta for three months out of the year, Rosalynn had to shoulder an even greater share of the business and family responsibilities, but she embraced the challenge. "I felt very, very important, because he couldn't have done it at all if I hadn't managed the business."[25] In the meantime, Carter established a solid reputation as a moderate progressive who opposed special interests, promoted educational reform, and sought to provide aid to the poor and needy. By 1965, he was regarded as one of the state's most influential lawmakers. Encouraged, he decided to run for governor in 1966.

"I never have been so surprised," recounted Rosalynn, when she learned of her husband's plans. She had assumed that he would run for higher office but expected it to be for lieutenant governor rather than governor.[26] Nevertheless, she supported his decision, and with the primary only three months away, she and the rest of the family helped Carter run an intense campaign. While Billy and his wife, Sybil, oversaw the peanut warehouse, Rosalynn, Jack, and Chip joined Jimmy on the campaign trail, each traveling separately around the state. Because Jeff was only fourteen, he went with his mom or with Lillian (despite the coldness between them, Rosalynn valued Lillian's help in watching over her youngest son). Jimmy estimated he and Rosalynn met some 300,000 voters. They were optimistic that they would at least get enough votes to take part in a runoff; instead, he finished third.

The loss was hard on Carter. He became depressed and found comfort in religion. Although he had always been religious, Carter had never been particularly devout. But now he found a renewed faith in God and declared himself a born-again Christian. He believed more than ever that it was his duty to serve God, which he could do best by serving humanity. His faith in himself and in the work he had to do was revived, and he immediately began preparations to run for governor again in 1970. If Carter felt confident that he could succeed the second time around, Jeff was even more certain. "We'll win the next time," he told his father shortly after the 1966 defeat, "because by then I can vote."[27]

In 1967, as the Carters were organizing their campaign, Rosalynn learned that she was pregnant. She and Jimmy had wanted another child for some time but had had no luck. An ovarian cyst may have been the problem, for not long after its removal, she received the exciting news. Having been surrounded by males since her marriage, Rosalynn hoped to have a daughter. Her wish was realized in October, with the birth of Amy.

In April 1970 Carter formally announced his candidacy for governor. Rosalynn was again involved in the campaign. Stumping meant leaving Amy behind, but she had Allie to help out. It also meant speaking in front of crowds. Although her confidence had grown over the years, Rosalynn was still shy when it came to public speaking. She had managed to avoid that duty in 1966 because her husband's campaign had been so short, but now she could not dodge public appearances. "I hated it," she remembered. "I would get physically ill."[28] However, she regarded it as her duty to help her husband win the election, even if it meant putting herself in the spotlight. In fact, she proved to be an able campaigner. She maintained a grueling schedule, rising before dawn and giving speeches and handing out flyers into the evening. She practiced by speaking before small crowds, and although she was nervous, she always tried to maintain a calm exterior. Together, the Carters shook hands with an estimated 600,000 Georgians. In November, Jimmy won.

The move to the governor's mansion brought mixed emotions for Mrs. Carter. On the one hand, she enjoyed the fact that all the children would be living there, and for the first time in four years, the entire family would be together. On the other hand, she was now the spouse of the most powerful person in Georgia—not an easy transition for her. She had to oversee events at the governor's mansion, appear at gatherings throughout the state, and even give speeches on a regular basis. And there were reports that Lillian intended to live with her son and daughter-in-law at the governor's mansion. According to some people living in Plains at the time, Mrs. Carter made it clear that she would not permit her mother-in-law to reside at the mansion: "This house isn't big enough for both of us, and I don't intend to leave." Whether this encounter actually occurred is not clear; Mrs. Carter denies that it did.[29]

In any case, being the wife of the governor of Georgia was not easy. Sometimes, out of frustration, Mrs. Carter would yell at the security guards, the servants, or even her children. She felt that she could not live a normal life and threatened to buy a wig so that she could go out incognito. One day, Jimmy suggested that she take a drive on her own, making sure that she knew how to use the police radio in case she needed help. Rosalynn took the car to visit Edna Langford, a close friend whose daughter, Judy, wed Jack Carter in November 1971. Langford was one of the few people from outside the family who had succeeded in entering the Carters' inner circle. Although the Carters had friends, they did not have many close relationships with non–family members. Both Jimmy and Rosalynn were largely introverts. In fact, while at the Naval Academy, the future president had been so reserved that many of his classmates did not even remember him attending the school. Rosalynn was similar. She would visit friends while Jimmy was at sea during his navy years, but they did not do much entertaining in their home. They preferred to stay at home together rather than spend time with others. Indeed, following Jimmy's successful bid for the presidency, it was not uncommon for individuals who worked for them, including some who had known them for years, to note the difficulty of achieving a status similar to Langford's.

Mrs. Carter found the opportunity to get out of the governor's mansion refreshing and began taking other steps to make her life more normal. Believing that the presence of a large contingent of police officers would intimidate her guests, she roped off the doorways to the family quarters, enabling her to reduce the number of guards. She began to dress more informally and to allow Amy to be a child. "I was neat and well groomed," she recollected, "but I didn't put on my makeup every single morning before I stepped out of my bedroom door."[30] She also found solace in religion, developing a closer relationship with God and believing that he would help her through any difficulties she might face.

One of those difficulties was entertaining guests. There, Mrs. Carter also found help from Ruth Gottleib, the wife of German consul general Roland Gottleib. Mrs. Gottleib had written a book entitled *Gracious Entertaining,* and she gave the state's new first lady useful advice on how to prepare for and host social functions. Jimmy's aunt, Emily ("Sissy") Dolvin, also provided much-needed assistance; with Aunt Sissy's help, Mrs. Carter held a reception for pianist Van Cliburn about three weeks after the inauguration. Although the event went off without a hitch, the first lady realized that she needed more help. She hired a housekeeper with a background in preparing food and overseeing a kitchen. The rest of the staff—all prisoners selected by prison officials to serve at the mansion—received training in cooking or waiting on tables. They practiced their serving skills on the whole family during breakfast, lunch, and dinner. The one exception was the governor, who did not join the family for the morning meal on weekdays. He announced after the election that he did not particularly enjoy breakfast and would prefer to skip it so that he could focus on his other work. Mrs. Carter, who had previously made him breakfast almost every day, later commented, "He could have told me a few years sooner!"[31]

In addition to a new housekeeper, Rosalynn hired Madeline MacBean as her personal assistant. MacBean had been recommended by Aunt Sissy's niece, and Mrs. Carter quickly took a liking to her new aide, who would become a close family friend and confidante. Like Mrs. Carter, MacBean had been raised in a poor family and had been forced to assume adult responsibilities at a young age: when she was ten, her mother had left home. MacBean acted as both a social and a press secretary for Mrs. Carter, and she kept Amy's schedules as well.

With the help of her staff, Mrs. Carter hosted numerous groups at the mansion, including mentally handicapped children and the elderly. The first lady made sure to place floral arrangements around the home to make it more inviting. She and MacBean also established a set of rules for entertaining, including not scheduling events that Rosalynn could not attend, not serving hard liquor, and auditioning all entertainment beforehand. Because of her limited entertainment budget, Mrs. Carter looked for ways to cut corners and save money. For instance, she realized that she and the other

Rosalynn Carter meeting with her personal assistant, Madeline MacBean. MacBean became one of the first lady's closest friends. Courtesy of the Jimmy Carter Library.

women in the family—Edna Langford; Jack's wife, Judy; Caron Griffin, whom Chip had married in 1973; and Jeff's girlfriend, Annette Davis—all wore the same size. When the need arose, they pooled their garments so that Rosalynn could choose among them, rather than purchasing something new for each occasion. Similarly, the first lady found that she could save money by having "large functions on successive days. The same flowers could be used, the menus could be coordinated, and it saved taking down tables and putting them up again."[32]

Both Rosalynn and Jimmy were fiscal conservatives who believed in using money—both their own and the state's—efficiently. Her desire to minimize spending came from growing up in a family with a limited income, particularly after her father's death. Jimmy's fiscal views were similar. His father had been an anti–New Dealer who considered Franklin Roosevelt's domestic program a waste of government money, as well as anti-business. Although not as tight with money as Earl was, Jimmy felt a need to cut unnecessary expenditures. As governor, Carter succeeded in getting the state legislature to pass most of his proposals for a reorganization of the Georgia government, which eliminated some agencies and consolidated others, thereby making the government more efficient and cost-effective. He also instituted "zero-based budgeting," whereby state departments had to reassess their programs annually to determine how much money they needed, rather than receiving an automatic increase in funding.

By the end of her first year as Georgia's first lady, Mrs. Carter decided that the task of overseeing the mansion had become organized enough that she could devote time to other projects. She enjoyed her independence and had become more confident in herself and her abilities. She also understood that any successes she might achieve with her projects would reflect well on the governor and his administration. With the boys in college in Atlanta or working for the state government, and with a nanny to help watch over Amy, Mrs. Carter could dedicate more time to her own agenda.

Of the issues Mrs. Carter championed, the most important to her was mental health. Her interest came from two sources. The first was personal: two of Jimmy's cousins suffered from mental disabilities. The second was political: during the 1970 campaign, a number of people had asked her what her husband would do, if elected, for their mentally ill or mentally handicapped children. One day, she decided to confront him on the issue. She joined a line of people waiting to see the candidate, and he automatically reached out to shake her hand before he realized who she was. "What are you doing here?" he asked. She replied, "I want to know what you are going to do about mental health when you are governor." Without missing a beat, he told her, "We're going to have the best mental health system in the country, and I'm going to put you in charge of it."[33]

Carter did not entirely keep his word. Following the inauguration, he established the Governor's Commission to Improve Services to the Mentally and Emotionally Handicapped, but he did not put his wife in charge of it. Rather, he made her a member of the commission, along with knowledgeable professionals in the field and other laypersons. To learn more about the subject, Mrs. Carter went to all the commission's meetings, volunteered one day a week at Georgia Regional Hospital, and visited other hospitals in the state.

Sometimes her emotions got to her, especially when visiting children with serious mental handicaps. But what she saw only made her more determined to help the mentally ill. After several months, the commission issued a report that called for "shift[ing] the emphasis away from the large institutions to the smaller, more intimate community health centers," thereby allowing some patients to live at home and others to receive care near loved ones. Carter agreed with the commission's recommendations, and as a result, the number of community health centers rose from 23 to 134 between 1970 and 1974. Mrs. Carter considered her efforts to help those with mental illness the most rewarding of her tenure as Georgia's first lady.[34]

Mrs. Carter found time for other projects as well, including her work with the Special Olympics. Lady Bird Johnson, a well-known environmentalist and champion of the 1965 Highway Beautification Act, helped Mrs. Carter establish a Georgia Highway Wildflower Program, the first time that a former and a future first lady cooperated on a major project. Mrs. Carter also worked with the Heritage Trust, which functioned to preserve natural habitat sites. With the cooperation of Betty Ford, the wife of Vice President Gerald Ford, Mrs. Carter oversaw the tour of the "Artrain"—a six-car train carrying works of art to communities that did not have access to museums—through the Southeast.

Georgia's first lady also supported passage of the equal rights amendment (ERA), which led to a fight with her husband. In 1974 Georgia was set to consider ratification of the amendment, and despite her support, Mrs. Carter realized that most voters in the state would not endorse it. When she learned that Gloria Steinem, a women's rights activist and ardent supporter of the ERA, was scheduled to visit Georgia and speak out in support of its passage, she told her husband that Steinem's visit was a mistake and would only increase opposition to the amendment. Just a few days before Georgia's vote on the ERA, adversaries of its ratification protested in Atlanta, and the governor met with some of them. During that meeting, he proclaimed his endorsement of the ERA but, in what Mrs. Carter later called a "bombshell," announced that his wife was against it. "How could you?" she asked him. It occurred to her that he had only "vaguely heard" her opposition to Steinem's visit and had mistakenly assumed that she opposed passage of the amendment. The following day, she made sure to wear an "I'M FOR ERA" button past the anti-ERA demonstrators to make sure that they knew her true stance.[35]

Mrs. Carter also took action on the matter of prisons. From the prisoners who worked at the governor's mansion, including Amy's nanny, Mary Fitzpatrick, Mrs. Carter learned that some individuals ended up in prison because they could not raise the money for a lawyer. Others had attorneys who demanded payoffs, claiming that without the money, the prisoners might not make parole. Fitzpatrick, who had been charged with murder, was told by her lawyer to plead guilty in return for a lighter sentence; instead, she received life in prison. (Fitzpatrick, who continued to work for the Carters during their years in the White House, was eventually exonerated.) The Carters created a work-release center for about sixty-five female prisoners and had women in the state's largest prison relocated to better quarters. Mrs. Carter also contacted the American Bar Association regarding those attorneys who had blackmailed their clients, but the lawyers in question received only warnings.

Promoting her agenda required Mrs. Carter to give occasional speeches, which continued to be troublesome for her. For a while, she refused all speaking invitations, but six months into her tenure as Georgia's first lady, she received an invitation to talk to the Georgia Association for Retarded Children. The governor saw it as a perfect opportunity to highlight his and Rosalynn's commitment to those with mental disabilities, and she reluctantly agreed. Although the speech went well, the experience left her drained and unwilling to attend another such event for months. In an effort to help her overcome her dread of public speaking, Carter gave his wife some valuable advice: "Write down a few words that will remind you of the things you want to say," he told her, "and then just get up and talk about them." When an opportunity to speak before the Atlanta Women's Chamber of Commerce about the governor's mansion presented itself, Mrs. Carter accepted. Using her husband's suggestion, she found not only that her speech was a success but also that she had no trouble answering questions from the audience. "I did it! I did it!" she excitedly told Carter. Although she remained nervous about speaking in front of crowds, she was gaining confidence.[36]

The ability to speak in public was about to become more important, for in 1972, Carter decided to run for the presidency in 1976, and he believed that he had a good chance of winning. Two of his advisers—Hamilton Jordan, who had worked on both gubernatorial campaigns and had become a good friend, and Peter Bourne, another friend and head of Georgia's drug abuse program—pointed out that new rules had changed the process of selecting the Democratic Party candidate. Under the old system, the party's leadership determined its candidate; under the new rules, the average voter had a greater say in that decision, and more states were using primaries to determine their choice for a nominee.

Meanwhile, the nation was experiencing a growth in both religious fervor and cynicism toward officials in Washington. The activism of the 1960s, particularly the women's rights and gay rights movements, had upset religious conservatives, for whom the right to abortion and legal protections for homosexuals were anathema. Simultaneously, a growing number of Americans questioned whether their representatives in the capital could solve the nation's problems, including unemployment, inflation, and poverty. The Vietnam War and, later, Watergate added to this lack of trust in those in Congress and the White House. If Carter could win some of the early primaries, he might be able to use the momentum from those victories, combined with his own religious devotion and his status as a Washington outsider, to win the election.

Carter's decision to run for president scared his wife, and it went way beyond the fear of public speaking. She recalled later that the very idea of being the wife of the most powerful person in the country "was just awesome to me."[37] Yet she agreed that her husband stood a good chance of winning, and she was determined to do her best to help him. For the two of them, capturing the White House would mean the opportunity to overcome Americans' lack of faith in their elected leaders; they would bring openness, honesty, and competence to government, and help to those in need. "For too long," Carter wrote in his autobiography, "political leaders have been isolated from the people.... Few have even seen personally the direct impact of government programs involving welfare, prisons, mental institutions, unemployment, school busing, or public housing."[38] Those words easily could have been Rosalynn's. For her, victory would represent the chance to involve the entire country in the agenda she had undertaken in Georgia. Lillian apparently did not believe that her son would even attempt such a bold move; when he told her of his plans, she reportedly responded by asking him, "President of what?" Only Amy, who did not like the idea of leaving her friends, opposed her father's decision.

The Carters agree that his decision to run for the presidency brought about the culmination of their burgeoning partnership. One Sunday while he was on the telephone, he asked her to pack his suitcase. "Do it yourself," she replied. "I have to get my own things ready." At the time, he did not appreciate her answer, but it forced him to examine their relationship. From that point on, he later wrote, "we carved out an unprecedented concept of equality and mutual respect." She concurred. "That was kind of the turning point. He's been packing his suitcase ever since."[39]

Amy sometimes traveled with her mother, but at other times she stayed in Plains with Allie or Lillian. It bothered Rosalynn to leave her youngest child behind, but she knew that Amy was in good hands (although she was not pleased that Lillian gave Amy sweets). For Amy, it was nothing out of the ordinary. "We've always come and gone," Mrs. Carter said. "Amy's used to it." Furthermore, she jokingly pointed out, her daughter did not enjoy listening to her mother give speech after speech. "I took her with me every third week and she liked it for about a day. She hates political speeches."[40]

Although Amy may have avoided the campaign trail, such was not the case with the rest of the family, who often traveled separately throughout the country promoting Carter's candidacy. Rosalynn's first stop, accompanied by Edna Langford, was Florida in April 1975. Armed with the *Florida Almanac of the Democratic Party,* the two of them located supporters, shook hands, handed out brochures, and visited media outlets. Realizing that few people outside of Georgia knew her husband, Mrs. Carter and Langford would stop by local newspapers or television stations and offer to give interviews; because this often caught the newspeople off guard, they would bring along a list of questions the interviewer could ask. They learned that visiting courthouses was a good way to not only meet people but also gather information. It was vital, for instance, for Carter to win the Florida state primary, particularly after finishing fourth in Massachusetts; a loss in Florida would almost certainly mean the end of his campaign. But to capture Florida, Carter would have to defeat

George Wallace, the former governor of Alabama who was also seeking the Democratic nomination. While touring Florida, Mrs. Carter and Langford heard that Wallace was losing support. They were right, and Carter captured the state in March. Whenever she was asked a question she could not answer, Mrs. Carter would make a note to discuss the issue later with her husband, with whom she kept in daily contact, so that they would be on the same page. The campaigning Carter family spent as many nights as possible at the homes of the "Peanut Brigade"—supporters who volunteered their time to help Carter's candidacy. Staying at private homes not only saved money but also provided the opportunity to develop a closer rapport with the voters.

As she had during the 1970 gubernatorial campaign, Mrs. Carter maintained a grueling schedule during the presidential race. Although Langford helped her in Florida, Mrs. Carter was often alone, waking up as early as 4:30 in the morning and traveling and giving speeches for sixteen to eighteen hours before calling it a night. A random selection from her campaign schedule during 1976 gives one a sense of what an average day was like: On 29 January Mrs. Carter left Atlanta shortly after 6:00 in the morning for Portsmouth, New Hampshire, arriving at 11:30. For the next nine hours, she gave four interviews, attended three receptions, visited a nursing home and the town shipyards, and oversaw the opening of a party headquarters in Dover before leaving for Portland at 8:30. The next day, she was busy from 8:30 in the morning to 10:00 at night, granting one interview, going to five receptions, and then attending a town meeting of the presidential candidates. On 2 March she delivered a speech at 7:00 in the morning at Fort Walton Beach, Florida, and was busy until at least 9:00 that night giving interviews and meeting with reporters. On 26 May her day started in Columbus, Ohio, at 6:15 in the morning and ended in Dayton at 9:00 that night.[41] During one week in September, Rosalynn, Jimmy, and other members of the family visited nearly 100 cities in twenty-seven states. Between 6 September and 1 November, Mrs. Carter alone traveled to almost 100 different cities throughout the nation. When asked how she handled the long days, the future first lady laughed. "You can't understand how you could do it between campaigns." More seriously, she said that what drove her was a desire to "make a difference."[42]

Although Carter no doubt read about his wife's speechmaking, he did not actually hear her stump for him until their campaign paths crossed in Trenton, New Jersey. As he sat on the platform, she told the crowd how the two of them had "scrimped and saved" to make a living, and then she listed all he had done as governor for the state of Georgia. Finally, she said, her husband was not tainted by scandal. What she said and the way she said it moved her husband to tears. When she finished, he stood up, hugged and kissed her, and then, still watery-eyed, he asked the crowd, "How many of you would like to have this woman as First Lady?" Following the boisterous approval of the crowd, he put his arm around her and declared, "I agree with you."[43]

In addition to giving speeches, Mrs. Carter helped plan the campaign strategy. Rosalynn and Jimmy always tried to get back to Georgia on the weekends, not only to spend time with Amy but also to discuss the state of the campaign and their next step. It was Mrs. Carter who convinced her husband to run in every primary, arguing that it would give him the best chance of success. She also analyzed the results of each vote and used that information to make recommendations on places that he might visit.

Mrs. Carter also coached her husband on his speeches. Trained as an engineer, Carter often had difficulty explaining complex issues in simple terms. Greg Schneiders, who worked for the Carters on the campaign and later became the president's deputy assistant for communications, recalled that during the campaign, the Carter team had interviewed voters to find out what questions they would ask the candidate if given the opportunity. According to Schneiders, "One of them was what he'd do about crime, and [Carter] went on in great detail about the root causes of crime and social issues. Rosalynn said, 'Jimmy, why don't you just say we'd put more criminals in jail?' And he said, 'Well, the fact of the matter is we don't even have jails to put them in, even if we could get all these people and could convict them all. We don't have any place to put them.' And she said, 'Well, I know that, and you know that, but I think you ought to just say it anyway.'"[44]

Mrs. Carter was not afraid to challenge her husband on personnel decisions either. She tended to be much more skeptical of people than he was. To the Carters, loyalty was vital, and people who knew both of them felt that Mrs. Carter had a better sense of who could be trusted. Schneiders recounted an event that took place during a meeting with an individual (whose name he could not remember) who was about to become a state coordinator during the 1976 campaign. Carter was immediately taken with the person, commenting that he was "a fine young man." Mrs. Carter responded, "I don't think so."[45]

Mrs. Carter's willingness to criticize her husband, when necessary, was demonstrated after his victory in the New Hampshire primary, when the future president flashed the "V" for victory sign. Recalling that Richard Nixon, now disgraced by Watergate, had often done the same thing (though with both hands), Rosalynn quietly turned to her husband and said, "Jimmy, please don't make that sign—and especially, please don't use both hands!"[46] In another situation, while campaigning in Pennsylvania, Carter commented that he saw nothing wrong with those in an ethnically homogeneous community trying to maintain their neighborhood's "ethnic purity." That phrase caused a firestorm and led African Americans to accuse him of racism. The Georgia governor, who could be very stubborn, remained adamant that he had said nothing wrong, charging the media with taking his comment out of context. Mrs. Carter, however, understood the damage he had done and, after an argument between them, convinced her husband to retract his statement.

Interestingly, Mrs. Carter's active role in the campaign brought a mixed reaction from feminists. They did not like the fact that she opposed abortion on moral grounds, even though she made it clear that she would oppose a constitutional amendment banning it. At the same time, she was the personification of what women could accomplish if given the chance. Rather than being the traditional governor's wife, Mrs. Carter had developed her own independent agenda and had become her husband's political partner, both in Atlanta and on the campaign trail. Mrs. Carter, however, saw herself differently. When she told voters that she would use her influence to give women a greater voice in the White House than they had previously enjoyed, she viewed this not as an example of women's liberation but as a continuation of the role she had maintained since childhood—that of supporting her husband and her family. These

{ *The Making of a First Lady* }

differing views on abortion and on a woman's role in the family would lead to growing tension between Mrs. Carter and feminists.

Throughout the campaign, Mrs. Carter was confident that her husband would win, and on the outside she seemed cool and collected. She developed a standard speech in which she talked about her husband's rural roots, his work as governor, and how his status as an outsider would bring positive change to Washington. The fact was, however, that she was nervous. Mary Hoyt, who became Mrs. Carter's press secretary in the middle of 1976, commented that the future first lady "was *really* terrified of public speaking" and would consistently comment, "I wish I didn't have to do this." Mrs. Carter herself admitted that sometimes she got so nervous that she would actually vomit before starting another day on the campaign trail, but she never showed her fear. "She's a tough lady," stated Hoyt. Mrs. Carter would "go into the bathroom, and she would say her speech out loud . . . and then she'd go out and give it." No one, she added, really knew how scared Mrs. Carter was.[47]

The media certainly did not know. Many reporters saw a woman who, assuming Carter won the election, would become another Eleanor Roosevelt, who was regarded as one of the most activist and influential first ladies up to that point. That Rosalynn's first name was Eleanor only fueled that belief. Indeed, the media began using the term "steel magnolia," first coined by Judy Klemesrud of the *New York Times,* to describe her. Although her slender, five-foot-five-inch frame and soft, southern voice made her appear feminine, fragile, and charming, she was, said reporters, as tough as nails and determined to win. *People* magazine remarked in March 1976, "Sometimes it's hard to tell which of the Carters—Jimmy, or his wife, Rosalynn—is running harder for President." One journalist referred to Mrs. Carter as "a Sherman tank in a field of clover." Even first lady Betty Ford seemed to share the media's perception of Rosalynn, calling her "saccharin sweet but always ready to stick a knife in your back."[48]

Sometimes, no doubt, Mrs. Carter felt like sticking a knife in someone's back. During the campaign, both Rosalynn and Lillian denied reports that they did not get along, but in fact, their relationship was tense. Lillian liked the media attention, and she enjoyed competing with her daughter-in-law for the press's favor. According to some reporters, this was one of the reasons for Rosalynn's long hours on the campaign trail. "Some intimates think," wrote Marie Ridder for the *St. Louis Globe-Democrat,* "that the need to prove herself more valuable to Jimmy than his mother is a reason that Rosalynn Carter has campaigned so hard."[49]

Nor did Mrs. Carter like those who were critical of her husband. One part of their campaign strategy was to stay vague on most issues, thereby allowing Carter to draw votes from both liberals and conservatives. Although he opposed an amendment to ban abortion, he declared that he might accept a law that limited the right to abortion. He also said that he wanted to work with the Soviet Union in curbing the arms race yet denounced Moscow for human rights violations. The lack of clarity, and even contradiction, in his statements led to criticism from both his rivals for the Democratic nomination and the media. Mrs. Carter strongly disliked the negative comments and blamed the Ford camp for suggesting that Carter was inconsistent, but she had learned over the years to accept such jabs as part of the game of politics.

The strategy of competing in every primary, having the family participate in the campaign, and assuming vague positions on the issues paid off. At the start of Carter's bid for the presidency, many voters had asked, "Jimmy who?" But by early 1976, many of them knew who he was. The result was victory in both the Iowa caucus and the New Hampshire primary, which led the media to identify Carter as the Democratic front-runner. The momentum from those successes carried him through the primary season, and by early June, Carter had the nomination locked up.

The next step was choosing a running mate. With Kirbo, Rosalynn, and other aides, Carter slowly whittled down the list of choices to Senator Edmund Muskie of Maine and Senator Walter Mondale of Minnesota. Of the two, Mrs. Carter preferred Mondale. Jimmy's cousin Hugh Carter reported that it was she "who tipped the scales" in favor of the Minnesotan,[50] but the fact was that Carter himself preferred Mondale. Because Carter had relatively conservative views, he wanted someone who could draw votes from liberals in the Democratic Party, and Mondale was more closely identified with the party's left wing than Muskie was. Also, because Mondale was the son of a minister, Carter felt that they would be able to relate on a religious level. Finally, Mondale insisted that if he became vice president, he wanted to play an active role, which corresponded with Carter's own vision for his administration. Carter announced his choice at the party's national convention in July, where he received its formal endorsement.

The Carter campaign now turned its attention to defeating the Republican incumbent, President Gerald Ford. At Carter's headquarters in Atlanta, maps of the nation kept track of each person's travels, with colored lines used to differentiate them: Jimmy's was green, Rosalynn's blue, Walter Mondale's red, Joan Mondale's yellow, and the Carter children's purple. Initially, it looked like clear sailing for Carter; polls taken after the Democratic convention found him with a 10 percentage point lead over Ford. But the president slowly pared it down by charging his challenger with being both vague and contradictory on the issues. Making matters worse was an interview Carter gave to *Playboy* magazine that appeared in September. The fact that an individual who regarded himself as religious would even give an interview to a pornographic magazine offended voters, particularly those who considered themselves devout. Carter's use of foul language and his comment that he had "committed adultery in [his] heart many times" only added to the furor. Carter's statements outraged Hoyt, but Rosalynn, though worried about their impact on the campaign, tried to downplay them. "It doesn't bother me," she said. "He's a human being. We have a very close relationship and I trust him completely." However, when reporters asked Mrs. Carter whether she too had lusted in her heart, she got angry. "I am not going to tell you my personal life," she stated, and reiterated her trust in her husband.[51]

Carter's faux pas did not help him in his first debate with Ford, which was held a few days after the *Playboy* interview became public. He appeared to ramble and, Mrs. Carter felt, gave too many statistics. She urged him to talk in simple terms, "like you were talkin' to me" rather than presenting a long, complex set of facts.[52] The candidate listened to his wife, but what helped him even more in the second debate, held on 6 October, was a mistake on Ford's part. When the president declared that there was "no Soviet domination of Eastern Europe," that statement was clearly incorrect. The momentum Ford had developed came to a halt; his support began to

President and Mrs. Carter walking down Pennsylvania Avenue during the inaugural parade. Courtesy of the Jimmy Carter Library.

slip, and the president did not perform well in the third and final debate held on 22 October. The campaign was not over yet, however. Ford continued to hammer away at Carter for waffling on the issues, but it was not enough. With a bare majority of the popular vote and 297 electoral votes to Ford's 240, Jimmy Carter became the thirty-ninth president of the United States, and Rosalynn Carter became the youngest first lady since Jacqueline Kennedy. Gerald Rafshoon, an advertising executive from Atlanta who had organized a media blitz for the Carter campaign, believed that Mrs. Carter had been essential to her husband's victory. New Hampshire's *Union Leader* seconded Rafshoon, commenting that although the other presidential candidates' wives had aided them in their campaigns, "none had the impact of Rosalynn Carter."[53]

On 20 January 1977, Jimmy and Rosalynn Carter took part in the inaugural parade. Rather than riding for the entire route, the new president had the Secret Service agents stop the car. He and Rosalynn got out and walked, hand in hand, the rest of the way.

For the crowd, their decision to walk to the Capitol came as a shock. For the Carters, though, it was an important symbol of how they viewed their roles and each other. First, it demonstrated that the Carters did not consider themselves special; they were no better than any other American. He was the most powerful person in the country, and she was going to be an influential factor in his administration, but they regarded themselves as average individuals who, with the help of other average individuals, had been given an opportunity to implement their new ideas for the country. Second, the walk symbolized their love for each other, which in 1977 was just as strong as it had been on the day they were married. Indeed, their contemporaries often commented about their open displays of affection—hugging, kissing, or holding hands whenever they were together. Finally, the Carters' decision reflected their equal partnership. "We had been married for thirty-one years and were full partners in every sense of the word," the president later wrote.[54] Walking toward their new life together hand in hand was a symbol of that relationship.

The Carters were indeed partners in every sense. The shy and insecure Rosalynn Smith had become a strong and independent woman, a caring mother, a shrewd businesswoman, and an able campaigner. As first lady of Georgia, she had realized that her own successes would reflect well on her husband and pay political dividends later. Carter recognized his wife's abilities and encouraged her to use them to the fullest. Together, they had built a successful business and, with the help of their family, had brought Jimmy Carter to the pinnacle of political power.

CHAPTER 2

CREATING A "CARING SOCIETY"

The institution of the first lady has undergone significant change since the end of World War II. With rare exceptions—such as Edith Bolling Wilson and Eleanor Roosevelt—first ladies largely stayed out of the spotlight, either because they desired to do so or because the media and the public lacked interest in them. This changed in the 1960s. John and Jacqueline Kennedy's arrival at the White House occurred at a time of expanding media coverage, particularly television. Consequently, the young, handsome couple piqued the interest of both reporters and the public. This greater scrutiny meant that, whether she liked it or not, the first lady's actions would create a public image of her—an image that determined how she was perceived by the American people. For Jacqueline Kennedy, the image was of a first lady who brought glitz and glamour to the presidential mansion. For her successor, Lady Bird Johnson, it was of a woman who believed strongly in environmental causes. Pat Nixon took an interest in volunteerism, and Betty Ford became known as a champion of women's rights and women's health, with a particular focus on breast cancer and substance abuse—both of which she battled personally.

Another change was the increasing public activism of the first lady. Again, with the exceptions of Mrs. Wilson and Mrs. Roosevelt and, to a lesser extent, Lou Henry Hoover, first ladies prior to the 1960s largely avoided publicity. Mrs. Kennedy, however, sought public support for her efforts to renovate the White House, and although she was generally ambivalent toward the media, she attempted to maintain good relations with the press. Mrs. Johnson actually courted reporters; indeed, she became the first first lady to formally appoint a press secretary to her staff. Mrs. Nixon generally avoided the spotlight, but Mrs. Ford's arrival in the presidential mansion meant a return of activism. She gave numerous interviews and statements in support of the equal rights amendment (ERA) and about the importance of having yearly breast exams.[1]

Thus, the office of first lady had experienced two significant changes by the time Rosalynn Carter moved into the White House: increasing media and public scrutiny, and a growth in activism. Like her predecessor, Mrs. Carter intended to be an active first lady. Even before the 1976 election, she had made it clear that, as she had in Georgia, she would be developing an agenda of her own, consisting of five projects: aid for the mentally handicapped, aid for the elderly, volunteerism, childhood immunization, and passage of the ERA. Mrs. Carter had several reasons for advancing this agenda. First, it would allow her to maintain the independence she had enjoyed for years. Second, the projects she chose would create, as she put it, a "caring society" in which various needy groups would receive help from their communities, their states, and the federal government.[2] It was, in short, a form of Christian compassion for those who were somehow disadvantaged. Finally, as her husband's partner, she wanted to be involved in programs that would complement what he was doing in the West Wing, with the hope that her successes would reflect well on him and his presidency. But promoting such a wide array of programs drew criticism from her contemporaries that she lacked an identifiable image.

Rosalynn Carter wanted someplace in the White House where she could focus on her projects, so she became the first first lady to have an office of her own in the East Wing. Because tourists regularly walked through the East Wing, she avoided them by taking a route through the basement in the winter or outside over the lawn when the weather was warmer. Her biggest complaint was not the tourists, however, but the temperature. When her husband took office, the nation was facing a burgeoning energy crisis, with higher energy prices fueling higher inflation. President Carter responded by urging energy conservation and, as a symbolic gesture, had the thermostats in the White House lowered. The East Wing became so cold in the winter months that Mrs. Carter was forced to wear long underwear. She pleaded with her husband to keep the thermostats at sixty-eight degrees, but he refused.

Eighteen staff members shared Mrs. Carter's fate and worked on her projects (the number was later increased to twenty-one). Heading the staff was Mary Hoyt, the first lady's press secretary since the middle of 1976 and, after the election, East Wing coordinator. An attractive, honey blonde–haired woman who looked significantly younger than her fifty-three years, Hoyt had extensive experience in Washington politics, having worked during the 1972 presidential campaign for both George McGovern and Jane Muskie, the wife of Senator Edmund Muskie of Maine; both men had sought the Democratic nomination that year. As Mrs. Carter's press secretary, Hoyt's job included overseeing the East Wing's press office, coordinating media coverage of East Wing events, and holding press conferences. As East Wing coordinator, Hoyt was essentially Mrs. Carter's chief of staff—similar to Hamilton Jordan's role in the West Wing. (Neither Jimmy nor Rosalynn Carter officially designated a chief of staff for their wings until 1979.) In addition to these duties, Hoyt acted as liaison to the West Wing staff.

Also important to Mrs. Carter's projects was Kathy Cade, director of the East Wing's Projects, Issues, and Research Office. Cade, a graduate of Radcliffe College with a master's degree in management from Yale University, had also worked for the Muskie campaign in 1972 and for the Carter presidential campaign. In 1973 she had produced documentaries on health and science issues for the Public Broadcasting System and the Science Program Group. Of the projects Cade worked on for Mrs. Carter, the one to which she devoted the most time was aid for the mentally ill. As first lady of Georgia, Mrs. Carter had made erasing the stigma surrounding mental illness a keystone of her agenda, and she had vowed that if her husband were elected president, she would take that effort to the national level. "I know that it has been 15 years since anyone has even done a report on mental health care," she had told an audience in September 1976, "and the programs have become so splintered that it's time we look at all of

Kathy Cade, Mrs. Carter's director of projects. She played a vital role in the first lady's mental health initiative. Courtesy of the Jimmy Carter Library.

them and give some direction to national health care for the mentally ill." By December 1976 she had convinced the president-elect to create a presidential commission to study the matter.[3]

To justify the urgent need for a commission on mental health, the White House cited a figure of 20 million Americans, or about 10 percent of the population, who were in need of mental health care. Further, whereas health insurance covered about 33 percent of general medical bills, it paid for only about 10 percent of mental health–related expenses. Earlier mental health initiatives had had varying degrees of success. In 1955 Congress had formed a mental health commission that had recommended, among other things, the establishment of community mental health centers—a proposal that had been implemented in the 1960s. Another commission formed in 1965 had suggested that more attention be paid to children's health needs, but that idea had gotten nowhere. In addition, none of these earlier commissions had addressed the mental health system in its entirety, and by the early 1970s, that system was disorganized. A variety of institutions—short- and long-term mental hospitals, nursing homes, community health centers, and self-help groups, among others—provided aid to those with mental illness, but there was no integration among them. Thus, a commission designed to examine the entire mental health system would be a unique step.

The process of establishing this new commission began even before the election. During the campaign, Peter Bourne, a close friend of the Carters who had worked with the future first lady on health issues in Georgia, consulted Thomas Bryant about matters of policy. Trained in both medicine and law, Bryant had worked for the Lyndon Johnson administration as head of the Office of Economic Opportunity's Emergency Food and Medical Services Program; he later became president of the Drug Abuse Council. Bryant, in turn, asked for help from John Gardner, who had been secretary of the Department of Health, Education, and Welfare (HEW) under President Johnson. Gardner suggested that the best way to begin a study of the national mental health system was to have Carter establish a commission to examine the subject. Bourne agreed. In December 1976 he sent Mrs. Carter a lengthy memorandum outlining what he thought should be the scope and makeup of the commission, as well as a timetable for its issuing of reports. He proposed a body established by executive order (because going through Congress would take too long) and made up of approximately twenty persons. The commission's focus would be on issues such as retardation, schizophrenia, and behavioral disorders. Because alcoholism and drug abuse fell under the purview of HEW's Alcohol, Drug Abuse, and Mental Health Administration, Bourne suggested that those subjects be avoided, "except where there is a direct overlap with mental health in service delivery, research or training." The commission would issue a draft report in November 1977, timed to influence the White House's "budget planning for the subsequent year." During the next six months, the commissioners would prepare and submit a final report to the president.[4]

One question for the new administration was who would chair the commission. Mrs. Carter wanted that role, but the 1967 Postal Revenue and Federal Salary Act banned nepotism in the hiring of employees or the promotion of individuals in the executive branch. First ladies were not exempt from the law, so Mrs. Carter could not serve in an official capacity; however, she could act as the commission's honorary chair. On 17 February President Carter, taking Bourne's advice, issued an executive order that established the President's Commission on Mental Health, with Bryant as its official leader. As it turned out, Mrs. Carter—displeased with merely honorary status, which she felt diminished her power—acted in all but name as the commission's head.[5]

In the early months of the administration, the East Wing received between 500 and 600 letters each week related to the first lady's projects, and many of them came from individuals who were thrilled that the Carter administration intended to give serious attention to an issue of personal importance to them. "We have a 28-year-old son who is mentally ill," wrote one couple. "He has been in the state hospital so many times, I've lost count. . . . The only things the doctors know to help him is to keep him drugged." A woman with schizophrenia explained, "All these years have been a waste in many ways for me. I don't enjoy life. I'm always sick. My work is a terrible effort and some things are impossible." She pleaded that the first lady advocate further research into schizophrenia.[6]

Others wrote to Mrs. Carter seeking to serve on the commission or recommending possible members. Lawmakers wanted constituents or friends appointed; Representative Barbara Mikulski (D-Maryland), for example, urged the first lady to consider a friend of hers. Numerous groups, including those advancing the interests of women, professionals, and racial and ethnic minorities, insisted on having representation on the commission. Still others suggested subjects that the group should study, ranging from the effects of working with mentally ill or handicapped individuals to an examination of psychological treatments for those with mental problems.[7] A screening committee set up by the White House and chaired by Gardner ultimately reviewed more than a thousand applicants for the commission, with twenty finally selected by the Carters. Gender, race, and ethnicity played a major role in their choices: twelve men and eight women, including three African Americans, one Native American, and two Hispanics.

The commission's job would not be easy. It had to examine a problem that affected millions of persons of both sexes, of all races and ethnicities, and in all parts of the country. Furthermore, the body had a limited budget. When he took office, President Carter had vowed to reduce an inflation rate that stood at approximately 6 percent, and as part of that goal, he sought to rein in federal spending. The original proposal for the commission advised a budget of $1 million, but Mrs. Carter, who wanted to start working immediately, suggested earmarking $100,000 from the president's emergency fund, pending further appropriations. Carter resisted. "I can't come into office and give my wife $100,000 for her pet project," he said. "I thought we were going to use volunteers for this."[8] Eventually, his wife succeeded in changing his mind. Finally, the commission also faced time constraints. In his executive order establishing it, the president called for the submission of a preliminary report by 1 September 1977 and a final report by 1 April of the following year.

Luckily, the commission found ample support. In addition to its twenty members and the two dozen paid staffers who helped Bryant, it could rely on more than 450 volunteers who worked on a number of panels that examined matters ranging from the prevention of mental illness to the impact of mental disabilities on specific populations. One-third of the paid staff came from HEW, which provided about $750,000, in part to cover those staff members' salaries. Individuals and private organizations provided additional financial support.

On 29 March the commission held its first meeting, during which each member presented what he or she considered the most pressing issues in the field. Ruth Love, superintendent of schools in Oakland, California, and the committee's vice chairperson, called for social services organizations, including schools, to do a better job in dealing with entire families. Franklin Vilas, an Episcopalian minister, focused on the failure among various groups, including the clergy and mental health workers, to collaborate in solving the mental health problems facing the nation. Both Glenn Watts, an official with the AFL-CIO who also worked with the White House Conference on Handicapped Individuals, and Priscilla Allen, a member of the National Patients Committee of the Mental Health Association, called for public education about mental illness. La Donna Harris, president of Americans for Indian Opportunity, added that it was important to fight the social stigma surrounding mental disabilities. Having obtained the views of each member of the commission, Bryant announced that he would convene four public one-day hearings so that the group could gather further information on mental health matters affecting the country.[9]

The commission held those hearings during May and June in different cities picked not only for their geographic locations but also for the demographics of the people living there. The first hearing, held on 24 May, was in Philadelphia, selected as a representative of other industrialized cities in the Northeast. The following day the commissioners heard testimony in Nashville, regarded as having a more rural populace. On 20 and 21 June they listened to witnesses in Tucson and San Francisco, who addressed the mental health issues affecting Hispanics, Asians, and Native Americans, as well as the elderly. Altogether, approximately 200 individuals appeared before the group, with another 200 providing written testimony.

The commission listened to a wide range of concerns: the fragmentation of the mental health system and the lack of funding, both of which made it hard for patients to get the help they needed; farm-labor contractors who enticed former patients to work for them but failed to provide mental health care services; the lack of doctors and programs in rural areas; the failure of Mexican Americans to properly use the services available to them; the deleterious impact of urbanization on Native Americans; and the lack of organized services for the elderly. The commissioners heard minorities complain that white health care workers had harassed or frightened them, and some witnesses urged the commission to make a better effort to hire mental health employees from minority groups. Others pointed to the lack of attention given to children with mental health problems and recommended that teachers be trained to help identify them.

Some of the testimony was heart-wrenching. Mrs. Carter recalled the story of a Haitian woman who had seen a therapist because she believed that "her husband's ex-wife had put a hex on her." Rather than considering the woman's culture, a doctor had determined that she was "paranoid and treated [her] with a powerful sedative." A college student hid the fact that she was going to a therapist for fear that she "might be labeled a 'crazy person.'" Richard D. Morrison of the Interagency Council on Migrant Services told of a woman who had recently been released from a mental hospital and got a job working on a farm. Unable to perform the jobs asked of her, her migrant, alcoholic coworkers forced her to provide them with sex. "When we encountered her," Morrison recounted, "she showed signs of repeated physical beatings." The woman was "forced to serve sexually 20 or more males a day. She was both severely retarded and actively schizophrenic." Morrison's testimony, according to a newspaper report, made Mrs. Carter "wince."[10]

Bourne had the job of coordinating the commission's report, which required going through thousands of pages of testimony and data. The commissioners also had to assess the findings of the various panels, which they did in a series of hearings between October 1977 and January 1978. Despite the work involved, the commission issued its preliminary and final reports on time. Both defined mental illness in fairly broad terms, including schizophrenia, depression, autism, alcoholism, drug abuse, and dementia. One of the final report's conclusions was that the previous estimate of 10 percent of Americans needing mental health care at any one time was probably low; it was probably closer to 15 percent. However, only about 12 cents of every dollar spent on health care went to the treatment of mental disabilities, and research on mental health had "been cut in half during the past decade." The commission found that four groups of Americans in particular lacked proper care: racial and ethnic minorities, children, the elderly, and those with chronic mental illness.[11]

The final report made 117 recommendations under eight headings: improving community support for those with mental disabilities; making the mental health system more responsive; providing better insurance coverage for those with mental disabilities; increasing the number of mental health workers, including minorities, and encouraging more mental health personnel to work in underserved

Rosalynn Carter chairing a meeting of the President's Commission on Mental Health, January 1978. Courtesy of the Jimmy Carter Library.

parts of the country; protecting the rights of those with mental disabilities; increasing funding for research into mental illness; establishing a Center for Prevention within the National Institute of Mental Health; and taking steps to eliminate the stigma associated with mental disability. The recommendations called for action not just by the federal government but by state and local governments as well. For instance, a number of suggestions focused on what could be done at the community level. Because most individuals who needed help were likely to seek it from family, friends, religious leaders, or local doctors who might have little or no training in mental illness, it was important not only to strengthen these support networks but also to provide better coordination between them and local mental health services. Moreover, because so much mental health care took place at the community level, it was vital to increase federal funding to establish community services where they were lacking and to improve existing services. Along these lines, the commission called for a revision of the Community Mental Health Centers Act, which had been passed in 1963 to establish community mental health facilities so that those who had been institutionalized could receive local care. Amendments added over the years required those centers to offer at least a dozen different services in order to be eligible for federal funding, which made it impossible for some communities to open facilities. The commission's report proposed that such centers receive funding even if they offered only one service. The commissioners reasoned that the communities themselves knew which mental health services were most vital, and offering just one service would provide the foundation for more comprehensive care later.

The first lady later called this report her greatest achievement, because she had "worked so hard on it."[12] However, Mrs. Carter knew that her husband would not accept recommendations with a high price tag, so she had told the commissioners to keep total costs low. Cade recalled the first lady telling the commission's members that they had "to tell the president how to use available resources more efficiently, not how to do more with more resources." Apparently, Carter liked what he saw in the final draft. "This will not be a costly program," he announced, "but it will be a program that can save enormous amounts of public funds" by providing treatment to those individuals who "[suffer] from mental illness unnecessarily."[13]

Although some of the commission's recommendations required no additional expenditures by the federal government, others involved significant amounts, including "at least $75 million for the first year . . . and $100 million for each of the next two years" for a program to provide better community health care, $85 million to encourage more people to work in the mental health field or to move to underserviced parts of the country, and millions of dollars to improve Medicare coverage for mental health care and to fund research into mental illness.[14] The trick was trying to implement all the commission's recommendations while simultaneously satisfying the president's desire to curb spending. Here, Bourne would have been useful, but in the summer of 1978, the public learned that he had provided one of his assistants with a prescription for Quaaludes and given her a pseudonym to protect her from scrutiny. The news about Bourne came at a bad time. President Carter was facing falling numbers in the polls, and the year before he had taken a political beating for standing by another friend, Bert Lance, whom Carter had appointed director of the Office of Management and Budget (OMB). Lance had come under investigation in the fall of 1977 for reportedly violating statutes requiring government officials to divest themselves of any financial holdings that might create a conflict of interest; specifically, the evidence suggested that Lance had failed to cut his ties to the National Bank of Georgia, which he had headed prior to assuming his position at the OMB. Despite his promise to restore honesty to government, the president, with the first lady's support, had stood by Lance, thereby causing Americans to question whether Carter had meant what he said. Finally, realizing that the scandal was hurting his administration, the president asked for and obtained Lance's resignation in September 1977. Not wanting to cause the president similar trouble, Bourne offered his resignation, which Carter promptly accepted. Without Bourne, wrote the first lady, "there was no senior-level advocate on the White House staff to guide the report through the day-to-day work necessary in translating a national commission report into policy."[15]

Responsibility for advancing the commission's recommendations fell on the shoulders of HEW and its secretary, Joseph Califano. As a result, Califano and his staff found themselves in the unenviable position of trying to please both of the Carters. The president had called for reform of the welfare system and the creation of a national health insurance program, and HEW was giving priority to those initiatives. The department also had to consider Carter's insistence that any new programs not involve a significant increase in expenditures. These issues of priorities and spending put HEW and the first lady at odds. In November 1978 Cade complained to Mrs. Carter that although HEW had estimated that the commission's recommendations would cost $400 million, it had allocated only $83 million for the 1980 budget and had not requested any funds to cover the proposed changes in Medicare. "Both Tom [Bryant] and I feel that this figure is inadequate and are concerned that your credibility and that of the Commission will be seriously jeopardized if additional monies are not allocated for implementation," Cade wrote. They recommended $175 million, or an additional $92 million in spending, "to make a credible start on implementing the report." Bryant suggested that the first lady contact James McIntyre, head of the Office of Management and Budget, and ask for his help in getting more money.[16]

Mrs. Carter resented HEW's lack of support, and meetings with Califano and his staff got her nowhere. "We hadn't put in all of those long hours and hard work just to see yet another national commission report gather dust on some busy Cabinet officer's bookshelf," she later wrote.[17] So she took Bryant's advice and brought her case to McIntyre, as well as to her husband. Although she did not get $175 million, she came close: the president allocated $150 million. At the same time, the president's budget proposal for 1980 was austere, and he continued to call for reductions in federal spending. Despite the administration's efforts, inflation had continued to rise, reaching 9 percent by the end of 1978. Some lawmakers questioned how the White House could propose spending $150 million on mental health while claiming that it wanted to keep expenditures under control.

To get congressional support, Mrs. Carter met with state mental health officials, representatives from the American Psychiatric Association, and various minority, women's, and children's advocacy groups, urging them to press lawmakers to pass her spending bill. Then, in February 1979, Mrs. Carter appeared before the Senate Subcommittee on Health and Scientific Research, becoming only the second first lady (the first was Eleanor Roosevelt) to testify on Capitol Hill. After discussing what she had learned during the commission's hearings around the nation, she pointed to the lack of facilities for those in need of mental health care and summarized the commission's recommendations for change. It was true that the administration wanted to curb spending, she explained, but "no other problem facing society touches so many families or leaves them so vulnerable."[18] Her testimony moved many of the attendees, among them Senator Edward Kennedy (D-Massachusetts), whose older sister, Rosemary, was mentally retarded. He promised to do what he could to help the first lady.

Yet there would be no money if Congress did not act. At the end of March, Bryant wrote to Mrs. Carter that "we are in far more trouble on mental health matters than we should be." He laid the problem at the feet of HEW, charging the department with delaying submission of the spending bill. Unless that legislation arrived on Capitol Hill and was reported out of committee before 15 May, Congress would not have time to act on it as part of the 1980 budget. He urged the first lady to press Califano, Domestic Policy Staff Chairman Stuart Eizenstat, and the White House's Congressional Relations Office (CRO) to take action. "I am convinced," he told her, "that without this kind of personal push by you, things will continue to drift, and 1980 will arrive without a great deal positive to report."[19] Apparently, Mrs. Carter intervened personally with her husband, and on 15 May the president submitted to Congress the Mental Health Systems Act. Senator Kennedy and Representative Henry Waxman (D-California) immediately endorsed the bill and promised its passage.

In addition to ensuring that the mental health bill arrived in Congress by 15 May, the first lady was determined to get rid of Califano. There is no doubt that by this time, she was fed up with the HEW head. Califano had also upset both the president and members of the White House staff; his liberal leanings did not mesh with the Oval Office's more conservative orientation. In July 1979, following discussions with his top advisers (including his wife), the president decided to shake up his cabinet, and he accepted the resignations of several people, including Califano. Although Mrs. Carter later claimed that she wanted the HEW secretary gone because he had been leaking information to the press, that was not the only reason. "She wanted beheadings," reported one White House aide, and "Califano was at the top of her list," in part because of his "tepid support for mental-health funding"—a statement that the first lady later admitted was true.[20]

News of the cabinet shake-up came as a shock to the HEW secretary. He was aware, as he put it, of the "cultural chasm between President Carter and me." Califano had long been a member of the Washington establishment and felt more "comfortable" in the capital than the president did. Still, he had no idea that he was about to lose his job until his seventeen-year-old son Mark, who was working at the *Washington Post* at the time, told him that two of the newspaper's leading correspondents had written a story to that effect. Nor did he learn until after he left the White House that Mrs. Carter had wanted him gone.[21]

Getting the Mental Health Systems Act passed also required Mrs. Carter's help. By August 1980 the bill was stuck in the House Commerce Committee, which was also about to consider Superfund legislation. The purpose of the Superfund, known officially as the Comprehensive Environmental Response, Compensation, and Liability Act (CERCLA), was to establish a fund to clean up hazardous-waste sites. It had been proposed in response to health problems among the residents of Love Canal, New York, caused by the dumping of toxic waste there. If the Commerce Committee did not act on the Mental Health Systems Act before CERCLA came up for consideration, Cade feared that the bill would die. To prevent that from happening, she called the CRO, which told her that it was more concerned with passage of the Superfund and urged her not to say anything to Mrs. Carter, "because it's critical that we get the Superfund bill out tomorrow."[22] As the staff member responsible for the first lady's projects, and knowing how important the mental health bill was to Mrs. Carter, Cade refused to stand pat. She wrote a memorandum to Mrs. Carter explaining the situation and suggesting that she contact the chairman of the Commerce Committee, Harley Staggers (D-West Virginia). That evening, the first lady phoned Cade at home. "I called Chairman Staggers," she said. "I think I woke him up." The next day, the West Virginia lawmaker shocked dozens of CERCLA lobbyists when he announced that his committee would consider the Mental Health Systems Act first.[23] Two months later, Congress passed the bill. It shifted the financing of mental health care from large hospitals to community programs, gave the states more leeway in providing grants for mental health care, and included a patients' bill of rights. Additionally, it authorized more money for mental health.

Passage of the Mental Health Systems Act was a major accomplishment for the first lady. She had participated in hours of testimony, assisted Bourne in coordinating the commission's report, and successfully overcame hurdles within both the executive and the legislative branches to get the measure passed. She had demonstrated her influence with the president and Congress to obtain what she regarded as an essential component of her agenda. She could be proud of the recognition she received from groups in the mental health field, with both the National Mental Health Association and the

District of Columbia Mental Health Association awarding her the title "volunteer of the decade" for her work.[24] She also hoped that the bill would reflect well on her husband, who was losing public support as a result of persistent economic troubles at home and his inability to free several dozen Americans taken hostage in Iran in November 1979.

Ronald Reagan, who defeated Carter in the 1980 election, cut much of the funding for the mental health program, and Mrs. Carter called the reduction in appropriations "a bitter loss."[25] Whether more funding would have made a difference is not clear, but studies have found a shortage of the type of community mental health programs supported by Mrs. Carter, meaning that many individuals with mental illness fail to receive the proper treatment.[26] Even so, the first lady left behind a legacy: she brought mental health to the public's attention. Furthermore, the National Institute of Mental Health established an Office of Prevention and revised its training program to make trainees more responsive to those mental disabilities.

The first lady's work on the mental health commission influenced another part of her domestic agenda: assistance for the elderly. She learned that there was a lack of mental health workers and physicians trained to meet the needs of older Americans. Traveling around the nation, she heard stories of older individuals who lived alone without anyone to care for them or who felt useless because of cultural attitudes or regulations that forced them to give up their jobs. With the increase in life expectancy and the growth of the nation's elderly population, there was clearly a need to give more attention to those individuals aged sixty and over.

Mrs. Carter also had personal connections to this issue. Following the death of her maternal grandmother, her grandfather had moved in with the family, and Rosalynn had seen how age affected him. During the 1976 campaign, she had joked with her mother, who, at age seventy, had just recently retired from her job as a postmistress. "I can't understand," Mrs. Carter said, "why anyone who has to get up and be at the post office at seven o'clock every morning for as long as I can remember wouldn't love to stay at home and sleep late and be leisurely for a change." Her mother responded, "No one thinks I can do good work anymore."[27] That comment had a powerful impact on Rosalynn. She could also point to the fact that her mother-in-law, Lillian, had joined the Peace Corps at age sixty-eight and that Jimmy's uncle was in his late eighties and still worked as a salesman. It was clear that elderly individuals could play an active and useful role in society. No doubt, stories like those of her mother and mother-in-law explained Mrs. Carter's determination to abolish mandatory retirement.

After the inauguration, Mrs. Carter maintained close contact with Nelson Cruikshank, President Carter's counselor on aging, who kept her informed of pending legislation affecting the elderly. In May 1977 she hosted a roundtable on the aged that included nearly two dozen experts and covered issues such as health care, nutrition, and mandatory retirement. Among those present was Claude Pepper, the seventy-six-year-old Democratic congressman from Florida. Pepper was a strong advocate of pending legislation to eliminate mandatory retirement, but the bill had been held up in committee. The conferees put together a pamphlet that they sent to the states and to various other groups, incorporating more than a dozen recommendations for helping America's aged.

Mrs. Carter did in fact lobby Congress to pass bills to help the elderly, and she had significant success. In 1977 Congress passed the Rural Health Clinics Act, which increased access to health care for recipients of Medicare and Medicaid. The following year, lawmakers did what Pepper (and Mrs. Carter) had wanted and added provisions to the 1967 Age Discrimination in Employment Act that banned mandatory retirement in the federal government and raised the mandatory retirement age in the private sector from sixty-five to seventy. Also in 1978, lawmakers amended the Older Americans Act, which consolidated several federal programs under one umbrella, increased funding for health and nutrition programs for the aged, and established an ombudsman program to investigate nursing home complaints.

The first lady's work for the elderly and the mentally ill had a direct effect on another part of her agenda: volunteerism. Back in Georgia, she had learned that programs to help those in need worked most effectively when "people in the community are interested in them, want them to work, and assume some kind of responsibility for them." The government could pour money into programs to help the poor, the needy, or the disabled, but "if there's not someone in the community that cares, well, the problem is not solved."[28]

With her attention focused on the other elements of her domestic agenda, as well as maintaining a busy travel schedule and attending to her traditional duties as hostess, Mrs. Carter had little time to devote to volunteerism during her first year as first lady. That fact drew criticism. "There are numerous local activities that could benefit from Mrs. Carter's attention and assistance," stated a *Washington Post* editorial in February 1978, such as improving local hospitals.[29] A week later, the first lady pledged to improve DC General Hospital, which both she and the hospital's governing board described as physically ugly. More serious were numerous violations of hospital standards, including poor record keeping and dangerous working conditions, that had caused the hospital to lose its accreditation in 1973. In May 1978 Mrs. Carter helped paint the emergency room at DC General. That same month, she was proud to learn that the hospital's accreditation had been reinstated.

Although the *Washington Post* editorial may have had an impact on the first lady's determination to help DC General, she was most influenced by her husband's program to provide help to communities in need of assistance. That program included the establishment of an Urban Regional Policy Group, chaired by Housing and Urban Development Secretary Patricia Harris. In line with his fiscal conservatism, however, the president did not want to pump large amounts of new funding into these communities; instead, he wanted to use existing funds more efficiently. Volunteerism was also a part of the urban program, and here the first lady saw a means of buttressing her husband's policies. Who better to determine the best way to help communities in need than the individuals and businesses in those communities? Moreover, getting people to improve their own neighborhoods and cities would not only develop an ethic of altruism among Americans but also save the federal government substantial sums of money. Finally, by promoting volunteerism, the first lady could add her own element to her husband's urban program, and if her call for volunteerism proved successful, it would reflect well on his presidency.

Mrs. Carter consequently instituted what the media called the Rosalynn Plan, a program designed to get Americans to volunteer

Volunteerism in action: the first lady painting at DC General Hospital, May 1978. Courtesy of the Jimmy Carter Library.

their time and money both for neighborhood beautification programs and to help those in need. Although she intended to focus most of her efforts on Washington, D.C., she decided to travel around the country as well, highlighting individuals and groups who were helping to relieve unemployment and improve community life. Her stops included Lorain, Ohio, where she met a group of workers restoring a theater; St. Louis, to participate in a ribbon-cutting ceremony for a new annex to a building for elderly citizens; and Springfield, Massachusetts, to meet with school volunteers.

This trip, which she took in 1979, served two additional purposes. One was to act as the president's "eyes and ears."[30] Mrs. Carter could speak with average Americans, learn their concerns, and report back to her husband. The second was to identify programs worthy of federal support. In July 1978 Mrs. Carter had met with about 300 representatives from various local groups that provided training to disadvantaged individuals so that they could find work. In the process, she had been able to evaluate the effectiveness of those programs and identify any that were deserving of the U.S. government's help. Her trip in 1979 gave her a similar opportunity. Although the president was still determined to keep tight reins on spending, the first lady could no doubt convince him to loosen them up a bit—as she had done in the case of mental health—for programs that had merit.

One of the projects that the president and first lady found worthy of federal support—and one that became a personal favorite of hers—was Project Propinquity (known later as Cities in Schools, and then renamed Communities in Schools in 1996), founded in the early 1970s by Bill Milliken. A devout Christian, Milliken had longstanding ties with the Carters. In the 1960s he had moved from New York City to Georgia, where he met Clarence Jordan, the uncle of Hamilton Jordan, one of President Carter's chief aides. Clarence, who led an interracial religious commune near the Carters' hometown of Plains, reinforced Milliken's own religious beliefs. The purpose of Project Propinquity was to help youth living in impoverished areas stay in school and to provide assistance to those who had dropped out or who had emotional problems or learning disabilities. Unfortunately, Milliken had trouble raising funds, so he turned to a friend, evangelist Ruth Carter Stapleton—Jimmy Carter's sister and Rosalynn's childhood friend. She arranged a meeting between her brother, who was then governor of Georgia, and Milliken. The Carters and Milliken hit it off, and with their help, he began to raise funds for his program. After Carter's election in 1976, Milliken found himself with access to the White House, including an office in the Executive Office Building. With Mrs. Carter's support, by 1977, he had raised nearly $3 million from U.S. government sources to help him finance Project Propinquity programs in Atlanta, New York, and Indianapolis, and he planned to expand the program to other cities. Indeed, as of 2007, the program had offices throughout the country.

Another of Mrs. Carter's favorite programs was Green Door, founded by Gail Marker and Ellen McPeake. Originating in Washington, D.C., its purpose was to take eligible mentally ill patients out of local hospitals and give them more normal lives. With the help of volunteers, these individuals obtained part-time jobs and housing, where they lived with fellow patients under supervision. The first lady, always desirous to help those with mental disabilities, quickly endorsed Green Door. By early 1979, Austin, Texas, had established a similar program. By 2006, Green Door had helped about 3,000 individuals in Washington, D.C., leave mental facilities and homeless shelters and lead more productive lives.

Mrs. Carter's interest in childhood immunization was an offshoot of her friendship with Betty Bumpers, the wife of Senator Dale Bumpers (D-Arkansas). Mrs. Bumpers had been working on a program to eliminate measles but had found little support in the Ford White House. She and Mrs. Carter began an intensive campaign to generate awareness of childhood illnesses and the importance of needing to immunize young children. By October 1979, the campaign had achieved its goal of immunizing 90 percent of all American children and all but eradicating measles; other childhood illnesses, such as diphtheria and tetanus, had been dramatically reduced. The first lady continued this program into her post–White House years.

If Mrs. Carter could claim success when it came to the mentally ill, the elderly, volunteerism, and childhood immunization, she had less luck with the final part of her agenda: passage of the ERA. The amendment's history began in 1923, when Alice Paul, a leader in the women's suffrage movement, drafted the document's language. Although women had obtained the right to vote in 1920, Paul argued that it did not guarantee women equal rights, thus necessitating her proposed addition to the Constitution. Adding an amendment required approval by two-thirds of both houses of Congress and ratification by three-fourths of the states. For almost fifty years, the efforts of the ERA's supporters had been fruitless, but that began to change in the 1960s: the number of women attending college increased; the 1963 Presidential Commission on the Status of Women found that, despite gains, women still faced discrimination both in education and in the workplace; and, most important, Betty Friedan's 1963 book *The Feminine Mystique* expressed the dissatisfaction that many women felt with an American culture that tried to relegate them to the home. All these factors played a part in the revitalization of the women's rights movement. That movement, along with elections between 1966 and 1970 that increased the number of female lawmakers supportive of women's equality, led Capitol Hill to give renewed attention to the ERA. In 1971 the proposed amendment reached the floor of the House of Representatives, where it was adopted; the following year, the Senate endorsed its language. Lawmakers then set a seven-year time limit for the amendment's ratification by the states, placing the deadline at 22 March 1979.

By the time Mrs. Carter became first lady, thirty-four states had already ratified the amendment. Thirty-eight was the magic number, but getting those last four states to vote in favor of the ERA was proving problematic. Matching the revived feminist movement was a new antifeminist campaign led by Phyllis Schlafly, a conservative political activist and founder of the organization STOP (Stop Taking Our Privileges) ERA. Schlafly contended that the ERA would subject women to the military draft, open the door to same-sex marriage, permit abortions, and take power away from the states. Mrs. Carter rejected those arguments. There was nothing in the amendment's language requiring women to be "drafted or forced to go to work." It would not force changes in "personal family relationships," nor did it endorse "unisex bathrooms [or] homosexual marriages." Rather, it would guarantee women equal rights. As she told one reporter, "To me the Equal Rights Amendment means that women have equal legal rights and should get equal pay for equal work. During my travels through the states I found some state laws where a woman could not even get auto insurance without a man's signature."[31]

Even before the inauguration, both Cade and Democratic officials had suggested that Mrs. Carter lobby lawmakers in those states where ratification of the amendment was coming up for consideration. In Indiana, for instance, the state senate was evenly divided over whether to endorse the amendment, prompting the state's Democratic senator, Birch Bayh, to call President-elect Carter and ask him to lobby for it. For some reason, Carter was unavailable, but Bayh did get hold of Rosalynn. She promptly contacted state senator Wayne Townsend, who was wavering on whether to endorse the amendment. The effort worked, and Indiana became the thirty-fifth state to ratify the ERA. Mrs. Carter had less luck convincing lawmakers in Virginia, Florida, and North Carolina to endorse the amendment. In fact, her phone calls caused some resentment among state officials, who did not appreciate her interference in their states' affairs.

Not surprisingly, the first lady's attempt to obtain passage of the ERA aroused anger among its opponents. In February 1977 Schlafly led a gathering of about 150 anti-ERA demonstrators outside the White House, charging that Mrs. Carter's phone calls violated Article V of the Constitution, which left the ratification of amendments to Congress and the state legislatures. More unexpected was that Mrs. Carter's work on behalf of the ERA did not generate widespread support for her among feminists. The relationship between Mrs. Carter and the feminist movement was strained in part because of the first lady's position on abortion. Both during and after the campaign, Mrs. Carter had declared that although she supported neither the overturning of *Roe v. Wade* (the 1973 Supreme Court decision that gave women the right to abortion) nor the passage of a constitutional amendment banning abortion, she was personally opposed to abortion because it violated her religious and moral beliefs. Feminists did not appreciate what they saw as only halfhearted support for such an important women's issue.

The first lady's image among feminists was not helped by her husband's apparent unwillingness to do more for women. Although he had a better record than any of his predecessors in terms of appointing women to high administrative posts, feminists believed that he had not gone far enough. Like his wife, the president personally abhorred abortion but was opposed to overturning *Roe*. However, he strictly enforced federal laws that limited the use of Medicaid funds to pay for abortions. In 1979 he fired Bella Abzug, an outspoken advocate of women's rights, whom he had appointed just the year before as cochair of the National Advisory Committee on Women (NACW). Mrs. Carter had opposed the appointment. Although both she and Abzug wanted the ERA to pass, the first lady feared that Abzug's outspokenness—which included publicly criticizing those who rejected its passage—would turn away potential support in states such as North Carolina and Florida. Ultimately, Abzug and the NACW angered Carter by criticizing his decision to increase defense spending while simultaneously cutting funding for social programs; they claimed that his actions would hurt those living in poverty, more than 60 percent of whom were women. In the end, even though Carter strongly supported the ERA, feminists believed that he relied too much on his wife rather than championing its ratification himself.

Added to all this was what feminists regarded as the first lady's overly traditional attitude toward gender relations. Mrs. Carter agreed that women had minds of their own and had the right to have their voices heard, and she repeatedly used her influence in the Oval Office to promote women's rights. But she refused to publicly disagree with her husband on issues that feminists regarded as important. Besides undermining any influence she might have over his decision making, the first lady contended, it would be "a tacky thing to do." Feminist Gloria Steinem rejected those arguments. "More than any other president's wife I have seen there is no independent thought or phrasing separate from his," she commented about Mrs. Carter. "I am disappointed in her altogether."[32] Overall, although feminists appreciated the first lady's efforts to get the ERA passed, they felt that she was not doing all she could for women.

This relationship between the first lady and the feminist movement reflected a problem that would plague Mrs. Carter throughout her tenure as first lady: image. Her predecessors had developed their images by focusing on one or two topics—environmentalism for Lady Bird Johnson, and volunteerism for Pat Nixon. Although Betty Ford's agenda had included at least three topics—the ERA, breast cancer, and substance abuse—the first two fell under the rubric of women's issues. It was impossible to do the same for Mrs. Carter, whose many projects were too diverse to place under one or two headings. Observers thus wondered what she was: a supporter of volunteerism? an advocate for the mentally ill? a proponent of women's rights? No one seemed to know. To Mrs. Carter, what mattered most was the success of her projects, whether that be passage of the Mental Health Systems Act or ratification of the ERA. She was less concerned with whether she came across to the public as a full-fledged feminist or a full-time volunteer.

Mrs. Carter also viewed her work as an extension of her husband's, and feminists had a problem with that attitude. How could she claim to be a supporter of the feminist agenda while never publicly disagreeing with her husband? How could a woman truly be equal if she saw herself as simply an extension of her spouse? Mrs.

Carter fought back by proclaiming that she had influence over her husband. "The President of the United States cares what I think," she told the New York Women in Communications in April 1979. She was also quick to point out everything Jimmy Carter had done for women: of the five female cabinet secretaries in U.S. history, he had appointed two; he had also named two of the four female undersecretaries, a total of fourteen assistant secretaries, and a number of other women to judgeships and ambassadorships.[33] Among other things, she could point to her own success at getting the military to allow women to serve in the White House military honor guard, to the president's support of the 1978 Pregnancy Discrimination Act, to his establishment of workshops to help female business owners obtain loans, and to his own determination to see the ERA passed. Nevertheless, feminists believed that the president only halfheartedly supported their agenda, and although they respected Mrs. Carter's efforts, they never really considered her one of them.

The first lady had no intention of allowing questions about her image stop her from seeing the ERA passed. In November 1977 she spoke before the National Women's Conference, urging the amendment's ratification. During 1978 she met with the wives of U.S. senators, lobbied for the amendment in Illinois, and issued a statement on Women's Equality Day. The following year, she discussed ratification of the amendment with representatives from the Religious Committee for the ERA and with Oklahoma state legislators, and she met with officials from a number of women's groups who were holding talks with Sarah Weddington, the president's special assistant for women's affairs.

These endeavors did not bear fruit. Failure to ratify the amendment in states such as Virginia and Florida led the National Organization for Women to fear that the 22 March 1979 deadline would not be met. Hoping to get the deadline extended, Mrs. Carter called lawmakers and urged women inside the government to push for an extension. Both the president and vice president joined this effort, and in October 1978 Congress extended the deadline to 1982, yet the ERA still failed to pass. Mrs. Carter called it the "greatest disappointment" among her White House projects.[34]

The question has been raised whether Mrs. Carter could have been more successful had she focused solely on one or two projects rather than several. Commented journalist Sally Quinn in June 1978, Mrs. Carter "has taken on one project after another, then dropped it and gone on to something else. The only one she has concentrated on is mental health."[35] It was true that the first lady had involved herself in several initiatives, unlike the vice president's wife, Joan, who focused solely on the arts. But Mrs. Carter did not drop one project and replace it with another. Hoyt had suggested that the first lady spend the equivalent of two days a week on her projects, but Mrs. Carter usually devoted about sixty hours to them each week. She also met with her senior staff once a week and the full staff once a month, allowing her to keep up-to-date on her agenda.

Tied to the criticism that Mrs. Carter tried to do too much was the observation that she had insufficient staff, and this point has some merit. In any situation, it takes time for staff members to get to know their boss, and this was true in the East Wing. For instance, it took a while to determine what information the first lady needed immediately and what could wait. Mrs. Carter and her staff eventually developed a procedure by which the most important items were red-tagged. Yet even with a paid contingent of twenty-one, as well as volunteers, there was only so much that the members of the East Wing staff could accomplish. They had to deal with an enormous amount of correspondence, averaging more than 500 letters a week. Some staffers complained that they were overworked, while others felt that Mrs. Carter was so busy that she was distant from them. The first lady herself blamed her staff "for not getting the word out more on her projects."[36] Hoyt commented in early 1978, "we simply do not have enough people to keep up with what Mrs. Carter does. In fact, we could do with about double the number of people we have here now."[37] But hiring more staff was out of the question. Mrs. Carter had already been criticized by some observers for having an overly large staff—a rather spurious argument, considering that Mrs. Ford had employed about twenty-six full-time staffers and Mrs. Kennedy as many as forty (more than any other first lady in American history). Further, the president surely would have rejected the hiring of more staff as too costly. Adding to the problem was high turnover: Ann Anderson, the first lady's deputy press secretary, left her post in August 1978 because of the long hours demanded of her; by early 1979, half of the original eighteen staffers had quit. If the first lady herself could complain that she lacked enough time to devote to her projects, it was certainly possible that her staff found it just as difficult to do so, in light of all their other responsibilities.

Even if the first lady had focused on only one or two issues and been given all the staffers she wanted, there was no guarantee that she would have achieved her goals. The ERA is a case in point. The amendment's opponents had several things going for them, the first of which was funding. Various businesspersons, including the owners of Coors and Amway; conservative organizations such as the Birch Society and the American Legion; and fundamentalist religious leaders all provided financial support to Schlafly's cause. Second, they could rely on coverage by the media, which felt obligated to give equal time to both the ERA's advocates and its opponents. Third, the anti-ERA movement had a much better grassroots organization, including antiabortion forces. Finally, the amendment's antagonists could point to any number of reasons why its passage would prove more harmful than good to women and to American society in general. When the ERA's supporters suggested that the amendment's ratification would allow women to serve in the military, its opponents charged that women could then find themselves in combat. If that accusation failed to arouse public condemnation, the ERA's adversaries could argue that the amendment would promote homosexuality, permit abortion, or lead to unisex bathrooms.[38] To overcome such a well-organized campaign with access to such a wide variety of arguments would have been arduous, even if the first lady had given all her attention to the ERA's passage.

What it came down to was that Rosalynn Carter was who she was. Giving up parts of her agenda to achieve a more focused program would have meant ignoring issues that were important to her and to her vision of a more caring country. It also would have meant leaving unaddressed matters that, if handled well, would reflect positively on her husband's presidency. In short, as Hoyt explained, had Mrs. Carter limited herself to just one or two issues, "we would have had a very unhappy first lady" who "would have felt unfulfilled."[39] Perhaps what is most impressive is that Mrs. Carter actually succeeded in accomplishing so much.

CHAPTER 3

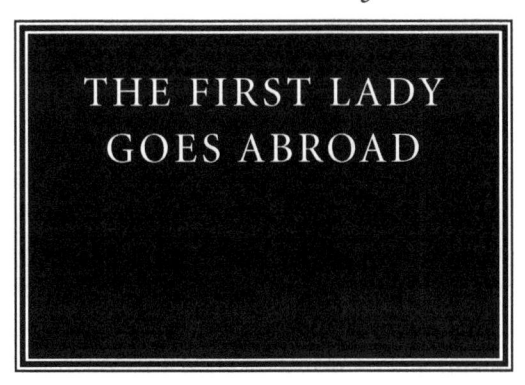

THE FIRST LADY GOES ABROAD

In addition to playing a significant role in the realm of U.S. domestic policy, Rosalynn Carter became a prominent participant in Jimmy Carter's foreign policy during her travels abroad. For a first lady to travel abroad was nothing new. Eleanor Roosevelt had inspected U.S. troops during World War II, Lady Bird Johnson had attended the funeral of the king of Greece, and Pat Nixon had traveled to Peru to witness relief efforts for earthquake victims there. Yet in each case, the first lady had traveled either with her husband or alone on a goodwill mission. In none of these cases did the first lady hold substantive discussions on matters of policy.

Rosalynn Carter was different. Like her predecessors, she too joined her husband on various trips or traveled alone as his personal representative. Unlike previous first ladies, however, Mrs. Carter's trip to Latin America in 1977 involved the discussion of serious policy issues with foreign heads of state. In addition, she acted as one of the president's key advisers, listening to his concerns and suggesting how he might respond to particular situations. Although he did not always take her advice, he often did. Mrs. Carter's diplomatic activity made her the target of criticism from both those who argued that she was overstepping the boundaries of her office and those who believed that she was not going far enough.

Since the end of World War II, U.S. foreign policy had focused primarily on relations between the West and the East. Jimmy Carter was determined to shift America's focus from East-West relations to those between the North and the South—that is, between the United States and less-developed nations. Among the regions of the third world, Latin America was of particular interest to the incoming president. Carter spoke Spanish, and as governor of Georgia he had sought to strengthen ties between his state and the nations of Central and South America. Moreover, he felt that the United States' historically paternalistic attitude toward Latin America had bred resentment among its southern neighbors. The first lady shared her husband's interest in Latin America. She had traveled with him to that part of the world, and though not fluent in the language, she had begun taking Spanish lessons after he became president.

That the Carters believed in giving more emphasis to U.S.-Latin American relations became clear even before the inauguration. In December 1976 Rosalynn joined a U.S. delegation led by Secretary of State Henry Kissinger that traveled to Mexico for the swearing in of that country's new president, José López Portillo. President-elect Carter was busy setting up his government and could not attend, but by having his wife go, he intended to send two messages. First, he wanted to show his preparedness to use Rosalynn as his personal representative on missions abroad, and second, he wanted to demonstrate his determination to develop a closer relationship with the United States' neighbors to the south. The new Mexican president understood the importance of Mrs. Carter's visit and honored her at a dinner prior to his inauguration.

But what would become the first lady's most important and most widely covered trip took place five months later, when she traveled to several nations in Latin America. The idea had been her husband's. President Carter had proved to be even more ambitious than his wife when it came to establishing broad-based initiatives. His proposals included promoting human rights around the world, signing a Strategic Arms Limitation Treaty (SALT) with the Soviet Union, achieving a comprehensive Middle East peace settlement, returning the Panama Canal to Panama, stopping the proliferation of nuclear technology, and normalizing relations with China. He also wanted to travel to Latin America to emphasize his desire to strengthen intrahemispheric ties. However, during the first months of his administration, the only trip his schedule permitted was to London to attend an economic summit in May. Accordingly, he asked Rosalynn to travel to the Caribbean and South America as his personal representative, and she immediately agreed to go.

The White House made it clear that this was not simply a goodwill mission; it would involve the discussion of substantive matters. That the president would send a woman, let alone someone who was not an expert in inter-American affairs, led to widespread criticism. State Department experts on Latin America believed that it was their job to maintain cordial relations with the nations of that region and feared that the first lady might damage their work. Representative Dante Fascell (D-Florida) declared, "The Latinos are macho and they hate gringos and women. What else do you want to know?" The *Washington Post* noted that Brazilian officials were "almost offended" when they learned that Carter had decided to send his wife, and "a Latin American diplomat [in Washington] (not from Brazil)" proclaimed it "'absurd' to think that a woman, particularly one with no expertise, could hold substantive discussions on hemispheric problems." Another Latin American diplomat commented, "If we were not so used to insults from the United States, we would make more of the insult and gall of a United States president sending his wife to talk with us."[1]

The Carters had no intention of allowing such criticism to derail the trip. The White House planned to send the first lady to seven nations: Jamaica, Costa Rica, Ecuador, Peru, Brazil, Colombia, and Venezuela. These particular countries had been chosen for several reasons. First, all were democracies or at least appeared to be headed in that direction. Second, by excluding states led by repressive, authoritarian regimes—such as Argentina, Chile, and Uruguay—the United States would be sending a message that it would not tolerate nations that violated the human rights of their people. Finally, the White House held that the Ford administration had not been supportive of countries such as Jamaica because, though democracies, they were leftist in orientation. The Carter administration hoped to show that it viewed Jamaica as a possible friend rather than a foe.

To prepare the first lady, administration officials and scholars from around the country gave her twenty-six hours of briefings. She received information on the culture, politics, and history of each nation she would be visiting.[2] Mrs. Carter also began sitting in on the president's daily foreign policy briefings by national security adviser Zbigniew Brzezinski. Interestingly, although Brzezinski was one of the individuals who prepared Mrs. Carter, he had concerns about the briefings, believing that the information might be more than she could handle.[3] Mrs. Carter proved him wrong, however. She took extensive notes, and when she was not in these briefing sessions or studying Spanish, she read as much as she could on Latin America to further prepare herself.

The first lady also sought recommendations on what approach she should take in the Latin American countries she visited. Following one briefing, she raised this matter with Jerome Levinson, counsel to the Senate Subcommittee on Foreign Economic Policy. Levinson told her that the trip had to be more than just symbolic. He advised her to avoid discussing matters that even the experts had been unable to resolve, such as U.S. tariffs on imports, and instead focus on the president's commitment to democracy and human rights. Although she would no doubt be accused of interfering in other countries' internal affairs, she could try to avoid that charge by being careful how she posed her questions. He ended by asking her, "How would you want the *New York Times* to summarize the outcome of your trip?"[4]

Mrs. Carter left on 30 May with Robert Pastor, the Latin American expert on the National Security Council (NSC); Assistant Secretary for Inter-American Affairs Terence Todman; Gay Vance, the wife of Secretary of State Cyrus Vance; and several individuals from the East Wing: chief of protocol Kit Dobelle, press secretary Mary Hoyt, and Rosalynn's personal assistant, Madeline MacBean. Their first stop was Jamaica, where the first lady held talks with Prime Minister Norman Manley. At the time, Jamaica was in the midst of a serious financial crisis generated by declines in both tourism and the sale of bauxite (a mineral used to make aluminum); to make matters worse, the country had to buy nearly all its oil from foreign sources. The result was a $350 million trade deficit in 1976 and an unemployment rate of at least 25 percent. Manley had sought U.S. financial help, but his leftist leanings and his favorable view of the communist leader of Cuba, Fidel Castro, had led the

President Carter seeing Rosalynn off on her trip to Latin America, May 1977. Courtesy of the Jimmy Carter Library.

Ford administration to view him with suspicion. Although Manley had calculated that his nation needed $250 million a year in economic aid, during the previous five years, the United States had provided a total of only $41 million.

When he spoke with Mrs. Carter, Manley explained that he had sought economic aid from Cuba because of the United States' unwillingness to provide him with sufficient funds. He even defended

Castro, denying U.S. charges that the Cuban leader was trying to spread communism to other countries. It was true, he admitted, that Cuba had sent troops to the African nation of Angola to help its leftist government, but Manley contended that that decision had been made in response to an invasion of Angola by South Africa. Mrs. Carter pointed out that the Cuban troops had left for Africa *before* South Africa's invasion. When Manley urged the United States to normalize relations with Cuba, Mrs. Carter replied that although such a policy was under consideration, Cuba's actions in Africa and its human rights violations would prevent normalization from taking place.

Despite their disagreements, the Jamaican prime minister was impressed not only with Mrs. Carter's knowledge of U.S. policy but also with the Carter administration's desire to improve U.S.–Latin American relations. He commented that with the change of government in the United States, "things were going to get better." The first lady understood the significance of that statement: "I realized that he was wooing me so I would put in a good word for him when I got back to Washington." It became clear that Manley viewed Mrs. Carter as someone who could speak with authority and who would present his concerns to the White House. Additionally, she believed that the prime minister really wanted closer ties with the United States. During a break, Mrs. Carter, MacBean, and Hoyt went to the women's restroom, where they passed notes to one another on a matchbook. "His economy is crumbling," wrote the first lady. Not only did Manley desire "$ from the U.S.," but he also wanted "to break away from Cuba." Mrs. Carter sent her findings to both her husband and the State Department, which would become her routine in each nation she visited.[5]

In addition to maintaining daily contact with the president, Mrs. Carter held meetings each morning with Pastor and Todman to discuss where they stood and to prepare for that day's talks. At times, she caused the assistant secretary some consternation. Todman recalled that he had told Pastor that, of the two of them (Todman and the first lady), he had been confirmed by the Senate and, as such, "if there ever came to be any issue where a final decision had to be made, I was going to make it."[6] But the first lady was clearly in charge, and she showed a readiness to go over the heads of Todman and the State Department. As Pastor explained: "Sometimes [Rosalynn] would ask me, 'Well, what's our policy on this subject?' and I would say, 'Well, to be honest, the policy is in the process of being made.' She said, 'Well, what do you mean by that?' 'I mean, you know, the State Department and the NSC are working on it, but we haven't put the proposal back before the president yet, so we don't really have a distinct policy.' She said, 'Well, tell me what the issue is and what you think should be done.'" Then Mrs. Carter would call her husband, inform him of the situation, and get him to explain what the policy was. When she would mention the new policy in her conversations with the leader at hand, State Department officials—including, no doubt, Todman—would challenge her, stating that there was no policy on that particular issue. She would reply, according to Pastor, "'Well, my understanding is the president makes policy, and he told me that this was his policy today. Do you have any problem with that?' and that sort of stopped them."[7]

Mrs. Carter's next stop was Costa Rica, where she was to meet with President Daniel Oduber. When she arrived, she found that he had invited his wife, suggesting that "he expected my visit to be a social one." And when she asked him questions, she noticed that he responded "to the men in our party."[8] The first lady, however, refused to be deterred, and after a time, Oduber began to talk to her directly. Like Manley, Oduber stressed his nation's economic problems. Although Costa Rica provided more beef, bananas, and coffee to the United States than any other Latin American nation, the White House had placed restrictions on Costa Rican imports, giving countries such as New Zealand and Australia "preferential treatment." Oduber also criticized the Carter administration's human rights policy, arguing that the White House should focus on rewarding those nations that upheld the rights of their people rather than chastising those that did not. One way of doing that would be to offer countries that supported human rights better trade agreements and economic aid. Following further discussion of trade matters, Oduber asked the first lady to tell her husband that a decline in the price of coffee could hurt the Costa Rican economy.[9]

Despite Oduber's initial rigidity, the meeting had gone well, but Mrs. Carter was upset when afterward the press focused most of its questions on Robert Vesco. A few years earlier, Vesco, an American financier, had been accused by the U.S. government of embezzling more than $200 million, prompting him to flee to Costa Rica. The first lady had purposely avoided being briefed on the Vesco affair, "so I could legitimately claim ignorance of the situation." Mrs. Carter considered the Vesco case a matter for the judicial system, and she explained to the reporters that she had no knowledge of the matter.[10]

Crowds of supporters had met Mrs. Carter in both Jamaica and Costa Rica, but such was not the case in Ecuador, where about 200 student demonstrators threw rocks, tires, and dirt at police, shouting, "Rosalynn Carter, go home!" and "Yankees want to reinforce their imperialism."[11] Unlike Jamaica and Costa Rica, Ecuador was led by a military junta, and after a review of the troops, the first lady headed to her meeting with the nation's military leadership. Mrs. Carter's objectives in Ecuador included an expression of American support for the regime's promise to return to democracy and an apology for the Ford administration's withdrawal of preferential trade benefits. (In 1973 the Organization of Petroleum Exporting Countries [OPEC] had imposed an embargo on oil shipments to the United States, and the White House had responded by withdrawing trade benefits to OPEC countries; Ecuador, though not a member of OPEC, had accidentally been included in the list of nations punished.) What Mrs. Carter found in Quito, however, was a rather acrimonious reception. Ecuadoran leaders were particularly irked by the Carter administration's decision to block the sale of two dozen Israeli Kfir fighter jets to Ecuador (because the Kfir had an American-made engine, this was within the president's purview). This was part of Carter's initiative to curb international arms sales, because the proliferation of weaponry only encouraged conflicts abroad. Ecuador had a long-standing feud with its neighbor, Peru. As a result of a war a century earlier, Ecuador had been forced to cede land to Peru; more recently, oil had been discovered in Ecuador, near the Peruvian border. Meanwhile, Peru was building up its military might with the help of the Soviet Union, and the Ecuadoran government viewed the White House's refusal to permit the Kfir sale not only as interfering in its internal affairs but also as endangering the country's security. What was supposed to have been a ninety-minute discussion lasted more than three hours. Each of the junta members requested weapons from the United States. They also talked about the United States helping Ecuador to develop "an effective air surveillance system" in lieu of offensive arms. The first lady promised to explain the Ecuadorans' concerns not only to her husband but also to the Peruvian leadership, and she praised the junta's plan to move its nation toward democracy. By the time she left Ecuador, she had developed a more cordial relationship with that country's leaders.[12]

From Ecuador, Mrs. Carter traveled to Peru, where she met with the military leader of that nation, General Francisco Morales Bermúdez. Mrs. Carter began by raising the administration's concerns about human rights and the prevention of war, and as promised, she passed on Ecuador's anxiety over Peru's military buildup. Apparently, Morales Bermúdez, like most of the Latin American officials she met with, had not anticipated a discussion of serious issues. Pastor recalled, however, that after Mrs. Carter began her statement, "Morales Bermúdez got up. He went to his desk, which was on the other side of the room, opened it up, and took out some detailed notes. Then he came back and said, 'I wasn't sure what kind of meeting this would be, whether it would be social or policy, but I prepared for policy, and now I can see it is.'" The Peruvian president then defended his nation's position on human rights, pointed to past troubles with Chile and Colombia to justify his arms buildup, and contended that the war with Ecuador had been the result of aggression on Quito's part. He declared that Peru's acquisition of weaponry was for defensive purposes only. Although it was true that Lima had obtained arms from the Soviet Union, that was only because Washington had rejected Peru's requests for weapons. When the first lady asked Morales Bermúdez to "send a clear signal, a demonstration that your intentions are defensive and not aggressive," the Peruvian leader replied only that meetings with Chilean and Ecuadoran officials had taken place. But he refused to stop his arms buildup.[13] The meeting ended with some discussion of the drug trade and prisoners being held in Peruvian jails. Morales Bermúdez stated that his government was attempting to stop the illicit drug trade, and as for the prisoners, he said, "They are all drug trafficers [sic] about to be tried." Although Mrs. Carter may not have been happy with that response, she was generally pleased with her encounter with the Peruvian head of state. "Of all the leaders I met on the trip," she later wrote, "I liked Morales Bermúdez the best," referring to him as "my favorite dictator."[14]

Mrs. Carter was proving herself an able diplomat. Early in the trip, there had been questions about her right to represent her husband in an official capacity. The first lady became angry after a reporter in Costa Rica asked her "what authority she had to speak for President Carter," prompting her declare that she was "the person closest to" him. But by the time she had completed her meetings in Peru, much of the original skepticism had disappeared. Newspapers in each of the countries she had visited, including Jamaica's *Daily News,* Costa Rica's *La Nación* and *Excelsior,* and Peru's *La Cronica* and *Correo,* gave her positive reviews. The *Washington Post,* for its part, reported that Rosalynn Carter was "wowing them in Latin America."[15]

Members of her delegation were also impressed. Todman and Pastor agreed that although the first lady had been nervous initially, she quickly found her confidence and demonstrated her abilities as a negotiator. "I have never," recalled Todman, "seen anyone prepare more seriously for anything than she did, for *every meeting.*" When Todman, Pastor, and Mrs. Carter met each morning to discuss the day's upcoming talks, "she would have gone over all the briefing papers again the night before so that she had questions and comments about every single thing. She's one of the hardest working people that I know."[16]

The first lady's next stop, Brazil, would be the most difficult. Relations between the United States and Brazil had become very tense, partly because of President Carter's human rights policy and the administration's denunciation of continued repression in Brazil, despite that country's pledge to restore democracy. When the State Department issued a report condemning the state of human rights in Brazil, the government of President Ernesto Geisel rejected a plan to purchase $50 million in military wares from the United States and canceled a military aid agreement with Washington. Another reason for the tension concerned President Carter's policy of nuclear nonproliferation. Since World War II, at least six countries had obtained nuclear weapons, India being the most recent in 1974. The president, whose navy background in atomic submarines gave him an understanding of nuclear power, wanted to prevent other nations from developing a nuclear capability. Accordingly, he opposed the West

German sale of a $4.7 billion nuclear power plant to Brazil. Not only did the proposed transaction violate the Nuclear Nonproliferation Treaty, he maintained, but Brasilia could use the facility to develop an atomic bomb. West Germany claimed that the sale did not violate the treaty; Brazil, which imported 80 percent of its oil, declared that it needed the plant to generate power; and both nations charged the U.S. president with interfering in their internal affairs.[17]

Nor did the Brazilian press think much of the first lady's visit. The São Paulo newspaper *O Estado* declared that "Mrs. Carter will lack the indispensable experience to negotiate with [Brazilian] authorities who have a tradition of negotiators which dates back to imperial times." Meanwhile, the *Folha de São Paulo* contended that "Todman and Pastor will be in charge of the real political discussions."[18]

Mrs. Carter arrived in Brazil on 6 June. She first met President Geisel, raising the issue of the nuclear plant. He refused to budge, insisting that he needed the facility to help Brazil meet its energy needs. He also rejected the first lady's request that Brasilia sign the Treaty of Tlatelolco. That treaty, signed in the late 1960s by a large number of Latin American countries, vowed to keep their part of the world free of nuclear weapons. Geisel said that he would not sign Tlatelolco until Brazil's neighbor, Argentina, ratified it. And he refused to endorse the American Convention on Human Rights, charging that it might allow other countries in Latin America to interfere in his country's policies. "In other words," Mrs. Carter later wrote, "they feared inspection of their human rights abuses." A discussion with Foreign Minister Antonio Azeredo da Silveira had the same result. Despite her failure to achieve any breakthroughs, the first lady's knowledge of the pertinent issues again made an impression. "I answered with some frankness questions I wouldn't have if she hadn't brought up the subjects," Silveira stated after Mrs. Carter's departure.[19]

Although Mrs. Carter's negotiating abilities had impressed Todman, her discussions with Geisel concerned the U.S. ambassador to Brazil, John H. Crimmins. During a dinner with the Brazilian president, MacBean told Mrs. Carter in private that Crimmins thought she "was pressing [Geisel] too hard" and asked whether she might engage in "light dinner conversation instead." The first lady agreed, but later, Geisel "continued on the same subject." Ultimately, the Brazilian president and Mrs. Carter "agreed to disagree."[20]

Despite her inability to move the Brazilian leadership, the first lady had no intention of backing down in demonstrating her concern about the situation in Brazil. When a group of university students gave her a letter charging the military government with human rights abuses, she promised to pass it on to her husband. She also arranged a meeting with two American missionaries, Thomas Capuano and the Reverend Lawrence Rosebaugh, who had been arrested by the government for "associating with delinquents." Although they had been released after a few days, they charged the government with maltreatment during their incarceration.[21]

From Brazil, Mrs. Carter headed to Colombia, where her talks focused primarily on the drug trade. Colombia supplied much of the marijuana and cocaine that came into the United States, and U.S. intelligence had information that a high-level official in the Colombian government was involved in that trade. Prior to her meeting with President Alfonso López Michelson, the first lady met with Todman and officials from the U.S. Drug Enforcement Administration and the U.S. embassy in Bogota regarding a Colombian request for helicopters to fight the drug trade. Mrs. Carter explained that her husband believed that "President López is turning his head to the corruption" in his government and that the United States should not provide him with "the helicopters until he demonstrates he is willing to do something." That comment immediately aroused concern among the embassy personnel, who concluded that an unwillingness to work with the Colombian government would lead a refusal to cooperate on Bogota's part.[22]

Having heard that López could be rather touchy, the first lady knew that she had to approach the issue of the drug trade carefully. Moreover, she was not sure how much the Colombian president really knew about the corruption in his government. When she raised the subject of narcotics, López explained that he had asked the United States for help in battling the problem, including the request for helicopters. Mrs. Carter pointed out the potentially corrupting influence the drug trade could have on the Colombian government and the need for their two countries to cooperate in solving the problem. López simply replied that it was an issue that should have been addressed years earlier. Realizing that she was getting nowhere, Mrs. Carter decided to drop the subject and leave further discussions of the drug trade to other U.S. officials.

Mrs. Carter also broached the issue of some sixty Americans incarcerated in Colombia on drug charges and the case of Richard Starr, a U.S. national whom Colombian guerrillas had captured. López stated that the jailed Americans were among some 8,000 cases pending and that the Colombian legal system was working as quickly as it could. As for Starr, he declared that sending soldiers to find him might actually make Starr's situation worse. (The guerrillas would finally free Starr in 1980.) Despite this response, the conversation ended on a high note when López praised a U.S. decision to ease restrictions on Colombian imports.

Mrs. Carter was finding acceptance among the leaders she met. Prior to her departure, López held a reception for her. Originally intended only for wives, by the time of the get-together, the guest list had been expanded to include both Colombian government ministers and U.S. officials. The State Department noted that this "reflected the growing Colombian realization that Mrs. Carter's tour is substantive and serious and not a flying coffee klatsch."[23]

The first lady viewed her trip to Venezuela, her final stop, as relatively informal, with the major purpose being to set the stage for her husband's visit a few weeks later. President Andrés Pérez strongly supported President Carter's administration and spoke highly of Mrs. Carter's trip. He did, however, protest Washington's decision to withdraw preferential trade benefits from his nation because of the 1973 OPEC oil embargo (unlike Ecuador, Venezuela actually was a member of OPEC). Pérez pointed out that during the embargo, Venezuela had actually increased its petroleum shipments to the United States. Mrs. Carter promised to raise the issue with her husband, but she warned that Congress had strong feelings against OPEC, and she could not guarantee the reinstatement of trade benefits.

Although the Latin America trip had been interesting, if not exhilarating, the first lady and her entourage were exhausted by the time they arrived in Venezuela. Hoyt remembered "sleep-walk[ing]" through much of the discussions and festivities. Thus, they were no doubt happy to be heading home. On the way back to the United States, Mrs. Carter received a message from her husband. Although the president could be distant from those in his administration, he was a loving husband and father, and he had a light sense of humor.

"The President of the United States requests the honor of your presence for dinner tonight," the message said. Mrs. Carter smiled and showed it to those accompanying her on the flight. "The First Lady accepts with pleasure," her reply read.[24]

Mrs. Carter returned to the United States on 12 June. In some ways, her trip had been highly successful. Despite the initial skepticism both abroad and at home, she had turned out to be a well-informed and skillful negotiator with the ability to represent the policies of the Carter administration, and she had proved herself willing to challenge both her own advisers and the leaders with whom she met. The *New York Times* commented that the impression Mrs. Carter left with officials in Latin America was "a favorable one."[25] Indeed, when the Peruvian foreign minister visited the United States in 1978 and discovered that President Carter could not see him, he turned down a suggestion that he see Secretary of State Vance and asked instead to meet with the first lady.

The U.S. public felt similarly about Mrs. Carter's trip. White House pollster Pat Caddell found that 70 percent of Americans "rated her journey as excellent or good," and a Roper poll stated that over half of Americans considered it "appropriate for a First Lady to represent the country on a diplomatic mission"—numbers that led President Carter to write to his wife, "don't run against your husband!"[26]

In addition to its symbolic impact, Mrs. Carter's junket apparently had real effects. In July the administration decided to provide Colombia with nearly $4 million in aid, including three helicopters to help with drug interdiction. The president did not authorize this aid until after talking with his wife about her meetings in Colombia. Later that year, Washington announced a $63 million economic aid package for Jamaica; although this was part of a larger program to develop the Caribbean's economy, it is likely that the first lady's reports on her visit to Jamaica had an impact. In other areas, Mrs. Carter had less influence. In July 1977 the administration rejected another Israeli request to sell planes to Ecuador, and there is no evidence that Venezuela's trade benefits were restored during Carter's term in office.

Yet, as some scholars have noted, the trip may not have been as successful as the Carters had hoped. Despite the poll numbers at home and the first lady's positive reception in many of the countries she visited, there were also clear indications of opposition both domestically and internationally to the idea of sending a first lady abroad to discuss policy with foreign leaders. During the remainder of her husband's term in office, Mrs. Carter's trips were of a more traditional nature, with her role being one of goodwill ambassador. The first lady claimed that her subsequent failure to venture into the realm of official diplomacy was because her husband was "able to go himself." But it was more likely that the Carters were disappointed with the results of the first junket. That Mrs. Carter's successors have not engaged in a similar type of mission suggests that the American public is not yet ready to accept the first lady in such a role.[27]

In November Mrs. Carter returned to Mexico, this time to Ciudad Juarez, where she met with her Mexican counterpart, Carmen de López Portillo. As before, the purpose was to promote closer U.S.-Mexican relations. Specifically, the two women celebrated the tenth anniversary of the settlement of a long-standing dispute over the location of a portion of the U.S.-Mexico boundary and discussed improving cultural ties between the two countries.

The following month Mrs. Carter joined her husband on an overseas trip. Their first stop was Poland. After World War II, the Soviet Union had forced the countries of eastern Europe, including Poland, Hungary, Czechoslovakia, Romania, East Germany, and Bulgaria, to adopt communist-led governments. But this did not mean that these countries did Moscow's bidding. Over the years, each had developed varying degrees of independence from the Kremlin, and some had adopted domestic policies more liberal than those of the Soviet Union. In September the White House decided that to encourage further divisions between Moscow and its eastern European satellites, the United States would give preferential treatment to those eastern European countries that had become more independent from Moscow or had given their people greater freedom than the Soviet people enjoyed.

Among the countries slated to receive preferential treatment was Poland. Brzezinski, as a native of Poland, had a personal interest in that nation, but there were also indications of liberalization there. Consequently, the NSC adviser had encouraged the president to make a stop in Poland. While the president held talks with Polish officials, Brzezinski and the first lady met with Cardinal Stefan Wyszynski, who had been fighting to protect the religious rights of Catholics. Originally, Brzezinski had wanted to meet with the cardinal as a symbol of American support for him, but the U.S. embassy in Warsaw feared that such a gesture might anger the communist government; therefore, the NSC adviser and the president decided to keep the State Department in the dark and announce afterward that the meeting with the cardinal had taken place spontaneously. Upon hearing of the proposed engagement with Wyszynski, Mrs. Carter decided to accompany Brzezinski. At first, Wyszynski did not recognize her and assumed that she was the NSC adviser's wife, but when it became clear that she was the first lady of the United States, the cardinal became very excited at the symbolic importance of her visit. In the meantime, President Carter offered Poland additional economic aid and denounced the Soviet Union's decision to put new nuclear missiles in Europe.

The trip also took the first couple to India. While the president met with Prime Minister Morarji Desai to discuss issues such as nuclear nonproliferation, the first lady laid a wreath where Mohandas Gandhi had been cremated.

These visits to Mexico, Poland, and India did not receive much media attention or arouse the kind of controversy that the first lady's trip to Latin America did. No doubt, this was because the president led the U.S. delegation to Poland and India, focusing the attention on himself rather than his wife. Furthermore, it is likely that many Americans viewed Mrs. Carter's role during these visits as acceptable: taking part in symbolic meetings on cultural or human rights issues, as opposed to holding discussions with foreign leaders on matters of policy.

In fact, Mrs. Carter was in a no-win situation. Although her engaging in symbolic rather than substantive matters pleased many Americans, it upset feminists. This was exemplified by their reaction to events at the Carters' next stop: Saudi Arabia. Following Arab custom, as the Carters left the plane, Rosalynn followed behind her husband rather than walk alongside him. The National Organization for Women (NOW) immediately criticized her, charging that her doing so demeaned all women. Not everyone agreed with NOW, however. Wrote columnist Georgie Anne Geyer, "As a feminist, I'll probably have to be explaining this away for years, but I have to say that President and Mrs. Carter did the only right and possible thing.... I do not believe it incumbent upon the world to excuse us, like children, from the grace of good manners toward other cultures on formal occasions."[28] The administration denied that the first lady had been forced to walk behind her husband. "Mrs. Carter was never asked to walk 6 feet behind the President," Hoyt wrote to the first lady's director of correspondence, Rhonda Bush. "The President always precedes Mrs. Carter at state arrivals, both here and abroad." Hoyt recalled that NOW contended that Mrs. Carter's actions in Saudi Arabia "negate[d] her credibility in women's rights.... If this hullabaloo weren't so fatuous," Hoyt continued, "I'd be churlish enough to inquire why the women aren't happy to have a President's wife who is diligent and able."[29]

Criticism of the first lady's activities did not stop her determination to act as her husband's advocate, surrogate, and adviser. This became clear later in 1978, when she helped in the effort to achieve ratification of the Panama Canal treaties. Since the 1950s, Panama had been the site of protests against U.S. control of the canal. In 1974 Secretary of State Kissinger and Panama's president, Omar Torrijos, had agreed in principle to return the canal to Panama. However, no further progress had taken place prior to the 1976 election. During the campaign, Jimmy Carter had declared his unwillingness to turn the canal over to Panama, but after the election, he changed his mind. Giving the waterway to Panama was morally correct, he argued, and it would improve U.S. relations with Latin America. Yet the majority of Americans, as well as most of the senators who would have to ratify a canal treaty, opposed Carter, arguing that the waterway was U.S. property and should remain so. It was because of this strong opposition that Mrs. Carter had encouraged her husband to put off a Panama Canal agreement until his second term. The president listened, but he disagreed. "If securing a second term was more important to me than doing what needs to be done," he told her, "then I'd wait."[30]

With her husband determined to negotiate a canal treaty, Mrs. Carter set out to help him do it. During her trip to Latin America, she had encouraged the leaders she met to support any treaty, once it was signed. That was the easy part, because there was already widespread support in Latin America for turning the canal over to Panama. Such was not the case in the United States. In September 1977 the United States and Panama signed two treaties: one would transfer control of the canal to Panama at the end of 1999, and the other gave the United States the right to defend the waterway from external threats. U.S. public opinion ran two to one against the treaties; there was similar opposition in the Senate, where the treaties would have to be ratified. To change the minds of the public and the senators, the White House began an intense public-relations campaign to convince Americans to support the agreements. Meanwhile, the president called each and every senator—sometimes more than once—to get their endorsement. The first lady helped in both endeavors. The Carters hosted a luncheon to which they invited thousands of influential individuals who might be able to convince the senators to support the treaties. Mrs. Carter also called the wives of Senators Edward Zorinsky (D-Nebraska) and Paul Hatfield (D-Montana) and asked them to help change their husbands' minds. The White House's campaign worked. By February 1978 a Gallup poll found that a plurality of Americans supported the treaties. The following month, the Senate ratified the first treaty; the second was ratified in April. Whether Mrs. Carter had any impact on the Senate vote is not clear, but Hatfield did vote in favor of the treaties (Zorinsky did not). There is no indication that the first lady's intervention aroused any public anger—in fact, it is likely that few people outside of Washington even knew about it—yet the first lady remained a controversial figure.

In July President Carter traveled to West Germany for the Bonn Summit, where leaders from the industrialized countries discussed such matters as the depreciation of the U.S. dollar, oil consumption, and inflation. In the meantime, Rosalynn and Amy toured Beethoven's home, and Rosalynn indulged in some wine tasting. Little notice was taken of these activities, but that was not the case when Mrs. Carter headed the U.S. delegation to the funeral of Pope Paul VI in August. Despite Vice President Mondale's expressed desire to fill that role, Brzezinski informed the president that he and others in the White House favored the first lady. The media immediately questioned why the president or vice president did not lead the delegation, and the White House replied that the first lady was "the president's closest representative."[31] But that response did not end concerns that Mrs. Carter was again crossing the line and assuming inappropriate responsibilities. Mrs. Carter did not like such criticism, of course, but she had become used to it, and she had no intention of backing down and becoming a traditional first lady. Indeed, in September she played a role in one of the most important foreign policy initiatives of the Carter administration: the Camp David accords, which established peace between Israel and Egypt.

Since 1948, Israel and its Arab neighbors—Egypt, Syria, and Jordan—had fought four major wars. In one of those conflicts, the Six-Day War of 1967, Israel had captured the Sinai Peninsula and the Gaza Strip from Egypt, the West Bank from Jordan, and the Golan Heights from Syria. In addition, tens of thousands of Palestinians became refugees after that war, and many of them fled to the West Bank and the Gaza Strip. Shortly thereafter, the United Nations passed a resolution calling on Israel to withdraw from the occupied territories; it also encouraged Israel to permit Palestinian self-determination. As of 1976, neither issue had been settled. President Carter hoped to resolve both these matters, but he faced strong opposition from Israel, which did not want to relinquish the captured territories and feared giving autonomy to the Palestinians. Egyptian president Anwar Sadat sought a breakthrough in November 1977 when he proposed a bilateral peace treaty between Egypt and Israel, which he hoped would set the foundation for a more comprehensive peace agreement. The two countries, however, were unable to overcome their differences, and President Carter decided that direct intervention was needed. Mrs. Carter had once suggested bringing Sadat and Israeli prime minister Menachem Begin to the presidential retreat at Camp David, and the president raised that idea with her again. "Are you willing to be the scapegoat?" she asked him. "What else is new?" he answered. When he wondered out loud what would happen if his efforts failed, she told him, "You can guarantee that you won't fail if you don't try anything. You can also guarantee that you won't succeed."[32]

The talks began on 5 September, and Mrs. Carter got them off to a positive start. Recognizing the religious devotion of the three men, she suggested that they open the conference with a joint statement asking the world to pray for a successful result. Carter, Begin, and Sadat enthusiastically adopted the idea. They all appreciated as well the political implications of their declaration. Unfortunately, that encouraging beginning did not carry through to the rest of the negotiations, which lasted for thirteen days rather than the three days anticipated by Carter. Although the first lady did not actively participate in the discussions themselves, she kept records of whatever meetings she did attend—ultimately typing nearly 200 pages of notes. The president kept her informed of their daily progress, and she provided him with moral support when it seemed that the negotiations might fail. When it appeared that Begin and Sadat had come to an agreement, she encouraged Carter to get the Israeli and Egyptian leaders to sign the document immediately, rather than giving them time to possibly change their minds. On 17 September Mrs. Carter was at the White House attending to some business when she learned of the signing of the Camp David accords. With that news, she, Dobelle, and her social secretary, Gretchen Poston, contacted the cabinet and the White House staff and prepared for the signing ceremony, while Hoyt and Carter's press secretary Jody Powell informed the media.

The peace process was not complete yet, however. The Camp David accords called for Egypt and Israel to sign a peace agreement within three months, but the 17 December deadline passed with no treaty signed. President Carter again decided to put his reputation on the line. He flew to the two nations in March 1979, accompanied by his wife. As before, the president kept her informed of the negotiations' progress. Later that month, Egypt and Israel signed a peace agreement, and Israel promised to return the Sinai Peninsula to Egypt. Although the Camp David accords and the Egyptian-Israeli peace treaty had their weaknesses, including vague language regarding Palestinian autonomy, there is no doubt that they represented a major accomplishment of the Carter administration.

President Carter could celebrate another achievement in June 1979 when he and Soviet premier Leonid Brezhnev signed the SALT II agreement, which called for significant reductions in the nuclear arsenals of both countries. But Senate ratification of SALT was in doubt. Many members of the upper house were critical of the treaty's failure to cut the Soviets' fleet of heavy bombers and questioned the United States' ability to verify Moscow's compliance with the pact. SALT's ratification became even more unlikely when, in

President and Mrs. Carter; Israeli prime minister Menachem Begin and his wife, Aliza; and Egyptian president Anwar Sadat meet prior to the signing of the Camp David accords, September 1978. Courtesy of the Jimmy Carter Library.

August, Senator Frank Church (D-Idaho) announced the "discovery" of a brigade of Soviet combat troops in Cuba. Although Church had supported SALT, he was facing a strong conservative challenge to his Senate seat and, fearful of losing reelection, raised the issue of the Soviet troops.

In fact, there had been a brigade of Soviet troops in Cuba since 1962. But Church's announcement placed the administration on the defensive and revived long-standing differences between Vance and Brzezinski. From early on, these two top foreign policy advisers had competed for influence over the White House's diplomacy. For instance, Brzezinski favored the early normalization of relations with China, whereas Vance believed that this would upset the Soviet Union—which had a tense relationship with China—and undermine the possibility of a SALT agreement. In the current crisis, the secretary of state, determined to protect SALT, took a hard line on the brigade publicly, believing that a show of strength would get the

Senate behind the arms treaty. Privately, however, he supported a softer, diplomatic approach to defuse the crisis. Brzezinski, who had less faith in the Soviets' willingness to abide by a SALT agreement, advocated a stiffer private position. Although he stopped short of demanding that the Kremlin withdraw its troops, he wanted the brigade broken up and called for the White House to challenge Soviet activities around the world. Mrs. Carter supported Brzezinski's more hard-line stance. The president, in a speech to the country in October, took a middle, and contradictory, position, though one that mollified most observers who were concerned about the brigade. He declared that the Soviet force posed "a political challenge to the United States," but he pointed out that the greatest threat to the nation was the arms race, not the troops in Cuba. He also vowed to increase surveillance flights over Cuba.

That the first lady supported Brzezinski was telling. Both Jimmy and Rosalynn Carter were closer to the NSC adviser than to the secretary of state. Brzezinski had been an early supporter of Carter's bid for the presidency and had acted as one of his key campaign advisers, whereas Vance had backed the short-lived candidacy of Sargent Shriver, the former U.S. ambassador to France. Ultimately, Vance and the president never developed more than an acquaintanceship. In contrast, Brzezinski joined the Carters for movies at the White House; he and his wife, Muska, had Jimmy and Rosalynn over to their house for informal gatherings. The NSC adviser, Mrs. Carter later commented, "was excitement, and the State Department [head] was staid." She agreed with Brzezinski on the need to take a harder line toward the Soviet Union, commenting that she wished her husband would "be a little demagogic sometimes." Brzezinski, for his part, valued his relationship with the first lady, commenting in 1982 that her support had been vital in his ultimately successful fight with the State Department for influence in the Oval Office (a point that neither the president nor the first lady denied).[33]

In August the first lady went abroad again, this time to represent the president at the inauguration of Ecuadoran president Jaime Roldós Aguilera. But the trip that would garner real attention took place a few months later, when she traveled to Thailand to investigate the conditions of refugee camps there. The situation in Thailand dated back to 1975, when the communist Khmer Rouge had seized power in Cambodia. Their leader, Pol Pot, had systematically killed at least a million Cambodians, while simultaneously intensifying a border dispute with Vietnam. In January 1979 the Vietnamese invaded Cambodia, forced Pol Pot out of power, and installed their own puppet government. The Khmer Rouge fled to the western part of Cambodia, along the Thai border, while tens of thousands of Cambodians trekked into eastern Thailand. As the media devoted more and more attention to the plight of the Cambodian refugees, the Carters discussed whether the United States could provide assistance. Around November, the first lady met with Hoyt, Cade, and Jane Fenderson, her appointments secretary, to discuss the situation, and Mrs. Carter decided to go to Southeast Asia to see the situation firsthand and then determine what needed to be done.[34] Similar to her trip to Latin America, Mrs. Carter was briefed beforehand by State Department and White House officials about the situation in Southeast Asia and specifically about the causes of the refugee crisis. She also learned that the Thai prime minister, Chamanand Kriangsak, had agreed to admit all refugees to Thailand—a decision that had upset many of his countrymen.

The first lady left on 9 November with Hoyt and a group of advisers. "Nothing," she later wrote, "had prepared me for the human suffering I saw in the refugee camps when I arrived." Visiting the Sakeo refugee camp, she encountered shelters made of plastic bags, the putrid smell of human excrement, and thousands of people dying from illness and malnutrition. Some people needed assistance to get to the ditches used as latrines. Relief agencies had sent volunteers, but they could not cope with the situation. Mrs. Carter kept her composure, but she recalled feeling "momentarily paralyzed by the magnitude of the suffering." She met one woman who had lost her husband and all her children. While at the camp, the first lady held a small baby; as she was departing, she learned that the baby had died.[35]

Mrs. Carter also visited two other sites: the Ubon refugee camp, populated by Laotians who had been there for about three years, and the Lumpini Transit Center in Bangkok, where emigrants passed through before leaving the country. Although the Thai authorities had cleaned up Lumpini prior to the first lady's arrival, she remembered it being "filthy."[36] Mrs. Carter then met the king of

In November 1979 the first lady visited the Sakeo refugee camp in Thailand. "Nothing," she later wrote, "had prepared me for the human suffering I saw." Courtesy of the Jimmy Carter Library.

Thailand, Phumiphol Aduldet, who had opposed Kriangsak's decision to allow the refugees into his country. She tried to convince him to open additional refugee camps, but the king seemed to be more interested in getting rid of his prime minister than in admitting more people. She then held discussions with officials from various international relief and volunteer organizations. Although these groups had agreed to cooperate to deal with the refugee crisis, there were serious logistical problems. Some groups lacked particular items, such as trucks to carry supplies, and there was a shortage of bridges, barges, and unloading equipment, making it hard to deliver the materials that were available.

On the way home, Mrs. Carter prepared a report of what she had seen. In addition to calling for more international support for the Thai government, she made a number of recommendations for the United States, including providing funds so the camps could purchase the food and services they required, beginning an airlift to assist the refugees, getting the United Nations Human Rights Commission to build new facilities for refugee emigration, increasing the number of volunteers assigned to the relief effort, and appointing a coordinator for refugee affairs to oversee the relief program. Once she arrived home, the first lady took action. She contacted UN Secretary-General Kurt Waldheim and asked him to appoint someone to coordinate the international relief effort; shortly thereafter, he named Sir Robert Jackson to that post. On 13 November President Carter called on the U.S. government, private organizations, and other countries to do more to help the Cambodian refugees. Meanwhile, Mrs. Carter gave speeches, made appeals on television, and testified before the Council on Foreign Relations.

The impact of these efforts was almost immediate. The president, assured of bipartisan congressional support, called for $69 million in aid for the refugees, with an additional $30 million if necessary. The U.S. government increased its yearly quota of refugees from Thailand. Notre Dame University president Father Theodore Hesburgh and representatives from more than forty American volunteer groups formed the National Cambodia Crisis Committee (NCCC), which sought to raise money from private sources to help the refugees. Various corporations, including Bristol Meyers and International Telephone and Telegraph, offered assistance, as did labor unions and individual Americans. The city of Rancho Mirage, California, raised $25,000, and the governor of Iowa, Robert D. Ray, established a relief program that raised more than $500,000. One boy even sent his allowance: 15 cents.

The international attention had a positive effect in the camps. Mike Blumenthal, the former treasury secretary, reported that the first lady's concerns had "brought a lasting improvement." In May 1980 Cade attended a conference in Geneva, Switzerland, where the attendees pledged enough money "to support relief activities through August with reasonable expectation that it can be sustained through the end of the year."[37] In the end, Mrs. Carter's trip and calls for help led the NCCC to raise $70 million from private sources, with another $120 million coming from the U.S. government and $300 million from foreign countries.

As Mrs. Carter worked on behalf of the Cambodian refugees, she kept informed about the administration's other foreign policy initiatives. During 1979, one matter that consumed an enormous amount of White House attention was the worsening situation in Iran. For decades, the United States had supported the government of the shah of Iran, Mohammad Reza Pahlavi. By the time Carter took office, however, the shah faced growing unrest. Although his economic policies had helped the Iranian economy to grow, they had also caused inflation. Moreover, the middle class derived little benefit from that economic growth, which bred resentment. Islamic fundamentalists, for their part, disliked the shah's willingness to bring Western ways into Iran, including styles of dress and the right to vote for women. Finally, many Iranians disapproved of Pahlavi's repressive rule, particularly his use of a secret police force called SAVAK (in English, the Organization for Intelligence and National Security), which terrorized the population. Many opponents of the shah gave their backing to the Ayatollah Ruhollah Khomeini, an Islamic cleric exiled by the shah in 1964 and an ardent proponent of Pahlavi's ouster.

Despite his goal of improving human rights around the world, President Carter had shown a willingness to make exceptions. For instance, the United States avoided pressing the human rights issue too hard with countries such as China, Cambodia, South Korea, the Philippines, Israel, and Egypt because of their strategic or political importance, even though most of them had repressive regimes. The same was true of Iran. In November 1977 the shah visited the president in Washington, and although Carter raised the human rights issue with Pahlavi, he did so quietly, fearful that any public criticism of the shah would create instability in Iran, which was vital to U.S. interests. Not only was the shah a pro-U.S. ally in the oil-rich Middle East, but the United States had posts in Iran that it used to spy on the Soviet Union. In fact, while privately expressing his concern about the human rights situation in Iran, the president provided the shah's government with a large amount of military assistance.

A month later, as part of their multicountry trip, the Carters visited the shah in Tehran. Mrs. Carter was key to this decision. When the president asked her where she would like to spend New Year's Eve, she replied that her top choice would be with the shah and his wife. At an exquisite banquet given for the Carters, the president toasted Pahlavi, calling him a great leader and referring to Iran as "an island of stability in one of the most troubled areas of the world." Many Iranians had hoped that Carter's stance on human rights would mean an end to the repressive regime of the shah, but the U.S. government's willingness to send military aid and the president's public praise for Pahlavi made it clear that they could not expect help from the United States. As a result, anti-American sentiment grew in Iran.

In 1978 the official Iranian press published an article critical of Khomeini, prompting demonstrations throughout the country. The U.S. State Department and the NSC split on whether the shah should respond with force, seek an accommodation with his opponents, or give up power. As the demonstrations grew more intense, the shah grew more unsure about what he should do. Finally, in January 1979, he left the country. Shortly thereafter, Khomeini returned to Iran, where he was greeted by huge crowds. In October Carter learned that the shah was suffering from cancer and wanted to come to the United States for treatment. He discussed the matter with the first lady. Both were concerned about how the Iranians might react, but Mrs. Carter endorsed her husband's decision to allow the shah into the country. To have sent the Iranian leader home, she later wrote, "would be a cowardly thing to do, and I knew if we sent him back to Iran he would be killed."[38] On 4 November a group of Iranian students, infuriated by Carter's decision, overran the U.S. embassy in Tehran and took fifty-two Americans hostage. What would become a 444-day-long siege led the first lady to comment later that she wished her husband had never allowed the shah into the country. At the time, however, the task at hand was putting pressure on Tehran to release the Americans. Carter thus froze Iran's assets in the United States and imposed economic sanctions on the Khomeini government. Mrs. Carter urged him to restrict imports of Iranian oil and discussed other options with him, such as mining Iran's harbors or bombing Tehran. Although he accepted the oil embargo, he rejected the other options on the grounds that the Iranians might respond by killing the hostages.

Even though the president had rejected stronger measures, many of his advisers believed that, based on her reputation as a hawk, Mrs. Carter might try to convince him to change his mind. A few days after the hostage crisis began, the president left a meeting with several of his advisers, including Brzezinski, Vance, Secretary of Defense Harold Brown, and Chief of Staff Hamilton Jordan, to take a call from the first lady, who was in Thailand at the time. Jordan commented to the others, "When he comes back he will probably declare war on Iran."[39] Although Jordan was obviously joking, the comment reflected how much influence Carter's advisers believed the first lady had on the president. It also reflected a first lady who, like Brzezinski, tended to be more hard-line than her husband. In fact, following the president's defeat in 1980, both Mrs. Carter and the NSC adviser commented that had Carter ordered the bombing of Tehran, he likely would have been reelected.

Determined that her husband "do something" to free the hostages, Mrs. Carter was pleased when she learned that he had approved a mission to rescue them.[40] Talk of such an operation had begun almost immediately after the hostages had been seized, but the president resisted the plan, fearful that it might lead to some of the captives' deaths. After months went by without any sign of a resolution, the president relented; in April, after speaking to several of his advisers, including Brzezinski and Rosalynn (although he did not tell his wife the specifics of the plan), he decided to give the go-ahead. Unfortunately, the commandos failed to rescue the American captives, and several of the soldiers died when one of their helicopters crashed.

Mrs. Carter was first informed of the unsuccessful mission while she was campaigning in Texas for her husband's reelection. The president called and asked her to come home, telling her only that the news was bad but refusing to give her any details, for fear that the telephone line might be tapped. Later that night, she learned what had occurred. The news evoked emotions similar to those she had felt when her father died. "Every time I woke up," she wrote, "I wanted to go back to sleep, hoping it would all go away."[41] But it did not go away, and a few days later, the administration received another blow with the resignation of Secretary Vance. Unlike Brzezinski, Vance had opposed the military operation, believing that a diplomatic resolution was still possible. Furious with the president's decision to go ahead with the rescue mission, the secretary of state quit.

Shortly thereafter, Mrs. Carter got into hot water when it was revealed that she had been part of a plan to use her brother-in-law's contacts with Libya to get the hostages out of Iran. Self-deprecating and jocular, Jimmy's younger brother Billy had developed a "good ol' boy image" in the United States. That changed in 1978, however, when he traveled to Libya,[42] which Washington regarded as an enemy state. The Justice Department began an investigation of Billy's ties to Libya, discovering in May 1980 that he had received a "loan" of more than $200,000 from the Libyan government. This news created a firestorm in the United States, and questions were raised whether Billy had attempted to use his contacts in the White House to get better treatment for the Tripoli government. Neither Jimmy nor Rosalynn Carter had known of the loan, and further investigation found no wrongdoing on the part of the president. However, reporters learned that Mrs. Carter had suggested using Billy's ties to Libya to try to secure the hostages' release. Billy had even set up meetings between Brzezinski and Libya's emissary in Washington, Ali Houderi. The first lady's attempt to use a questionable mode of diplomacy to free the American captives did not sit well with the public. The president tried to deflect the criticism, declaring that it had been his decision to use his wife's suggestion as a means of freeing the hostages.

Mrs. Carter continued her travels, joining the president on another trip to Europe, but she spent most of 1980 at home, campaigning for her husband's reelection. The president eventually lost to Republican Ronald Reagan in November. Despite his defeat, President Carter continued his efforts to get the hostages released. Ironically, the news that the hostages had been freed and were on their way home came on the day of Reagan's inauguration. The first lady wished that news had come sooner, prior to the election.

Rosalynn Carter ended her tenure as the most active, if not the most influential, first lady in the realm of U.S. foreign policy. She had traveled all over the world, visiting thirty-six nations by the end of 1979. In some cases, her role on those trips was not merely wife of the president but rather his personal representative, taking his place at official functions, explaining U.S. policy to foreign leaders, and attempting to convince them to change their nations' policies. She also acted as the president's sounding board and adviser, listening to his concerns and making suggestions. Her efforts were not always successful, and sometimes they even backfired. She could not convince Peru to stop its arms buildup, Brazil to reject nuclear power, or her husband to take a more "demagogic" attitude toward the Soviet brigade in Cuba. Her involvement in the attempt to use Billy Carter's Libyan connections to free the hostages brought censure on the White House. Yet she had proved herself to be an able and well-informed diplomat who could gain the respect of foreign leaders, even if they disagreed with her. She played an important role in the administration's decisions to supply helicopters to Colombia and to provide aid for the Cambodian refugees in Thailand.

Unfortunately for Mrs. Carter, no matter what she did, she was the subject of criticism. During her trip to Latin America, detractors charged her with crossing the line of acceptable behavior for a first lady, noting that serious political discussions should be left to the foreign policy experts. When she appeared to adopt a more traditional role, as in Saudi Arabia, she became the target of angry feminists. In short, there remained a certain ambivalence about the first lady's appropriate role in the realm of foreign policy.

CHAPTER 4

HOSTESS AND HOME LIFE

One traditional role of the first lady is to act as White House hostess, putting on various social functions such as teas, dinners, and dances. Another is to effect changes in the White House decor that reflect her tastes and make the presidential mansion more comfortable for her family and more inviting to guests. As first lady, Rosalynn Carter did both. Yet even in this traditional realm, her activities, particularly with regard to planning and supervising events, generated controversy. Her reluctance to serve hard liquor and the Carters' unwillingness to involve themselves in the Washington social scene raised eyebrows in the capital. Mrs. Carter's own comments led some to charge her with being a reluctant hostess. In the meantime, her desire to protect her family's privacy did not please those who wanted to know more about those who lived in the White House.

Although individuals walking by on Pennsylvania Avenue can see that the White House is large, it is actually much bigger than it appears. Its six stories encompass more than 50,000 square feet, much of it (two stories) underground. Most people are aware of the top four stories: the ground, first, second, and third. The ground floor has several rooms, including the China Room, where visitors can see collections of china used in the White House; the Vermeil (Gold)

Room, used as both a display room and, for formal events, a ladies' sitting room; the library; and hallways to the West and East Wings, where Jimmy and Rosalynn Carter had their respective offices. The top two stories—the second and third—are the first family's residence, with offices, a kitchen, a workout room, a living room, and bedrooms, among them the famous Lincoln Bedroom.

White House events take place on the first floor. Entering through the South Portico, one goes directly into the Blue Room, which is used as a reception room. Looking toward the White House from the South Portico, the Red Room, used as a sitting room, is to the left of the Blue Room; the Green Room, to the right, has served a variety of functions. To the right of the Green Room is the East Room, where many formal events take place. To the left of the Red Room is the State Dining Room, often used for formal dinners; directly behind it is the Family Dining Room, which, despite its name, is used primarily for small official functions. Situated between the two dining rooms and the East Room, and behind the three colored rooms, are the entrance and cross halls, as well as the Yellow Room, where the president meets guests prior to state dinners, and the Grand Staircase, which leads into the East Room.

Unlike her predecessor, Betty Ford, Mrs. Carter had time to prepare for her first state event. Almost immediately after Gerald Ford had been sworn in as president after Richard Nixon's resignation, Mrs. Ford had received word of the impending visit of the king and queen of Jordan. Mrs. Carter had the luxury of deciding who her first guests would be and when they would come. Nevertheless, the process of preparing for an event was both time-consuming and stressful. Once the date and time of the event were set, invitations had to be mailed out and arrangements made for media coverage, food and music (if necessary), seating, flowers, and any other details necessary to make the guests feel welcome and comfortable during their stay. The Carters and their staffs also had to learn White House etiquette—from where to stand to the proper order in which to greet guests.

To help her plan these events, Mrs. Carter relied on her staff, particularly her social secretary, Gretchen Poston. Poston had worked in the convention-planning industry and had helped raise funds for Jimmy Carter's presidential campaign. Mary Hoyt, the

Gretchen Poston, Mrs. Carter's social secretary. She was essential in planning and supervising functions at the White House. Courtesy of the Jimmy Carter Library.

first lady's press secretary and East Wing coordinator, had received recommendations from several people that Poston be hired as the first lady's social secretary, including one from Joan Mondale, the vice president's wife. As social secretary, it was Poston's job to supervise the Social Office, which oversaw event planning.

Another important person was Jane Fenderson, Mrs. Carter's appointments secretary. She had worked with Hoyt for the Muskie campaign, where she had managed scheduling for the Democratic candidate. Fenderson's job at the White House was to screen invitations and to block out Mrs. Carter's calendar, ensuring that any events the first lady attended did not overlap with those of the president or vice president.

Events involved not just planning but also etiquette, and here, President and Mrs. Carter relied on a member of the West Wing staff, Evan Dobelle, the White House chief of protocol. At age twenty-seven, Dobelle had been elected mayor of the town of Pittsfield, Massachusetts—the youngest person to serve in that office. In 1976 he and his wife, Edith ("Kit"), had met Jimmy Carter during the presidential candidate's visit to Pittsfield; both had been taken with him and worked for his campaign. In return, Carter appointed Dobelle to the protocol post. When Dobelle left the White House staff in April 1978 to become treasurer of the Democratic Party, Kit took his place.

The process of putting together an event was complex. It began with the president, the first lady, or both deciding on the date and time of the event, the type of function it would be, and the guest list (with input from the National Security Council, the State Department, the Office of the Congressional Liaison, and the Press Office). The Social Office would then spring into action, compiling selections of food, music, and flowers, as well as a list of social aides to assist the guests. Once a draft plan had been put together, Poston would take it to the Carters (although Rosalynn was the White House hostess, Jimmy enjoyed having a hand in the planning of events.) At first, Poston met with Mrs. Carter about once or twice a week, but as she became accustomed to the Carters' tastes, these meetings became less frequent. Once the Carters had approved the details of the event, the Social Office took over, coordinating guest lists, having the invitations engraved and mailed, keeping track of who accepted and declined those invitations, and deciding where people would sit. The Social Office also helped deal with matters of protocol.

In the meantime, the Press Office was concerned with media coverage of the event and with how the office staff should conduct itself. "We are *not* guests," Hoyt told her subordinates in preparation for the Carters' first state visit from the newly elected president of Mexico, José López Portillo, and his wife, Carmen, in February 1977.

"We should not stand around and be visible to guests, but we must somehow always be available to the Press." It was important, wrote Hoyt, for the press staff to maintain "a low profile."[1]

The Carters chose the López Portillos as their first state visitors because the president was determined to improve relations with Latin America. The new administration regarded Mexico, with its common border and extensive trade with the United States, as one of the most important countries in the region. To help prepare themselves for their first formal White House event, the Carters watched a film of the arrival ceremony for West German chancellor Helmut Schmidt during the Ford administration. Everything "was planned down to the very second," recalled the first lady. According to the schedule of events, the Carters would meet the López Portillos and stand at attention while the two countries' national anthems were played by the Marine Band. The two presidents would review U.S. troops on the lawn. Then they and their wives would head into the Blue Room for a reception, after which officials from the two countries would go to the West Wing for meetings.[2]

All went well until the entourage arrived at the Blue Room. According to protocol, state visitors were supposed to walk to the right of the Carters. Instead, the first lady found Mrs. López Portillo standing on her left. When Mrs. Carter brought this to the attention of a military aide, he told her not to worry about it, which calmed her down. She quickly learned that which side one stood on was less important than "warmth and putting your guests at ease."[3] By the time of the evening's festivities, Mrs. Carter had concluded that entertaining at the White House would be enjoyable. The remainder of the evening went off without a hitch. Mrs. Carter joined her husband to greet their guests and escort them to the Yellow Room to talk. From there, they went to the Grand Staircase and then to a reception in the East Room, where they met the guests in protocol order.

Mrs. Carter later wrote that, in terms of entertaining, the transition from state senator's wife to first lady of Georgia had been more difficult than that from first lady of Georgia to first lady of the United States. In Georgia, Mrs. Carter and her secretary had had to train the prisoners who staffed the governor's mansion, because her predecessor had not done any entertaining. In the White House, people and procedures were already in place, making life significantly easier. The staff took care of the flowers and the food, the chef and his assistants oversaw the making of the meal, the social aides helped the guests, and "the valet had even laid out Jimmy's tuxedo! Entertaining in the White House, I decided, was going to be fun."[4]

In what would become an important part of state visits, the first lady and her social staff researched the interests of their guests. For instance, having learned that Mrs. López Portillo played the piano and enjoyed the works of pianist Rudolf Serkin, Mrs. Carter had asked Serkin to perform at the White House during the López Portillos' visit. She showed similar consideration for other official guests. In April, when King Hussein of Jordan came to Washington, Mrs. Carter made sure that the table decorations reflected his love of sea sports. Three months later the Carters hosted West German chancellor Helmut Schmidt and his wife, Hannelore. Hearing that Mrs. Schmidt liked crape myrtles, Mrs. Carter had the flowers placed around the White House.

Despite the success of the first state visit, Hoyt decided that there was still a lack of coordination and efficiency in event planning. Accordingly, in March she informed the staff that once the first lady had agreed to an event, Fenderson would report to several top individuals in the East Wing, including Hoyt; Poston; Madeline MacBean, Mrs. Carter's personal assistant; and Kathy Cade, the first lady's director of projects. The principal figures would then meet and choose one person to oversee the event. "At least two days before the event all papers will be sent to Carol Benefield," a member of the first lady's staff, who would then send them to Hoyt for review. Following Hoyt's approval, Benefield would send the papers to the entire staff.[5]

These alterations did not solve the problem of coordination between the East Wing and the West Wing. According to one story, shortly after the inauguration, Rosalynn called the White House operator and asked to be connected to Jimmy. "Jimmy who?" the voice on the line asked.[6] Although that problem was quickly remedied, Mrs. Carter found that West Wing staff members were scheduling activities without letting her know. In July both she and Hoyt wrote to West Wing senior personnel, asking that they contact Poston before setting up any functions. Hoyt also provided a list of the names

{ *Hostess and Home Life* }

and job descriptions of those individuals in the East Wing with whom West Wing staff would most likely have contact.

These efforts at coordination did not guarantee that every event went off without a hitch. For example, Ohio governor James Rhodes arrived at the Carter administration's first governors' dinner in March 1977 with two grandchildren in tow. When "an aide told him there was no place for the children," Rhodes left. Upon learning of the incident, the Carters immediately ordered the staff to find the governor and tell him that the children could play with Amy, but unfortunately, he could not be located. In April 1978 the band playing at the arrival ceremony for Romanian president Nicolae Ceaușescu accidentally played the wrong national anthem, unaware that it had recently been changed.[7]

This lack of coordination led to reports of a larger conflict between the East and West Wings. "The boys [referring to press secretary Jody Powell and key presidential aide Hamilton Jordan] never had a great rapport with Rosalynn Carter," declared journalist Sally Quinn. Furthermore, she wrote, the president "basically sees his wife as wife, mother, hostess." Finally, Quinn reported that Powell disliked Hoyt and even suggested that she be fired. There is no evidence to substantiate such claims. By all accounts, Jordan and Powell looked fondly on the first lady and understood the influence she could have on her husband. "Whenever I think the President is pursuing an unwise course of action and I strike out with him," said Jordan, "I try to get her on my side." Clearly, the president saw her as an equal and as someone he could trust. As for reports of trouble between the East and West Wing staffs, Greg Schneiders (deputy assistant for communications in the White House), Powell, Hoyt, and Faith Collins (Hoyt's deputy) all denied its existence. Schneiders mentioned that Hoyt might periodically do something that Powell disagreed with, but he never saw anything to suggest "an ongoing, significant breach between the two staffs." Collins seconded her West Wing colleague, calling the media reports "overblown."[8]

Mrs. Carter made some staff changes in the summer of 1979. She named Kit Dobelle, the White House chief of protocol, as East Wing coordinator, replacing Mary Hoyt. That left Hoyt to concentrate on her duties as press secretary and head of the Press Office. The first lady explained that every time she traveled, her top aides, including Hoyt, had to go with her, leaving no one behind to oversee affairs in the East Wing. By appointing Dobelle—whose official title was chief of staff—Mrs. Carter could be assured that someone would be there to oversee her projects and to maintain contact with the West Wing. Hoyt admitted that initially she was "pique[d]" at having her administrative responsibilities taken from her, but that feeling was quickly replaced by a sense of relief. Doing double duty as both coordinator and press secretary had been draining, and she was still grieving over the loss of her son, Steve, a lobster fisherman who had died in an accident at sea the previous September. To be able to focus solely on the Press Office was, she explained, a welcome change.[9]

The Dobelle appointment also created a brief uproar among journalists, who wanted to know why Mrs. Carter needed a chief of staff, let alone one who was paid $56,000 a year—the same as Brzezinski and Jordan (whom Carter had recently named *his* chief of staff)—at a time when the president wanted to rein in the budget. But Carter stood by his wife's decision, explaining that she needed the help. In fact, after Dobelle assumed her post, coordination between the two staffs improved.[10]

If mix-ups caused by poor communication marked the least enjoyable aspect of Mrs. Carter's role as hostess, her most rewarding task involved choosing the entertainment for White House events. This "was always a thrill and a job I enjoyed doing myself," she wrote, although the president helped finalize these decisions. Determined that performers who came to the White House "should reflect the broad spectrum of American creativity,"[11] those invited included John Denver, the Charlie Daniels Band, Beverly Sills, Itzhak Perlman, Isaac Stern, Shirley Verrett, Mikhail Baryshnikov, and the Guarnieri String Quartet. Not all these individuals actually performed *in* the White House. The Carters loved the outdoors, so, weather permitting, they often held galas outside. In fact, it made sense to hold some events outdoors, such as when the White House rooms were too small to accommodate all the guests. One of these large outdoor events took place in May 1978 when the Carters hosted a picnic and concert for more than 700 lawmakers and their families. Conductor André Kostelanetz led the concert, which included music from Mozart, Mendelssohn, and Tchaikovsky. The final performance, Tchaikovsky's *1812 Overture*, ended not with cannons but with a huge fireworks display.

One of the most exciting outdoor events took place the following month: the White House Jazz Festival. Ever since the Kennedy administration, U.S. presidents had held jazz concerts at the White House, but the Carters, who were jazz enthusiasts, took it to a new level. An audience including the Carters, Vice President Walter Mondale, and members of the cabinet and Congress watched performances by more than fifty artists from around the country, including Stan Getz, John Lewis, and Gerry Mulligan. During the final number, Dizzy Gillespie invited the president to join him on stage, where the two of them sang a most appropriate song, in light of the president's background: "Salt Peanuts."

In September the first lady hosted stock-car night. During his days as a peanut farmer, Carter had sold tickets at the Atlanta Speedway; in 1976 he kicked off his presidential campaign at the same locale and promised to invite the drivers and their crews to the White House if elected. Almost 500 guests listened to Willie Nelson and his band play while they enjoyed a southern-style dinner that included ham, roast beef, potato salad, and strawberry shortcake; miniature racing cars on plastic strips served as centerpieces for each table.

A far larger event took place in October 1979 when Pope John Paul II visited Washington, D.C. Officials from all over the country requested invitations for themselves or their constituents to the reception for the religious leader. A total of 10,000 people attended, forcing Mrs. Carter to hold two separate outdoor receptions for the pontiff—one on the north side of the White House and another on the larger South Lawn. As the National Symphony played, the pope walked through the crowd, blessing numerous individuals.

If the first lady was proud of her ability to carry off large events, she also took pride in a series of televised Sunday performances in the East Room. The first one, held in February 1978, featured Vladimir Horowitz. Gerald Slater, the executive vice president of WETA, the Washington, D.C., affiliate of the Public Broadcasting System (PBS), had learned that the famous pianist would be playing at the White House and asked Poston if he could televise the recital. Mrs. Carter agreed to the idea, believing that the American people should share in the occasion. It became a regular event, with the

In October 1979 a huge crowed gathered on the South Lawn during Pope John Paul II's visit to Washington. Courtesy of the Jimmy Carter Library.

performances of other artists—all of them chosen personally by the Carters—such as Andrés Segovia, Isaac Stern, Dave Brubeck, Billy Taylor, Mstislav Rostropovich, and Leontyne Price being broadcast to the public. In the fall of 1979, however, PBS canceled the series. With the upcoming campaign season, PBS executives decided that showing the concerts would require the station to give equal time to the other candidates.

Sometimes social events took place on the spur of the moment. One such function that was particularly difficult to arrange was a banquet to celebrate the signing in March 1979 of the Egyptian-Israeli peace treaty. Although some planning had taken place beforehand, it was unclear whether the pact would ever be signed. Once it became obvious that the two nations would reach an agreement, however, the first lady and the Social Office acted quickly. Invitations were sent as mailgrams to save time, and Mrs. Carter had telephones put in her office, where volunteers handled the responses. "We brought in army trucks with refrigerated trailers to cool the salads and desserts," Mrs. Carter recalled, "and rowboats filled with ice to chill the wine." Each country provided entertainment for the 1,800 guests under a tent on the South Lawn.[12]

Another impromptu event took place in June 1978. British prime minister James Callaghan and his wife had come to Washington for a meeting of the North Atlantic Treaty Organization, and they stopped by the White House on their way to a reception. Although the Carters had planned to have a family dinner in the President's Dining Room, they asked the Callaghans to stay. The meal was southern fare, including ham, corn bread, collard greens, and okra. The Callaghans loved it. They stayed for a movie afterward, to which the Carters also invited British ambassador Peter Jay and his wife and daughter. The Carters remembered this spur-of-the-moment get-together as one of the most enjoyable during their stay in Washington.

This informal dinner with the Callaghans pointed to another aspect of entertaining at the Carter White House: a desire to make it more open and family-friendly. To the Carters, the White House was not just a place of business but also a home. Besides Jimmy, Rosalynn, and their daughter Amy, other family members living in the White House included Chip and Caron and their young son, James Earl IV, as well as Jeff and his wife, Annette. (Jack, Judy, and their son, Jason, lived in Georgia.) To make the White House feel more like home, the Carters had a tree house built in the backyard for Amy, and she often had friends spend the night (where they might stay up late in the Lincoln Bedroom hoping to see the ghost of the former president).

A similar attitude pervaded more formal events. Whenever possible, the first lady sought to invite not just members of the Washington elite or the White House staff but also what Hoyt referred to as "people-people": ordinary citizens who had done something nice for the Carters, such as those who had extended their hospitality during the 1976 campaign. Mrs. Carter also tried to include children in as many events as possible. For instance, the Carters' first Easter egg roll—a tradition that dated back to the 1870s—was a major success, with clowns, puppets, animals for the children to pet, and a human-sized Easter Bunny. In December, Mrs. Carter hosted a party attended by Amy and more than 400 children of foreign diplomats, during which they watched New York's Pixie Judy Troupe perform "The Littlest Clown." According to the script, the play ended with a new littlest clown, and to her surprise, the actors brought Amy up on the stage and dressed her up for the part. "I've

The Carters' oldest son, Jack, wife Judy, and son Jason. Jack and his family were the only members of the immediate family who did not live at the White House during Carter's presidency. Courtesy of the Jimmy Carter Library.

one thing to say to you, Miss Amy Carter," the play's narrator, Helen Hayes, said: "You're a real trouper."[13]

Before their second Christmas in the White House, the Carters had entertained almost 5,000 people in a series of functions that included members of the Secret Service, the press corps, and the White House staff. One of the last events the first lady hosted was for about fifty members of the White House staff and their families, who enjoyed playing in man-made snow.

However, not all the events hosted by Mrs. Carter had the purpose of providing entertainment for guests or relaxing with friends. Mrs. Carter repeatedly made it clear that she wanted to be more than a traditional first lady; she regarded herself not only as the president's wife but also as his advocate, and she considered it her duty to promote his policies. Believing that her husband was not receiving proper coverage in the press, she persuaded him to host a series of informal dinners with journalists, including the anchors of the three major networks' nightly news programs: Walter Cronkite, Tom Brokaw, and Frank Reynolds.

During the 1980 campaign, Mrs. Carter hosted a Valentine's Day dance in the East Room attended by 500 guests. Although the White House characterized the event as "not political," the guest list suggested otherwise: most of the attendees were Democrats who supported Carter over his Democratic rival for the party nomination, Senator Edward Kennedy.[14]

In September of that year, the first lady hosted 1,000 African Americans on the South Lawn for a meeting of Blacks in Government. Although African Americans had supported Carter in large numbers in the 1976 election, relations between the White House and blacks had quickly soured. African Americans criticized the president for not supporting their interests, charging that he had failed to increase funding for programs to develop urban areas, create new jobs, and provide low-income housing. In fact, Carter had appointed more blacks to federal judgeships than any of his predecessors, increased the number of government contracts for minority companies, and strengthened the enforcement of laws protecting voting rights. But it was also true that most of his actions benefited middle- and upper-class minorities rather than those in the lower classes. And Mrs. Carter had inadvertently made things worse during a July

1979 speech before the National Urban League. Even though many of the attendees blamed her speechwriters rather than the first lady, they disliked her failure to address the broader interests of blacks in the country, as well as her use of the phrase "happens to be black" when referring to several African Americans appointed by her husband to government positions.[15] Hosting the Blacks in Government meeting represented an attempt to rally black support for her husband, if not undo the damage done the previous year.

The first lady also understood that hosting social events at the White House could be beneficial to her own projects. For example, for her first Christmas in the White House, Mrs. Carter's holiday display included a twenty-foot fir tree in the Blue Room decorated with 2,500 ornaments, each made by a mentally handicapped individual. She hoped that the tree would help erase the stigma surrounding mental disabilities. "We wanted to show that retarded citizens have talents," she commented. "Everyone should have the opportunity to go as far as he can."[16] In May 1978 she hosted a luncheon for the wives of current or retired senators, encouraging them to help achieve passage of the equal rights amendment (ERA).

The number and variety of events the Carters hosted amazed observers. During the 1976 campaign, one newspaper had commented that if she became first lady, Mrs. Carter would likely bring square dancing to the White House — and indeed, she did. However, Mrs. Carter also demonstrated an understanding of the dignity of the building; moreover, both she and her husband wanted the events held at the White House to reflect the diversity of culture in the United States. In 1977 alone, the first lady hosted nineteen arrival ceremonies, nearly forty receptions, fifteen luncheons, eight picnics, and eight dinners. Poston later commented that during President Carter's term in office, Mrs. Carter "was the instigator and major creator of over 5,000 events and entertained in the neighborhood of 100,000 people."[17]

It did not take long for observers who might have been worried about the propriety of Carter-style entertainment to heap the first couple with praise. *U.S. News* commented that the variety of events the Carters hosted "adds up to a mix of entertainment that, while still all-American in most cases, offers more variety than the White House has seen for years." The *Baltimore Sun* wrote that "no first lady, including Mrs. Kennedy, has graced a state dinner with more warmth and charm."[18]

Feminists were no doubt pleased with one change the Carters made to state visits. During such events, the president and the visiting leader would review the U.S. military honor guard from a platform. In the past, the first lady would stand to one side, away from her husband. But beginning with the López Portillos' visit, the two wives stood next to their husbands, symbolizing the equal status of spouses.

But the Carters also faced criticism. Although they hosted a number of formal events, some in the capital missed the sort of glitzy, white-tie affairs offered by their predecessors, such as John and Jacqueline Kennedy. Mrs. Carter tried to brush off such comments, but they bothered her. Another complaint was the length of events. To allow them to devote more time to their work, the Carters served dinner at 7:30 rather than 8:00 and ended all functions by midnight. Another reason for keeping such functions short was financial: both of the Carters were fiscal conservatives who sought to cut the budget (this also led the president to carry his own bags rather than hire someone to do it for him). Members of the establishment who were used to parties that lasted into the wee hours of the morning did not like the new "curfew."

Others in Washington complained about the lack of hard liquor. The Carters did not drink much, and as first lady of Georgia, Mrs. Carter had served liquor only rarely, such as at formal dinners for visiting dignitaries. She carried this policy into the White House, which, she said, was "not a place to drink." In addition, the first lady argued, she saved the taxpayers some $1 million by not having to buy liquor or hire bartenders to serve it. Her explanation, however, did not silence the critics, such as Washington satirist Byron Kennard. Playing on the nicknames of other first ladies who had instituted dry policies, such as "Lemonade Lucy" Hayes, he called her "Rosé Rosalynn." Mrs. Carter disliked the nickname, complaining, "They make me sound like a real prude. I'm not a prude!"[19]

The first couple's fiscal conservatism affected events in other ways as well. Generally, when deciding on a menu, the first lady would select the least expensive items (and for family meals, the first lady instructed the housekeeper to take advantage of sales at the grocery store and urged the kitchen staff to serve leftovers). Also, she usually divided the guest list: half the guests would be invited to attend the dinner, and the remainder would be invited only to the reception afterward. A similar attitude applied to gift giving. Traditionally, presidents and first ladies exchanged pricey gifts with state guests. By law, gifts from foreign officials could not be valued at more than $100, although it was not uncommon for state visitors to undervalue the gifts they presented (such as the $250,000 urn given to President Carter by the archbishop of Greece, who claimed that it was worth only $99). Yet even $100 gifts could add up to a lot of money over the long term. The Carters therefore limited their gifts to official visitors to a photograph of Jimmy and Rosalynn together in a frame with the presidential seal.

Finally, the Carters faced charges that although they were prepared to host events at the White House, they were unwilling to participate in Washington society. For instance, according to tradition, the day after the president held a dinner and reception for a visiting official, the guest would reciprocate with a dinner and reception. President Carter considered this a waste of time and decided to limit state visits to just one dinner. At the time, the first lady defended their position. "When Jimmy was governor," she stated, "we weren't involved in Atlanta society. We were busy. And when we had an evening at home we wanted to be at home, like any other couple that works."[20] Moreover, if they went to one event, then they would be expected to attend others, limiting the time they had for work and family.

This is not to say that the Carters never ventured out into the capital for social events; however, there was often a political purpose. In April 1977, for instance, the first lady spoke before the 2,300 members of the Women's National Democratic Club, where she touted her husband's policies. In February of the following year she represented her husband at the Pan American Union, where she praised the Inter-American Commission of Women for its support of human rights. In December 1979, while the president remained at the White House to monitor the hostage crisis in Iran, she spoke at the Kennedy Center Honors, an awards ceremony for "lifetime achievements in the performing arts."[21] Though busy campaigning for her husband during 1980, she found time to attend a sixtieth birthday celebration at the Kennedy Concert Hall for Isaac Stern.

{ *Hostess and Home Life* }

The truth was that if Rosalynn and Jimmy Carter had to choose between going out to socialize with others and having them come to the White House, they preferred the latter. According to Schneiders, who had known the Carters since the 1976 campaign, he and the president's other aides "would actually set up opportunities, not for them to go out places but for people to come in." Furthermore, such functions "had to be put on the schedule and had to be sold to them because it was not anything that they would naturally do." Despite her statements at the time, Mrs. Carter admitted after leaving the White House that she and the president had made a mistake by not taking a greater part in the Washington social scene and making more extensive connections in the capital. Still, she added, "if he went back he would do it the same way." This was indeed an error on the part of the first couple. "When it came to the politics of Washington, D.C.," commented House Speaker Tip O'Neill (D-Massachusetts), Carter "never really understood how the system worked. And . . . he didn't want to learn about it, either."[22]

Because of her own comments about being more than simply a traditional first lady, and likely because she and the president seemed to shun Washington society, Mrs. Carter was accused of not enjoying being a hostess. "If you had a choice between sitting in a corner and listening to a Cabinet meeting or staying over in the White House and serving tea, wouldn't you prefer to listen to the Cabinet meeting?" she asked the *Saturday Evening Post*. Similarly, she told the *Shreveport Times*, "For me to just sit at the White House and act as a hostess, I think, would be a terrible waste." Further, the chapter on her role as hostess is the shortest one in her memoirs, suggesting how she felt about that duty. Schneiders supported the claim that the first lady was a reluctant hostess. The Carters, he said, were private individuals who enjoyed spending a quiet evening at home with family more than hosting large events or involving themselves in the capital's social scene.[23]

Yet Mrs. Carter also stated in her memoirs that she had fun hosting White House events, and others confirmed this. For example, Joseph Califano remembered a first lady who enjoyed entertaining. Likewise, members of the East Wing staff vehemently denied that Mrs. Carter disliked planning and hosting events. The first lady, stated Hoyt, "*loved* those parties [and] being hostess!"

Poston agreed. "I'm always amazed, a little confused, and certainly amused by the fact that the words 'reluctant hostess' are used with Mrs. Carter." Poston added that the first lady "understood the importance of entertaining. She paid a lot of attention to it, and I am sure that the people who were fortunate enough to be invited to the White House certainly will always remember her style of entertaining."[24]

The truth appears to lie somewhere in between. There is no doubt that Mrs. Carter preferred playing a nontraditional, political role within the administration, but there were aspects of hostessing that she enjoyed. And she realized that she could combine both roles—hostess and political activist—as she did to promote mental health and the ERA or to seek African American support for her husband.

Those who were invited to White House events no doubt noticed Mrs. Carter's decorative touches, although, busy with other matters, she did not make any substantial changes until 1978. Because the government does not provide funding for furniture or artwork, the first lady turned to private individuals and to a warehouse used to store items used by past first families. Mrs. Carter also worked closely with the Committee for the Preservation of the White House, a body established by President Lyndon Johnson in 1964. This committee includes the curator and chief usher of the White House, the secretary of the Smithsonian Institution, the chairperson of the Commission on Fine Arts, and other members chosen by the president; the first lady serves as honorary chair.

Mrs. Carter found two chairs and an ottoman in the warehouse that she put in the president's study so that he would have a place to read; the fireplace added to the room's coziness. Her central project, however, was the solarium, where she was aided by daughter-in-law Annette, who had a degree in interior design. Considered the family room of the White House, the solarium is an octagonal, twenty- by thirty-five-foot room with south-facing windows. Mrs. Carter had the walls painted an off-white, and rather than purchase new furniture, the first lady decided to reupholster the two sofas and two chairs already in the room. She chose a blue-white-yellow striped fabric for the former and a cloud pattern for the latter. In addition, there were six Spanish-made chairs, chinoiserie-style lamps, a white

{ *Hostess and Home Life* }

The Carters' youngest son, Jeff, and his wife, Annette. Annette had a degree in interior design and helped Mrs. Carter decorate the White House. Courtesy of the Jimmy Carter Library.

cabinet to hold the television and stereo, and a small statue of a horse made in Nigeria. Finally, the room had an octagonal rug and a Lucite-and-glass table that, it turned out, had been designed by Eden Rafshoon, the wife of President Carter's assistant for communications, Gerald Rafshoon.

Mrs. Carter's decorating ideas caused one brief fight. During the first few months of the new administration, donors reclaimed certain items that they had loaned to the White House. The New York State Historical Association wanted back its portrait of Abigail Adams that had hung in the Red Room for fifteen years, and the Metropolitan Museum of Art repossessed some other paintings. Then, in mid-1977, Senate Majority Leader Robert Byrd asked to move the second-floor Treaty Room chandelier to one of his offices. Clement Conger, the White House curator, rejected his request, contending that it was "an integral part" of the building. Mrs. Carter agreed.[25] Their refusal strained relations with the Senate leadership, and Mrs. Carter finally relented in September 1978 and let Byrd have the chandelier.

Mrs. Carter also sought to make decorating alterations and additions to the White House that the public could enjoy on their tours. In 1978, in conjunction with the preservation committee, Mrs. Carter began a multimillion-dollar fund-raising drive that would establish a trust fund to cover the costs of such refurbishments. What made this fund-raising drive different was its target audience. In the past, wealthy donors had quietly provided funds to purchase new items for the White House. Now, Mrs. Carter requested donations from anyone who was willing to give. Using the money from that fund, Mrs. Carter purchased "a bronze bust of Benjamin Franklin," William Michael Harnett's painting *Cincinnati Enquirer, 1888*, and a portrait of Andrew Jackson, among other works.[26]

Planning and hosting events and overseeing the redecoration of the White House took up a lot of time, and that did not include the hours Mrs. Carter spent on her other projects or the days and weeks she was away from home traveling with her husband or acting as his personal representative. When she was in the presidential mansion, Mrs. Carter maintained a long workday that usually began at 9:00 in the morning. For a while, she spent three hours on Tuesdays, Wednesdays, and Fridays learning Spanish; however, her other responsibilities gradually cut into the time she could devote to these lessons. She would take half an hour for lunch, which she would have with her husband or other members of the family. She met twice a week with her staff. If the weather was nice, she tried to end her workday at 4:30, after which she and the president would play

{ *Hostess and Home Life* }

tennis, swim, take a walk, or use the White House bowling alley. Sharing her husband's belief in keeping physically fit, their exercise regimen also included jogging or a game of softball (one of the president's passions). Some days, however, Mrs. Carter stayed in her office until 6:30, in which case she and the president would watch the evening news and then try to spend the rest of the evening with the family, sometimes taking advantage of the White House movie theater. The Carters were also interested in self-improvement, and they used their free time toward that end. To help them increase the amount of material they could read, they both took a speed-reading course.[27] The first lady also remained intensely religious and prayed several times a day, and she still enjoyed sewing.

Rosalynn and Jimmy Carter spent numerous weekends at Camp David, the presidential retreat in Maryland. They had fallen in love with the place after their first visit in February 1977. They took walks along the nature trails, played tennis, jogged, and swam in the pool—if the weather was warm enough, sometimes jumping in still wearing their sweaty clothes. The president also liked to go there because his cabinet secretaries and staff tended to leave him alone, sensing that he wanted to relax. In fact, the president enjoyed the place so much that he set aside his fiscal scruples. As he told Bert Lance, director of the Office of Management and Budget, "Don't tell me how much it costs to maintain Camp David. I don't ever want to know."[28]

The connection between Jimmy and Rosalynn Carter was very close. "When she goes off for a few days, he just has a long face around here," commented an aide. "And when she comes back, that day, he'll be like a little boy—so excited to see her." They openly displayed their affection for each other, hugging, kissing, and holding hands while walking together. She chose his clothes, commenting that what he wore mattered less to him than to her. Because they made so many decisions together, Jimmy and Rosalynn had lunch together every Thursday, during which they discussed matters ranging from policy to personnel. Light eaters, they preferred soup and sandwiches to the large meals served at state functions. Some contemporaries pointed to their affection for each other as further evidence of their partnership. Others made fun of it, such as a *Saturday Night Live* "news" segment that showed a picture of them cheek to cheek. "In an effort to show their solidarity," stated cast member Chevy Chase, "President and Mrs. Carter have epoxied themselves to each other."[29]

Of the children, Amy naturally received the most attention from her mother. She was the Carters' only daughter and much younger than her brothers, all of whom had families of their own. Mrs. Carter stated, "When my boys were growing up, we [she and Jimmy] were very busy too, but I was always there. . . . Now I [have to] make time to be with Amy where I didn't with them because we were together all the time."[30] Other than Amy's having to leave her friends in Georgia, Mrs. Carter had little concern about moving her daughter to Washington. Amy knew what it was like to live in the spotlight. Even so, Mrs. Carter wanted to make sure that her daughter's life was as normal as possible. The first lady ate breakfast with Amy before going to her office, and she took a half-hour break before dinner to play with Amy or help her with her homework. Mrs. Carter also took violin lessons with her daughter.

The Carters encouraged Amy's interest in learning. As a child, Jimmy and his siblings had been allowed to read at the dinner table, and the president (with Rosalynn's support) permitted their children to adopt that habit as well. ("Anyone who doesn't like to read is dumb," the Carters' daughter once said.)[31] Amy attended a public school only a few blocks from the White House, making her the first child of a president to do so since Theodore Roosevelt's son, Quentin. Having Amy attend public school sent two messages: that the Carters were not above their fellow Americans, and that they were serious about curbing spending.

Amy also received the most press attention of the Carter children. This was not surprising: she was the first preteen in the White House since the Kennedys. Amy took the attention well, having been in the public spotlight for most of her life. But there were limits. The first lady stopped permitting her daughter to grant interviews because the reporters "kept asking her questions that made her look stupid. And she wasn't." The first lady also strongly resented reports that she and her husband "exploited" their daughter by allowing her to attend state dinners and show her boredom by pulling out a book to read. Mrs. Carter explained that when her husband had been governor of Georgia, Amy would sometimes have to accompany

Rosalynn, Jimmy, and Amy Carter. Of the Carter children, Amy received the most attention from the American public. Courtesy of the Jimmy Carter Library.

them to events that held little interest for a child, and she would bring a book to keep herself occupied. In the case of state dinners, Amy would see her mother getting dressed up and would ask to dress up and go with her. Knowing that her daughter would probably get bored, Mrs. Carter let her take along something to read. As mentioned earlier, it was common practice for the Carter children to read at the dinner table, and state dinners were no exception. "We let her go to state dinners because we like her to be with us. We don't make her go," she said.[32] Administration insiders confirmed this. Schneiders recalled that the first time he had dinner with Jimmy, Rosalynn, and Amy during the 1976 campaign, "I was astounded and didn't know what to do because I sat down and the three of them sit down and take out books." Likewise, commented Hoyt, if Amy "had an interest in something," such as going to a state dinner, her parents "let her do it." Amy was, she continued, a curious child, and her parents supported their daughter's desire for knowledge.[33]

There is no evidence that Mrs. Carter's duties that took her away from Washington had any negative impact on her daughter. If Amy could not travel with her mother, Rosalynn kept in touch by telephone. In fact, talking to her daughter could calm the first lady during tense times. For example, during the Israeli-Egyptian negotiations at Camp David, Mrs. Carter recalled, "It was a relief for me to hear Amy's voice on the telephone. Talking with Amy made my life seem normal again for the moment." In addition, Amy had numerous friends, "so many," commented Hoyt, "that you couldn't pick [her] out of a block of kids."[34]

Some critics charged that her doting parents had created a spoiled child who always got her way. Diana McClellan, a columnist for the *Washington Star,* claimed that when Amy's relay team failed to win race against another school, she pouted and demanded a trophy. According to McClellan, a Secret Service agent whisked away the first-place trophy from the winners. Jody Powell called the report "absurd," adding, "it is impossible to imagine a teacher and a Secret Service agent becoming involved in such foolishness."[35] Amy was, in fact, anything but spoiled. Her parents loved her, of course, but they had no intention of giving her everything she wanted. Mrs. Carter, for instance, tried to keep Amy out of her makeup. She also refused to let Amy watch the movie *Saturday Night Fever* because of its content. (Rosalynn made it up to Amy two years later by having the star of the movie, John Travolta, come to the White House for her twelfth birthday.)

Amy was, however, different from others of her age: she was the daughter of the president of the United States. As a result, there were limits on what she could do. In Georgia, the Carters had enjoyed taking Amy to places such as the zoo; that was not possible in Washington. That became clear when they went to the Smithsonian Air and Space Museum one day and found themselves mobbed. After that, the Carters decided to spend most weekends at Camp David.

The Carters' older children had lives of their own. Jack, Judy, and their son lived in Georgia, where Jack worked for a grain company. Annette, in addition to being an interior designer, was an avid photographer, a love that she and Jeff, who worked as a computer consultant, shared. Chip had a job with the Democratic National Committee and, during 1978, worked for the nonprofit organization Cities in Schools.

Although the public knew a lot about the Carters, there was much that was private, and Jimmy and Rosalynn wanted to keep it that way. When Barbara Walters interviewed the Carters just a month after the election, she asked personal questions, including what irritating habits they had, what type of bed they slept in, and what type of relationship the incoming first lady had with her mother-in-law. The Carters avoided direct answers to the more intimate questions, and outwardly, they appeared calm and collected. Inwardly, however, they were furious over what they regarded as requests for unnecessary and invasive information. Later that year, the White House refused to explain the reason for Mrs. Carter's gynecological surgery, prompting the media to speculate that it might have been cancer related. To further protect the family's privacy, Mrs. Carter did not permit tourists and only rarely allowed the media onto the second and third floors of the White House.

The Carters' contemporaries noted their desire for privacy. Even individuals who had known them for some time pointed out that Jimmy and Rosalynn were generally loners who had few intimate friends. Schneiders recollected eating supper in Plains with the Carters and Jody Powell during the presidential campaign and being told by the future press secretary that it was only "the second or third time that he had ever had dinner in the house." So, added Schneiders, "they didn't even invite close [friends like] Jody over for dinner."[36]

When Chip and Caron separated in November 1978, Rosalynn refused to discuss the matter. Her friends stated that both she and the president had tried to keep the couple together, but failed. Nor would she comment on an April 1979 *Washington Post* article that claimed that Jeff and Annette had smoked marijuana in Arlington, Virginia, at the home of Annette's college roommate. She would only say that Jeff was a hard worker and she "felt anger that they were portrayed as irresponsible." In response to reports that Jimmy's brother Billy was an alcoholic, Mrs. Carter commented simply that "he's ill" and that she "disagree[d] with some of the things he says." Even what the Carters talked about over the dinner table was a matter of speculation, with aides saying that the evening meal was generally informal and that the family might get into arguments "on everything from politics to sports." The media disliked the lack of access to the Carters' private life. Lee Thornton, CBS's White House correspondent, summed it up by declaring that Rosalynn Carter knew what being in the presidential mansion "was all about," and "all this talk about loss of privacy is just so much hooey."[37]

Thus, even when performing traditional first lady roles, such as hosting White House functions, and performing traditional wifely and motherly duties, such as protecting her family's privacy, Mrs. Carter raised controversy. In some respects, Mrs. Carter was a reluctant hostess. Although there were aspects of planning and hosting social events that she enjoyed, she clearly preferred politics and promoting her domestic agenda to overseeing parties at the White House. At times, Mrs. Carter combined the two, taking advantage of these social events and using them for political purposes to further her own agenda or that of her husband. Because tradition required the first lady to act as hostess at the presidential mansion, Mrs. Carter did so, and even skeptics were impressed with the variety of entertainment and the warmth of their hostess, notwithstanding the lack of hard liquor or the midnight cutoff of the festivities.

Likewise, Mrs. Carter's attempt to maintain her family's privacy was not without controversy. As public figures, they could not avoid the media spotlight, but she considered certain aspects of their lives off-limits. The media referred to Rosalynn Carter as the "steel magnolia," meaning that although she appeared feminine, kind, and warm, she could also be tough and cold. The contrast between the charming White House hostess and the icy woman determined to protect the intimate details of her life no doubt fed that reputation.

CHAPTER 5

THE FIRST LADY AND THE MEDIA

Rosalynn Carter had a love-hate relationship with the media. On the one hand, the press was impressed with her ability to engage in multiple initiatives, including working on behalf of the mentally ill and the elderly, traveling to Latin America, giving speeches in support of the president's programs, planning and hosting a wide variety of White House events, and still finding time for her family. On the other hand, many journalists criticized her fashion sense, her assumption of improper roles for a first lady, the size of her staff, and the poor relations between the East and West Wings. The first lady, meanwhile, attacked the media for not giving her programs, such as mental health, the attention they deserved because they were not "sexy."

The nature of the relationship that Rosalynn Carter would have with the media became apparent during the campaign. Reporters almost seemed in awe of the intensity of her efforts to get her husband elected. *U.S. News & World Report*, for example, commented that incumbent first lady Betty Ford was "more likely to lean toward ceremonial appearances than old-fashioned campaigning." And although Mrs. Ford's daily schedule was by no means "leisurely," she "limit[ed] the number of her daily engagements" and rarely spoke before large audiences. Mrs. Carter, in contrast, was a "whirlwind," a "political wife who can match her husband's pace on the campaign trail." During one three-day period, she campaigned for thirteen hours a day, visiting eight cities and giving fourteen speeches and well over a dozen interviews. Moreover, her addresses were politically oriented, lamenting the American people's lack of trust in their elected officials, advertising her husband's honesty and fiscal conservatism, and promoting her own agenda of initiatives.[1]

Yet reporters disliked the fact that Mrs. Carter seemed to repeat the same things her husband said during the campaign, and she managed to avoid slipups. Whereas the president's off-color interview in *Playboy* magazine had been a major gaffe, his wife made no such errors. Writer Gail Sheehy commented, "It drove [reporters] crazy that throughout the campaign she never made any of the juicy mistakes he did, not once," leading correspondents to comment that she had been "programmed" and "packaged."[2] Mary Hoyt, Mrs. Carter's press secretary during the campaign, rejected those assertions. Years later she said, "If you [interview Mrs. Carter] and think that there's any way that that woman's going to be packaged, I want you to call me."[3] Indeed, there is no evidence that Mrs. Carter was forced to do or say anything; rather, it was a matter of political sagacity. She believed that her successes would reflect well on her husband and, conversely, any lapses in judgment or errors would have the opposite impact. She simply did not want to give the media a story that might undermine Jimmy Carter's bid for the presidency. Rosalynn Carter did not like to lose, and if her husband was defeated in the election, she did not want to be responsible for it.

Following Carter's victory in November, a number of reporters shifted their focus to the incoming first lady's wardrobe. Even during the campaign, journalists had noted Mrs. Carter's preference for simple outfits, but the incoming first lady found questions about her wardrobe irrelevant and "silly." She admired the response of Margaret Trudeau, the wife of Canadian prime minister Pierre Trudeau, when faced with a similar situation: "If I were a man, would you be asking me where I got my suit made?" But Mrs. Carter kept her cool and defended her choices. Having sewed for much of her life, she saw no point in buying expensive clothes when she could make her own. (Indeed, she brought her sewing machine with her to the White House, although she admitted that she was too busy to do more than "hemming skirts and stitching blue jeans and fixing Amy's clothes.") Furthermore, being on the campaign trail for long hours every day made simple, comfortable outfits a practical choice.[4]

This preference for simple clothing and economy aroused controversy following the election. During the campaign, Mrs. Carter had stated that if her husband won, her gown for the inaugural ball would be the same beaded, blue chiffon dress she had worn to his gubernatorial inauguration—and that is exactly what she wore. This caused a stir among fashion correspondents and fashion industry executives. The former bemoaned the fact that the first lady was abandoning the glitz and glamour of the inauguration, and the latter feared that her fashion choices might affect taste in apparel nationwide, causing them to lose business. Put on the defensive, and no doubt hoping to turn media attention away from her wardrobe to more substantive matters, she purchased some designer items, including a cape to throw over her inaugural gown and a blue-green dress with a matching coat for the inauguration itself.

The first lady's fashion sense, though, continued to draw attention. The purchase of a few designer outfits could not hide her affinity for simple (even homemade) clothing with long sleeves and high necklines. Although the 50 million Americans who enjoyed sewing, along with the pattern and fabric industry, applauded the first lady, the fashion industry did not. Designers, however, had little to worry about. What the first lady wore had little if any impact on the country's fashion sense. And, as one reporter stated, in light of the fact that both of the Carters had worked in the business world, it was "unlikely that either one will ignore the fourth largest industry in the country."[5] Even so, Mrs. Carter's wardrobe continued to draw attention, and in their reports on her activities, correspondents often mentioned what she was wearing.

The worlds of fashion and journalism came together on 23 March 1977, when the first lady visited New York City's Seventh Avenue—also known as "Fashion Avenue"—and ordered several designer outfits. *Women's Wear Daily*, a fashion newspaper, provided a detailed report of the shopping spree, and other media outlets picked up the story. News of the New York visit was embarrassing and potentially damaging to the White House. With inflation being such a major a problem, Mrs. Carter's seemingly frivolous expenditures appeared to fly in the face of President Carter's efforts to avoid unnecessary spending. *Women's Wear* tried to keep the story alive when it reported on 25 March that a representative from the first lady's Press Office had asked the newspaper to cease its efforts to determine exactly how much Mrs. Carter had spent. *Women's Wear* responded by publishing the estimated retail value of the outfits—approximately $7,000. There is no evidence that anyone from the Press Office or the East Wing had contacted *Women's Wear.* As Hoyt put it, doing so not only would "have made me the laughingstock of Washington"[6] but also would have blown out of proportion a matter that the White House preferred to downplay. In fact, the story of the shopping spree quickly disappeared from the headlines—at least for a while.

The dispute with *Women's Wear* reappeared briefly in May, when Mrs. Carter left on her seven-nation tour of Latin America. According to reports, it was *Women's Wear*'s article on the New York shopping spree that led Hoyt to exclude that paper's reporter from the group of correspondents who accompanied the first lady. Hoyt strongly denied this claim, although she admitted having a poor relationship with *Women's Wear,* dating from her work on Senator Edmund Muskie's 1972 presidential campaign. During the campaign, Kandy Stroud, a journalist with *Women's Wear,* had written a somewhat unflattering story about the candidate's wife, Jane, including that she called her husband "Big Daddy." *Newsweek* magazine picked up the article, as did other media outlets throughout the country. Mrs. Muskie subsequently received numerous letters stating that her husband should not be president because he was married to her. Hoyt later commented that Stroud's story had seriously damaged the Muskie campaign. "So," she concluded, "I had this terrible experience with *Women's Wear,*" but she claimed that neither the Stroud article nor the March report on the shopping spree had played any part in her decision not to invite a *Women's Wear* correspondent to join the first lady's entourage.[7] Rather, the aircraft that Mrs. Carter would be flying on had a limited capacity, and because the trip was one "of international importance," the press secretary decided that she had to get "tough" and give the "people who have reason to go aboard—the [New York] Times, the [Washington] Post—some priority."[8] It just did not make sense to include the representative of a publication that focused on fashion.

After this brief squabble, the majority of media attention prior to and during Mrs. Carter's Latin America trip focused on the topics she discussed and the difficulties she faced in some of the countries she visited (such as Brazil). The major newspapers, including the *New York Times* and the *Washington Post,* often questioned the seriousness of her trip, however. They reported that she was going to be holding "substantive talks," but they made sure to put quotation marks around that phrase. Other journalists questioned whether her journey crossed the line of proper behavior for a first lady. Meg Greenfield wrote in *Newsweek* that if Mrs. Carter intended to act as an official representative of the United States, then she had to be accountable for her actions, and Bob Wiedrich of the *Chicago Tribune* advised the president to "stop using members of his family as ex officio representatives of the American people who voted him into office." Others were more supportive. "After one week of her trip," stated an *NBC Nightly News* report on 6 June, "Mrs. Carter has played the role of the wife of a head of state while discussing the fine points of foreign policy with foreign leaders." Similarly, the *Richmond Times-Dispatch* remarked that although the first lady was not an expert on Latin America, "when one considers the hash experts have made of U.S. relations with much of the world, this may not be a bad thing."[9]

What bothered Mrs. Carter was that her domestic agenda did not receive the same kind of press attention as her trip to Latin America or even her visit to Thailand two years later. She pointed out, for instance, that although the *New York Times* reported on the establishment of the President's Commission on Mental Health, the *Washington Post* said nothing, choosing to comment instead on her decision not to serve liquor in the White House. In mid-1978, *Time* magazine also noted this lack of coverage: "After 18 months in the White House, Rosalynn Carter remains something of an enigma, her public statements rare, her public activities largely ignored. She seems to be the First Lady nobody knows."[10] In light of the number of interviews and press conferences she gave, the comment about her lack of public statements is questionable. But it is true that her public activities were not given high priority by the media, and the question becomes why.

There are several likely reasons. One was the nature of the activities involved. Mrs. Carter representing her husband in substantive discussions with foreign leaders or traveling to Southeast Asia to confront an international crisis were major news stories and, in the case of Latin America, something that no other first lady had ever done. Fighting for passage of the equal rights amendment (ERA), promoting volunteerism, advocating immunization for children, or working to aid the mentally ill and elderly were less newsworthy because these issues were more traditional ones on which any first lady might focus: women's rights, morality, and caring for others.

A second factor that affected coverage of the first lady's agenda was reporters' perception that she was not giving them a story worthy of attention. It was, in short, a continuation of the claim of "packaging." Mrs. Carter never disagreed with her husband publicly, claiming that to do so would undermine her credibility and influence with him, and she rarely made major mistakes that might draw unwanted media attention. Journalist Sally Quinn wrote in June 1978 that the president's aides had tried "to package" Rosalynn during the campaign, "and they're still doing it." Some of Quinn's colleagues disagreed with this assessment. For instance, Stroud wrote that Mrs. Carter was "not about to allow herself to be programmed or packaged."[11] Nevertheless, journalists looking for a story seemed to agree that the first lady was not the place to find one.

Third, editors seemed to be unsure where to put stories about Mrs. Carter. Traditionally, articles about the activities of the first lady appeared in the "lifestyle" section, where one would find information on fashion, furniture, and art. But with Mrs. Carter involved in matters of domestic and even international politics, editors were torn: should the articles go in the style, local news, or national news section? Sometimes, an article that Mrs. Carter felt belonged in the front section ended up buried in the style section or was not published at all. This lack of coverage frustrated the first lady. How, she argued, could she combat the stigma surrounding mental illness or promote volunteerism if those issues remained hidden from the public?

Finally, the sparse media coverage had to do with an issue that feminists had already pointed out: image—or, more precisely, the lack of one. Because Mrs. Carter agreed with her husband on every issue, because she was involved in so many different projects, and because she saw her role as one of actively assisting the president rather than being a traditional first lady, she had failed to develop her own identity. "She's too goddamn normal," stated a reporter for the *Washington Post*. Helen Thomas, a journalist for United Press International, declared, "There's no ferment, no mystique" about Rosalynn Carter. "She creates neither love nor hate."[12] Without an image of her own for reporters to grab on to, the press seemed unsure how to deal with the first lady.

Some journalists believed that Hoyt only made matters worse. They charged the first lady's press secretary with putting a wall around her boss, making it hard for the media to contact Mrs. Carter or to get to know her better. Faith Collins, Hoyt's deputy, emphatically denied the charge, as did Hoyt herself. "Why," asked the press secretary, "would I want to keep the press from Rosalynn?" Just as it was impossible to package the first lady, she declared, it was also impossible to "put her in a box."[13]

If there was a lack of access, it was not because Hoyt was keeping the first lady away from reporters; it was simply a matter of time. In an effort to increase efficiency, Mrs. Carter had cards printed with her signature to respond to requests for autographs, and she compiled a free pamphlet that answered frequently asked questions about the presidential mansion. But even so, there was only so much she could do. Mrs. Carter, pointed out her press secretary, "gets 2,000 letters a week and 500 invitations. She's more active than any first lady I know of."[14] Still, Mrs. Carter found time for 154 press interviews in her first two years as first lady.

Maybe because Mrs. Carter did not create an image for herself, the media created one for her: she was the new Eleanor Roosevelt, one of the most powerful first ladies ever. The fact that Mrs. Carter's actual first name was Eleanor added to the persona. Rosalynn Carter "is likely to be the most influential First Lady since Eleanor Roosevelt," wrote the *New York Times*'s William Shannon a few months before the 1976 election.[15] Throughout Mrs. Carter's tenure as first lady, reporters tended to make comparisons with Mrs. Roosevelt and, to a lesser extent, Edith Bolling Wilson, who largely assumed her husband's role after Woodrow Wilson's debilitating stroke in October 1919.

Journalists found evidence to support this image during the first year of the Carter administration. Mrs. Carter admitted that she acted as her husband's sounding board and that they discussed almost every issue facing the administration; she would even offer

Mary Hoyt, Mrs. Carter's press secretary and, for a time, East Wing coordinator. She was falsely accused by the media of keeping reporters away from the first lady. Courtesy of the Jimmy Carter Library.

her opinion without being asked for it. Jimmy Carter called her "a perfect extension of me" and his "political partner." Linda Charlton of the *New York Times* commented that such language "might have been applied to Mrs. Roosevelt and, to a degree, to Lady Bird Johnson but to few other Presidents' wives."[16]

Although Mrs. Carter looked up to Mrs. Roosevelt, she also admired other first ladies, including Jacqueline Kennedy and Lady Bird

Johnson. Indeed, there is no evidence that she ever aspired to become another Eleanor Roosevelt, and she consistently denied media reports to that effect. "I've read that I've tried to be like Eleanor Roosevelt, but that's absolutely false.... I've been doing the things I think are important, and I've not tried to copy anybody."[17] Rather, Mrs. Carter saw herself as no different from many other women, assuming an active role in the well-being of her family and maintaining the partnership she had developed with her husband.

For those reasons, Mrs. Carter felt justified in advising and attempting to influence the president. She thought, for example, that he was trying to do too much too fast. In addition to his vast array of foreign policy initiatives, the president had a number of domestic policies that he was pursuing, including implementing a comprehensive energy program, containing hospital costs, cutting a number of water projects proposed by members of Congress, passing ethics-in-government legislation, reorganizing the executive branch, and reforming the tax code, the welfare system, and Social Security. Mrs. Carter, who did not like to fail, believed that her husband was spreading himself too thin and could not possibly implement all his proposals.

The first lady also advised her husband on his speeches. She often read drafts of them, listened to tape recordings of them, and suggested changes. As was the case during the 1976 campaign, she urged him to speak in simple terms. For instance, she criticized an early draft of Carter's July 1979 address on energy, telling him that it was too complex and confusing. The American people "don't want to hear about a new program that will allocate energy to the elderly at a lower cost. They just want to be told that everything is going to be all right and that somebody understands the situation and has it under control."[18]

And Mrs. Carter often made her opinions known with regard to personnel decisions. Aside from her opposition to Bella Abzug's appointment to the National Advisory Committee on Women and her desire to see Joseph Califano removed as secretary of Health, Education, and Welfare, she convinced Gerald Rafshoon to join the administration as communications assistant in 1978, urged Carter to name Robert Strauss as chief negotiator for the Middle East peace talks in 1979, and encouraged her husband to hire Anne Wexler as deputy undersecretary of commerce and Sarah Weddington as special assistant to the president.

The first lady was not always successful, however. The president rejected her concerns about his trying to do too much, declaring that "it was better to get 95 percent of something than it was to get just an awful 5 percent of what you really wanted."[19] Nor did he see eye to eye with her on other matters, such as turning up the White House thermostats, mining Iran's harbors during the hostage crisis, or approving a series of tax breaks for business (which she opposed). But she did have an important, if not decisive, impact on other matters, including obtaining more funding for the Mental Health Systems Act and using Billy Carter's contacts with Libya in an attempt to free the hostages in Iran.

Just how much influence Mrs. Carter had, or should have had, split journalistic opinion. Shortly after the election, for instance, Hoyt announced that Mrs. Carter would participate in advising the president while at the same time developing her own agenda. That comment immediately brought criticism. "Would you cool it a little on all that big talk about how you fully expect to share in making United States policy decisions?" declared an editorial in the *Cleveland Press*. It was fine for Mrs. Carter to help the mentally ill and the elderly, the newspaper continued, "but please, Miz Rosalynn, when it comes to picking ambassadors, the Arab oil talks, the United States, the internal problems of Chile, banning the bomb and trying to figure out Anwar Sadat, cool it—and leave the driving to Jimmy and elected members of Congress." The *New York Times* disagreed. Taking note of Mrs. Carter's work during the campaign, the paper wrote that her husband's "reliance upon her was as predictable as his reliance upon Hamilton Jordan or Jody Powell." Being first lady "does not automatically endow her with governmental skills, but neither should it be a disqualification. Her power and influence are derivative, but so is that of half the appointees of any President."[20]

Besides their comparisons of Rosalynn Carter with Eleanor Roosevelt, reporters developed another image of the first lady: a steel magnolia. The term, which had first been used during the 1976 campaign, reflected that fact that, on the outside, she was sweet, gracious, feminine, and even shy, but underneath she could be hard and unforgiving. Protective of her family, she criticized those who called the president weak or inconsistent and advised reporters that they should be focusing on all the good things he was doing for the nation. Criticism of her husband's failure to solve the energy crisis prompted her to blame the Republicans for it. She also rejected reports that President Carter was a micromanager who wanted to know everything that was going on in every department. "Unlike you might believe," she declared, "he does NOT sit down and study every minute. He does NOT go back to the office at night."[21] She felt free to contact reporters if she thought that they had misconstrued what she and her husband were trying to do, and she refused to discuss personal issues, such as the breakup of the marriage Chip and Caron.

The press sometimes got the story wrong. For example, the *New Republic*'s John Osborne claimed that West Wing officials had to "muzzle" Mrs. Carter during a trip to Latin America with the president because she had so upset Latin American leaders during her 1977 visit. A furious Hoyt contacted Osborne, who apologized, blaming his article on sloppy reporting.[22]

But the media also got some stories right. The president's policies could be inconsistent, even contradictory. Upon taking office, he had pushed an economic stimulus package that included a $50 rebate for every taxpayer, only to change his mind after he had lined up congressional support. He had promised honesty in government, yet he initially supported Bert Lance, bringing that commitment into question. He called for repressive governments to stop mistreating their citizens, yet he gave economic and military assistance to some of those same governments, including Iran and South Korea, claiming that it gave him leverage. He had a tendency, especially in the first two years of his administration, to combine the Soviet policies advocated by Secretary of State Cyrus Vance, who favored taking a soft line toward the Kremlin, and the more hard-line stance of Zbigniew Brzezinski; thus, the president might berate Moscow for some indiscretion while at the same time stating that he wanted better U.S.-Soviet relations. These inconsistent and contradictory positions caused confusion and anger in Congress. For instance, his change of heart on the tax rebate led Al Ullman (D-Oregon), chairman of the House Ways and Means Committee, to comment, "It was a little less than fair to those of us who support[ed] it against our better judgment and worked hard to get it

The Carters' middle son, Chip, wife Caron, and son James Earl IV. The first lady refused to discuss the breakup of Chip and Caron's marriage with the media. Courtesy of the Jimmy Carter Library.

passed." About giving aid to human rights violators, Senator James Abourezk (D-South Dakota) declared, "There is no rationale that I can think of or that anybody has offered me that would militate for giving the Administration what they claim in flexibility to negotiate with these countries about their human rights situation."[23]

It was also true that President Carter was a micromanager. His handwriting file in the Carter Library shows a president who wanted to be involved in much more than policy; he even had an opinion on how many pens should be provided at signing ceremonies. Carter had originally planned to wake up at 6:00 each morning and spend fifty-five hours a week working; soon, however, he pushed his wake-up call back to 5:30 and was spending eighty hours at work, including some nights. "Look, we are trying to do too much," Powell told his boss in April 1977, but he had no luck changing the president's ways.[24]

That Mrs. Carter would deny her husband's inconsistency or his micromanaging led some in the media to believe that she was losing sight of reality. By the end of 1977, polls showed a president with falling support as a result of the Lance scandal and rising energy prices and inflation. When Mrs. Carter responded by declaring that her husband had "had a better first year than any president in recent history," Vera Glaser of the *Detroit Free Press* wrote that the first lady seemed "oblivious to the political facts of life affecting her husband."[25]

Mrs. Carter admitted that the president had made some mistakes. While she blamed herself for not campaigning harder for the ERA, she noted that her husband could have done a better job in improving relations with Congress. It appears that her defense of her husband and his policies was just a natural reflex in response to criticism of him. As his wife, she felt free to comment on his mistakes, but she did not want anyone outside the family doing it.

This impression of a tough woman who would do what it took to protect and support her husband took on a new dimension when journalists discovered that Mrs. Carter had started to attend cabinet meetings. To the first lady, this seemed to be a natural outgrowth of the partnership she had developed with her husband—and it was his idea. Mrs. Carter had become frustrated with the media's reporting of administration activities, and she wanted to know whether the news stories were accurate. The president recommended that she attend cabinet meetings and see for herself, which she did starting in February 1978. Mrs. Carter did not actively participate in these meetings; rather, she sat to one side and took notes (although she reportedly sat in the vice president's chair one day when he was not present). Moreover, during the Carter presidency, cabinet meetings were not where the major decisions were made. It was more "like show and tell," commented Schneiders, where each member of the cabinet would explain what was happening in his or her department or agency. The transcripts of those meetings, many of which are available to researchers, attest to that fact. Indeed, after leaving the White House, Brzezinski said that he regarded cabinet meetings as a waste of time.[26]

To reporters and the public at large, however, news that the first lady had taken the unprecedented step of sitting in on cabinet meetings provided further proof that she was indeed a very powerful and influential force within the administration. As early as June 1977, Meg Greenfield of *Newsweek* had referred to Rosalynn Carter as "Mrs. President," and by the middle of 1978, others were calling her "the first woman vice-president," the "co-president," and the "second most powerful person" in the capital. *McCall's* magazine asked in March 1980, "Is Rosalynn Carter Really Running the Country?"[27]

Statements by the president and the first lady only fed the controversy. The president commented in an August 1978 press conference that "with the exception of top-secret material, where security restrains me, I share almost everything with her." When asked how much influence his wife had on him, the president replied, "I would hate to admit how much." Commenting on the cabinet shakeup in July 1979, Mrs. Carter seemed to mix up her pronouns: "I just . . . uh . . . we . . . I . . . uh, Jimmy thought, and I agreed with him, that it was better to do it fast."[28]

Correspondents continued to be split over whether the first lady's influence was a good thing or a bad thing. The *Christian Science Monitor* urged her to stop being "a public prop for a President who has to stand on his own two feet." Joan Beck of the *Chicago Tribune* seconded the *Monitor*, accusing the Carters of running the country like a "mom-and-pop shop." She added that the president's "chief adviser should be someone who knows more than peanuts." The *Manchester Union Leader* stopped short of telling the first lady to limit her role to that of hostess but stated that she "might be advised to stay a little further away from the actual seat of government for this country than she has in the past."[29] "Who elected her?" became a popular refrain.

Mrs. Carter still had her defenders, however. Richard Cohen, writing in the *Washington Post*, stated that some of the accusations made against Mrs. Carter were the result of sexism. Moreover, he said, her accusers should keep in mind that her support of her husband and her willingness to speak her mind to him were no different from what any other wife might do. The *Washington Star* asked, "What disservice has this woman done to the president's supporters? How has she misconstrued his purposes? . . . The complaints about an overly dynamic First Lady seem like a case of hollering before you're hit." Columnist Carl Rowan's endorsement of the first couple may have been the strongest: "I'll be damned if I ever want my country run by a president who is too dumb to consult his wife."[30]

Public opinion polls reflected the media's ambivalence. A *New York Times*–CBS poll taken in the fall of 1980 gave Mrs. Carter a 46 percent favorable rating, versus 9 percent unfavorable; this compared with a 44 percent unfavorable rating for her husband. However, Mrs. Carter's approval rating was still 25 points lower than that of Betty Ford at about the same point before the 1976 election.

Of interest, though, is that even some of Rosalynn Carter's critics seemed to be in awe of her. In this case, they were impressed not by her influence but by how much she was able to accomplish. In March 1978 *U.S. News & World Report* published a "partial list" of the first lady's activities in 1977. The magazine noted that she had spent 71 days traveling, during which she visited 21 cities in the United States and 16 foreign countries; she had attended more than 220 meetings and spent 71 hours in foreign and domestic policy briefings; and she had devoted 250 hours to working on mental health initiatives and 10 hours to improving her speed-reading skills. In November 1979 it provided a similar list, showing that the first lady had attended nearly 650 briefings, visited 36 foreign nations and 150 U.S. cities, given more than 150 press interviews, and delivered nearly 250 speeches. Vera Glaser, who had criticized the first lady for losing sight of reality, added, "All this in addition to her Spanish-language studies and responsibilities as a wife and mother of four, including 10-year-old daughter Amy."[31]

The public felt the same way. In a December 1980 Gallup poll, Americans cited Mrs. Carter as the woman they most admired, tied with Mother Teresa. Thus, like the media, Americans greatly respected Mrs. Carter, but they did not love her. They recognized that she was a good person who wanted to do good things for her country, but they questioned whether, in the process, she had overstepped the boundaries of the proper role of a first lady.

Editors' confusion over where to put stories about Mrs. Carter and journalists' debate over her influence in the White House reflected the same concern raised by her trips abroad as her husband's official representative: what is the proper role of the first lady? That Rosalynn Carter took an active part in her husband's administration was actually nothing new. A recent study that examined the presidencies of George Washington through Bill Clinton "found that at least 31 first ladies discussed politics with the president, 26 were confidantes or advisers . . . and 14 'influenced' the appointment process."[32]

But what made Rosalynn Carter different was that her activism and involvement rose to new levels. Never before had a first lady traveled as her husband's official representative abroad to discuss substantive issues; never before had the president's wife appeared to have such an influential role in the Oval Office. The result was a dichotomy: On the one hand, it was easy to accept what Mrs. Carter was doing; she personified women's efforts to be heard and to be treated as equals, whether in the public or the private arena. On the other hand, she had not been elected and had no formal political training, yet she was involved in issues that affected the country's domestic and international affairs. Mrs. Carter was, in short, a transitional first lady at a time when gender relations were undergoing great change. How far that transition should be allowed to go when it came to the office of the first lady was an issue on which the public and the media were unable to agree.

CHAPTER 6

THE UNFINISHED AGENDA

In his 1998 work *The Unfinished Presidency,* historian Douglas Brinkley contends that Jimmy Carter regarded his postpresidential years as an opportunity to continue the policies he had started but failed to complete while in the White House.[1] Key among these initiatives was the promotion of world peace. Rosalynn Carter saw her post–White House years in a similar light. She remained committed to creating a "caring society" and, in addition to continuing the programs she had championed during her years as first lady, joined her husband's efforts to foster peace and halt the spread of disease.

By the middle of 1979, it appeared that President Carter had little chance of winning a second term in office. Criticism of the administration's policies, such as its handling of revolutions in Iran and Nicaragua and the Soviets' machinations in Africa; of its pragmatic human rights policy; and, most important, of its inability to solve problems at home, such as inflation and unemployment, sapped the president's support. Believing that Carter could not be reelected, a growing number of Democrats urged Massachusetts senator Edward Kennedy to seek the party's nomination. Kennedy, in fact, had lost patience with the president's fiscal conservatism and his refusal to support a comprehensive national health insurance program that the senator favored. Indeed, a poll taken in May 1979 found that Democratic voters preferred Kennedy over Carter by 23 points.

Rosalynn Carter was one of the first in the White House to see Kennedy as a danger to her husband's chances for reelection, yet she had no doubt who would win. "We would rather have [Kennedy] on our side," she stated. "But if he runs we'll beat him.... It will be difficult, but we *will* prevail."[2] The first lady had good reason to believe this when Kennedy announced his candidacy on 7 November 1979. The senator had chosen an inauspicious time to throw his hat in the ring—three days earlier, Iranian militants had taken hostage several dozen Americans working at the U.S. embassy in Tehran. Americans rallied around the president, and his approval rating skyrocketed to 61 percent. In the meantime, Kennedy had given rambling answers during a CBS interview with correspondent Roger Mudd on 4 November. Then, after the seizure of the hostages, Kennedy attacked the shah of Iran for his repressive policies and the Carter administration's decision to admit the Iranian leader into the United States for cancer treatment. An angry president responded that the shah was not an issue; the focus should be on freeing the American hostages.

Thus, when Carter announced his candidacy on 4 December, both he and his wife were confident that he would receive his party's nomination. They had even more reason to feel self-assured following the Soviet invasion of Afghanistan later that month. The president's tough response, which included the imposition of a grain embargo against Moscow, further rallied Americans behind him. This support was evident in the first caucus of the election season, held in January 1980 in Iowa. Despite the adverse impact of the embargo on their economic well-being, farmers in that largely agricultural state overwhelmingly voted for Carter. The president's victory in Iowa suggested that he would easily defeat Kennedy.

This time, President Carter had not campaigned in Iowa. Rather, he had decided to stay in Washington to monitor the hostage crisis. Thus, unlike in 1976, the 1980 campaign fell largely on Rosalynn's shoulders, although Chip and Lillian helped. The first lady ran an intense campaign, spending upwards of twelve hours each day traveling and giving speeches and interviews. When she flew, she used a DC-9 jet that had two sections. In the front were two tables, chairs, and a row of aircraft seats where Mrs. Carter, press secretary Mary Hoyt, personal assistant Madeline MacBean, and their staff worked. Behind a curtained partition was a typewriter and a copy machine, along with thirty additional seats for reporters, Secret Service agents, and anyone else who was along for the ride. With the help of that plane, between September 1979 and October 1980, Mrs. Carter spoke in more than 160 cities in nearly forty states to diverse groups ranging from the elderly to factory workers. Between June and November 1980 alone, she raised some $1 million for her husband's campaign.

During the campaign, the first lady developed a standard address that usually began with an explanation of her husband's determination to stay in Washington. She then turned to his achievements, including his promotion of human rights, the Camp David accords, the Panama Canal treaties, efforts to reform both Social Security and welfare, and the creation of the Departments of Education and of Energy. She also made sure to customize each speech, emphasizing certain points that would appeal to her audience. Thus, before congregants at a church in Harlem, she focused on her husband's religious devotion; to a group of senior citizens, she highlighted all the president had done to provide federal assistance to the elderly. The intensity of the first lady's drive led journalist Myra MacPherson to comment that Mrs. Carter had again become "the quiet battler of 1976. And no one can mistake that she means business."[3]

It was one thing, however, to "mean business" and quite another to convey a convincing message. With inflation hitting 18 percent in February 1980 and unemployment on the rise as well, the first lady attempted to reassure Americans that her husband had the courage to face the country's troubles. But sometimes her rhetoric missed the mark, such as when she compared the United States' current economic difficulties with those of the Great Depression. She apparently forgot that Americans had refused to reelect President Herbert Hoover, who, like Carter, seemed to be unable to bring economic stability to the nation.

In fact, those economic problems worried Carter's advisers. If the president could not bring inflation and unemployment down, his sudden rise in the polls could collapse. The foreign policy situation added to their concerns. If the hostage crisis dragged on, and if the

Soviets refused to withdraw from Afghanistan, Americans would have all the more reason to doubt the president's abilities. For the time being, however, Carter had the support of the American people. For that reason, his wife convinced him not to debate either Kennedy or California governor Jerry Brown, who had also thrown his hat into the ring for the Democratic nomination. Her public explanation was that "partisan politics now might endanger the hostages" by suggesting to the Iranian militants that U.S. public opinion was divided.[4] The main reason, however, was political. With Carter's lead in the polls, his victory in the New Hampshire primary in February, and news that Kennedy's support in the South and Midwest were declining, it made no sense for the president to engage the Massachusetts lawmaker in a debate that might resonate in the latter's favor.

In March, however, Carter suffered two significant defeats in Connecticut and New York. Part of the reason was a mix-up involving a vote in the United Nations. Earlier that month, the United Nations had considered a resolution to call on Israel to stop the construction of settlements in the territory it had captured from neighboring Arab nations in the 1967 war, including in the city of Jerusalem. Although not happy about the settlements, Carter realized that pressuring Israel to stop its activities in Jerusalem would anger the American Jewish opinion. Therefore, he had instructed the State Department to vote in favor of the resolution only if it was silent on Jerusalem. The United States subsequently voted in support of the resolution, discovering only after the fact that the reference to Jerusalem had not been cut. The president repudiated the vote, citing faulty communication, and the first lady told members of the Jewish organization B'nai B'rith that although the vote was "unfortunate," her husband had "moved immediately, as soon as he realized what had happened to correct the mistake."[5] Nevertheless, angered by the UN vote, Jews in Connecticut and New York overwhelmingly gave their support to Kennedy.

The UN vote was not the only reason for the president's losses, however. As his advisers had feared, Carter's support in the polls was soft. The continued crises in Iran and Afghanistan, along with the sick economy, caused the president's numbers to decline. The president's decision (over his wife's objections) to try to control inflation by cutting funding for a variety of social programs supported by New York voters did not help matters. Thus, the results in Connecticut and New York were seen as a vote against Carter's policies in general, not just a statement against U.S. support for the UN resolution on Israel. Mrs. Carter later wrote that the outcome in the two northeastern states "gave new life to Kennedy's lingering candidacy which would in the long run cause us and the Democratic party to suffer interminably."[6]

Serious damage had already been done. By early April, seven out of ten Americans opposed Carter's reelection, and for the first time, a plurality supported the likely Republican contender, former California governor Ronald Reagan. The failed mission in April to rescue the hostages in Iran, Secretary of State Cyrus Vance's resignation in protest of that mission, and persistent concerns over the economy led Americans to question Carter's competence to lead the nation. Realizing Americans' doubts, the president decided to give up his Rose Garden strategy and go on the stump. By June, Carter had rounded up enough delegates to guarantee himself the Democratic nomination, and Brown had pulled out of the race. But Kennedy had won primaries in enough states, including Pennsylvania, Michigan, California, and New Jersey, that he could continue his campaign all the way to the Democratic convention in August. And with the polls showing Carter lagging farther behind Reagan, it appeared that the president stood little chance of reelection.

Despite her efforts to maintain a positive attitude, there were rare occasions when Mrs. Carter let loose her frustrations. Paul Costello, one of the first lady's aides, remembered one summer night at an airport. Just as she was leaving for her next stop, Mrs. Carter received word from the Secret Service that she had a telephone call from her husband. He asked how the campaign was going, and the first lady responded, "It's really rough. Everybody's beating up on you." Rather than listen, he interrupted her, saying, "Rosalynn, I don't want to hear any of this." Angrily, she replied, "You can just go to hell," and hung up on him.[7]

Reagan received the Republican nomination in July; the following month, the Democratic Party held its convention in New York. Kennedy had called for an open convention, meaning that the delegates could vote their conscience rather than sticking to their previous commitments to either Democratic candidate. Between the two of them, the Carters contacted each delegate, successfully convincing them to reject the senator's proposal for an open convention. With no chance of winning the nomination, Kennedy formally withdrew from the race. To try to placate Kennedy and his supporters, the president agreed to incorporate into the party platform several planks favored by the senator, including a public works program and an agreement not to use unemployment or higher interest rates as a way to combat inflation. In a further attempt to demonstrate party unity, the president wanted Kennedy to join himself, Rosalynn, Vice President Walter Mondale, and Mondale's wife, Joan, on the platform. When the senator arrived, recalled Mrs. Carter, he shook hands with everyone and then "stood awkwardly to one side." The first lady suggested that the president walk over and shake the senator's hand to make Kennedy feel "more at ease," and Carter did so. But to Mrs. Carter's consternation, the media reported that the president had "'chas[ed Kennedy] around on the platform' to get his attention and support." Moreover, at the earliest opportunity, Senator Kennedy left the convention hall. Reagan, who had watched the events on television, commented, "If that's the best they can do in unity, they have a long way to go."[8]

Despite the problems at the Democratic convention, polls showed that Carter had cut into Reagan's lead. A Harris survey, for example, reported that the former California governor was only 6 points ahead of Carter, versus 20 points prior to the convention. Believing that Reagan was vulnerable, the Carter campaign developed a strategy that it hoped would lead to success. First, the president would not participate in any formal debates. The presidential race in 1980 was actually among three candidates: Carter, Reagan, and Representative John Anderson (R-Illinois), who ran as an independent. The president was under pressure to engage in a three-way debate with his opponents, but he recognized that whatever he did, it was a no-win situation. If he refused to face Reagan and Anderson, his political adversaries would charge him with running scared. But if he agreed to a debate, the two other presidential contenders could gang up on him. The president decided on the first option, and his wife (using the first person plural) justified his decision. "We've never been assured of a one-on-one debate with Governor Reagan," she stated, and for that reason, her husband would not agree to take part in a televised debate.[9] Although the president's decision was criticized, the political impact was minimal, with the polls showing little change.

Simultaneously, the president and first lady focused on Carter's accomplishments and the threat that the Republican candidate posed not only to traditional Democratic constituencies but also to world peace. Mrs. Carter declared that her husband had passed an energy program, had done much to help the elderly and women, and was working hard to get the economy on its feet. Meanwhile, she charged that Reagan opposed Medicare and would make Social Security voluntary, thereby endangering the welfare of the nation's elderly. She rejected Republican claims that Carter had weakened the U.S. military, pointing out that defense spending had increased every year he had served as president. Conversely, her husband was not a "trigger-happy" individual like Reagan, whose policies might drag the country into military conflict. Although the hostages had not yet been released, Mrs. Carter explained to an audience in South Carolina, "we could have been at war with this crisis if we did not have a level head in the White House." To voters in Fort Worth, Texas, she called her husband the "president of peace," adding, "not a single U.S. serviceman has lost his life in combat since he has been in office." Reagan, however, "has said some things that need to be looked into."[10]

Sometimes the first lady made exaggerated claims. For instance, she argued that her husband had "saved the Social Security system from bankruptcy and put it back on a solid foundation," despite a report issued earlier in 1980 that stated that the continued weakness of the economy would compromise that program's solvency. She also contended that her husband "has a better relationship with Congress than anybody has in a long time,"[11] when in fact, quite the opposite was true. Carter had achieved a number of successes in Congress, including passage of energy legislation, establishment of the Departments of Energy and Education, and ratification of the Panama Canal treaties, but Capitol Hill did not appreciate Carter's view of himself as a trustee of the American people, whose bidding should be carried out by lawmakers. Even members of his own party disliked his decision to give inflation priority over unemployment.

How much impact Mrs. Carter had on the campaign is a matter of debate. In a poll taken shortly before the election, 90 percent of Americans said that their vote would not be affected by a candidate's family members, including his wife. Yet some observers believed that Mrs. Carter made her influence felt. B. Drummond Ayres of the *New York Times* commented that at least portions of the first lady's speeches "almost always" appeared in the local media. "And many voters say that they find Mrs. Carter disarmingly effective." Indeed, stated one Pennsylvania newspaper, "If President Carter is elected to a second term, it may well be largely because of the efforts of the First Lady."[12]

Whether the first lady's speeches had an impact or not, the polls showed the president gaining on his Republican opponent. Carter joined his wife in attacking Reagan as someone who might lead the country into war, putting the former California governor on the defensive. Reagan also hurt himself by making a number of gaffes, such as when he said that the explosion of the Mount St. Helens volcano in Washington State in May 1980 had caused more environmental damage than automobiles; a day later, the Environmental Protection Agency released statistics belying that claim. Three weeks before the election, polls showed that the president had moved slightly ahead of Reagan. Of further concern to the Republicans were indications that Iran, which in September had been invaded by neighboring Iraq, wanted to find a solution to the hostage crisis. If Tehran freed the hostages before election day, it would almost surely guarantee Carter another four years in office. In response, the Reagan camp warned of a possible "October surprise." In October 1972, one month before the election, the Nixon administration had announced that it was close to reaching an agreement with North Vietnam to end the highly unpopular Vietnam War—an announcement that helped Richard Nixon win reelection. It was not until early 1973, however, that the agreement was finally signed. Republicans did not want the Carter administration to make a similar declaration with regard to the hostage situation as a means of getting votes.

In the meantime, Reagan had agreed to a one-on-one debate with Carter. Although some of the president's advisers worried that the former California governor's background as an actor would give him an advantage in a televised contest, there was general recognition

*Rosalynn Carter on the campaign trail, 1980.
Courtesy of the Jimmy Carter Library.*

that they had no choice but to agree to the debate, particularly because Carter had been insisting on such a face-off for months. Thus, the only debate was held in Cleveland on 28 October. Carter did well, demonstrating a knowledge of the issues and explaining his differences with Reagan. He made only one serious mistake: he said that he had asked his daughter, Amy, what she thought was the most serious issue facing the nation, and her response had been nuclear arms. The comment led some reporters to jest that Amy was running the country. Roger Staubach, star quarterback of the Dallas Cowboys, also had a daughter named Amy, and he jokingly stated on national television that he had asked her opinion about his team's loss in a recent football game, "and she said the number one problem was the bomb."[13] Even Mrs. Carter admitted that her husband should not have brought up Amy. As the president's advisers had feared, however, what hurt Carter the most was Reagan's style. The Republican nominee was relaxed and humorous, and he too appeared to be knowledgeable about the issues. And his question to voters, whether they felt that they were better off than they had been in 1976, resonated with them.

A few days later, the president announced that a significant breakthrough had occurred in the hostage crisis, making it appear that he was attempting an "October surprise" after all. Americans made their feelings clear by electing Reagan, who received 51 percent of the popular vote and 489 electoral votes to Carter's 49.

The outcome of the election came as a shock to the first lady. Even after the debate, she had still felt assured of victory. Not until a couple of days before election day did she begin to have doubts. Early Sunday morning, she received a call from the president, who said that he was heading to Washington because of new developments in the hostage crisis. "I don't know what is going to happen," he told her. "This could cause the election to go either way." She spent the remainder of that day and all day Monday campaigning, ending that evening in Huntington, Alabama. Just before her plane was ready to leave for Plains, Mrs. Carter called the White House to get the latest news. She was unable to reach her husband but did talk with Pat Caddell, the administration's pollster, who told her that the numbers did not "look too good." She arrived in Plains early on election day morning, got a few hours' sleep, and then met her husband at a nearby helicopter landing pad. Carter knew by that time that he had lost, but he wanted to break the news to Rosalynn himself. So it was at that moment that Mrs. Carter learned that they would not be spending another four years in Washington.[14]

Depressed by the outcome, the first lady had wanted to concede the election right away, but the president waited a few more hours. He finally gave his concession speech at around 10:00 that night; that he did so before the polls had closed on the West Coast angered Democrats, who blamed Carter for the defeat of some Democratic legislators. Mrs. Carter rejected the criticism of her husband's decision, later writing, "we just assumed that anybody interested in the news already knew that we had lost and that Jimmy didn't really need to concede at all."[15]

Mrs. Carter had always found it difficult to lose, and she commented years later that her husband did a much better job of handling defeat. She admitted feeling "bitter" toward just about everyone: the Iranians, the Republicans, and the media. In fact, the president felt similarly, but, wrote Mrs. Carter, "I was the only one who admitted it."[16] The president could not afford to dwell on his loss, however, for he still had not secured the release of the hostages. The Carters returned to the White House a few days after the election, and the president and his advisers continued the negotiations with Iran, with Algeria acting as an intermediary. Mrs. Carter no longer kept a regular schedule, using her time to read, relax, and watch movies with her husband most evenings.

Mrs. Carter acknowledged that she cried upon learning of the election results, but it was not until ten days later that the defeat really hit her. While going through the briefcase she had carried with her on her last day of campaigning, she heard a loudspeaker outside. Looking out the window, she saw her husband on the lawn standing next to Israeli prime minister Menachem Begin. It was at that point that she "began to cry—really cry, to sob—for the first time. It all seemed so unfair. Even the Middle East peace process that Jimmy so wanted to complete was ending for him, and maybe for the people in that war-torn part of the world. He should have been re-elected."[17]

Two rumors spread by the media—that Reagan's wife, Nancy, wanted the Carters to leave early so that she could begin decorating the White House and that she planned to remove a wall in the Lincoln Bedroom—only added to Mrs. Carter's frustration. Mrs. Reagan called Mrs. Carter to deny the rumors, but it appears that both were true. The incoming first lady believed that the Carters had not treated the White House well and that it was time to make changes to bring "class and dignity" to the presidential mansion. The reports hurt the Carters, who believed that they had done much to enhance the prestige of the White House, such as increasing the size of the presidential art collection and inviting internationally renowned artists to perform there.[18]

By the time the Carters left the White House to attend Reagan's inauguration, U.S. and Iranian officials had overcome the last hurdles to the hostages' release. The former captives had been put on jets ready to head for Germany and freedom, but the aircraft still sat on the tarmac in Tehran. The Carters then realized that the Iranians would not let the planes take off until Reagan had taken the oath of office, an act that Mrs. Carter later called "despicable."[19] After the inauguration, a Secret Service agent walked up to Mrs. Carter and let her know that the planes were on their way. Happy with that knowledge, Rosalynn and Jimmy Carter boarded Air Force One for the last time for their flight home to Plains. The following day, the now former president traveled to Germany to greet the hostages. When he returned home, the Carters, exhausted and depressed, spent ten days vacationing in the Virgin Islands, where they fished, hiked, sailed, slept, and learned how to windsurf. Then, back in Plains, they faced the uncertainties of post–White House life.

One of those uncertainties was whether they even wanted to live in Plains. Having spent the past fifteen years involved in first state and then national and international politics, they both feared that living in a small, rural town might be exceedingly boring. Another question was what to do about Amy, who was used to city life and was not happy about being in Plains. Also, the Carters had to repair their home, find a place to put all the materials they had accumulated during their years in Atlanta and Washington, and figure out how to raise $25 million for Carter's presidential library. Finally, and most important, they had to confront some serious personal financial problems.

The first two concerns—boredom and Amy's future—proved to be the least problematic. The Carters decided, with Amy's approval, to send her to a boarding school in Atlanta. Although they would miss their daughter, they knew that it was what she wanted. Meanwhile, Jimmy and Rosalynn found life in Plains anything but dreary. Numerous dignitaries came to visit, including Begin, Egyptian president Anwar Sadat, Japanese prime minister Takeo Fukuda, and French president Giscard d'Estaing. The Carters also took pleasure in jogging, riding their bicycles, and walking through the woods and gathering various fruits that grew near the trails. "Gradually," they later wrote, "we began to feel that life in Plains might turn out to be satisfying."[20]

Fixing up their house was another matter. The Carters had not lived in their home in Plains on a regular basis for a decade. Upkeep of the yard had amounted largely to raking the leaves; nothing had been done to keep the soil from washing away. Inside, the attic needed a new floor. After the election, White House staffers had pooled their money and purchased a complete set of tools and machines for Carter so that he could do his own woodworking, and he put them to good use. First, Carter laid a floor in the attic, which gave the Carters somewhere to store their boxes of possessions. He also moved a wall to make the master bedroom larger. Of the other three bedrooms, the Carters left Amy's alone but turned the second into a dressing room and the third into an office for Rosalynn. Carter then turned the garage into an office and library and, so their children would have a place to stay when they visited, built an apartment over the garage. Finally, they glassed in the back porch. While her husband managed the renovations on the inside of the house, Mrs. Carter oversaw the yard work, including the planting of a garden.

As they worked on the house, Jimmy and Rosalynn began thinking about his presidential library. Neither of them wanted it to be just a "lifeless memorial" to his time in office; rather, they envisioned an institution with a larger purpose. The question was what that larger purpose would be. The answer came to Carter one night in early 1982. After tossing and turning in bed, he suddenly sat up and excitedly told his wife, "I know what we're going to do with the library. We're going to make it a place to resolve conflicts."[21] With the purpose of the Carter Center now determined, the president began raising funds, finding financial support from individuals, from corporations such as Coca-Cola, and from private foundations, including MacArthur, Carnegie, and Ford.

Of all the concerns the Carters had, the most serious was their personal financial well-being. Following the 1976 election, the Carters had put their finances into a blind trust. Shortly after the 1980 election, they learned that their main asset, the peanut warehouse, was $1 million in debt. The embarrassed former president had no choice but to sell it, although he retained about 2,000 acres of land outside Plains. The Carters were still short of funds, however, so to make money, they signed lucrative contracts to write their memoirs.

Signing the contracts was one thing; actually writing their memoirs was quite another. Whereas Jimmy planned to write about his presidency, Rosalynn eventually decided to make her work an autobiography. She had originally intended to use her monograph to defend her husband's policies, but she changed her mind when biographer Edmund Morris gave her some sound advice: "Don't try to make your place in history. It's already made."[22] This gave Mrs. Carter the freedom to write a book about her own life. She talked with members of her family to learn more about her own background—she discovered, for instance, that her grandmother had eloped rather than marry in a church—read her friend Edna Langford's account of the 1976 campaign, and perused numerous documents from her years in the White House. Although Jimmy's book, *Keeping Faith,* appeared in print in 1982, hers took significantly longer; putting words to paper was not an easy task for her.

Another, perhaps unexpected, problem was living in the same house with her husband. They had lived together in the White House, of course, but the presidential mansion was massive, and Rosalynn and Jimmy had had their own separate offices in the East and West Wings. Now, they had to coexist in a small house with little free space. They decided to make the kitchen and den, which lay between their offices, into "neutral ground," keeping their office doors shut when they were busy.[23] Still, closing their doors did not stop interruptions. Believing that it was her duty as a good wife to give her husband peace and quiet, Rosalynn answered telephone calls, entertained guests, and oversaw the cooking, in addition to trying to write her memoirs. It eventually became too much for her. One August morning, Mrs. Carter sat down to work, but numerous interruptions had prevented her from writing a single word by mid-afternoon. Frustrated, she went into the backyard and cried. Her husband and daughter-in-law, Judy, came to the rescue. Witnessing her aggravation, they created a sign that read, "WORKING HOURS 9–12 A.M.[*sic*]—DO NOT DISTURB" and put it on the door to Rosalynn's office. "It worked," recalled the ex–first lady. "My secretary stopped calling until the afternoon. Family members knew when to come see me. It was wonderful."[24]

Another type of interruption was physical. Rosalynn had been working on her book for only a few months when she began to experience severe pain in her legs and back; the pain then spread to the rest of her body. Aspirin helped, but even then, she could write only for short periods before she had to get up and move around. When her doctor could find nothing wrong, she went to Emory University, where the physician diagnosed her with polymyalgia rheumatica, which causes the muscles to become inflamed. Her doctor believed that the condition would eventually resolve itself, and with the help of exercise, it did. But combating the illness slowed down the writing process.

Additionally, Rosalynn was less disciplined than Jimmy—something that she readily admitted. He would spend eight to twelve hours each day writing. He woke up at 5:00 and worked until 7:30, at which point Rosalynn was just getting up. They would have breakfast together, and then he would head back to his office to continue writing. Rosalynn would take a long bath, and by the time she was ready to start writing, "he was ready for a coffee break!"[25]

Finally, there was the issue of speed. As the Carters later discovered when they decided to write a book together, Rosalynn would brood over every sentence, which slowed her writing. Fearful of criticism, she would not let anyone see her memoirs for a long time. Finally, she allowed Judy, who was a professional writer, to look it over. "It's pretty good," Judy declared, and her daughter-in-law's response gave Mrs. Carter a much-needed boost of confidence.[26]

Thus, it was not until 1984, some two years later than originally expected, that Rosalynn's memoir, *First Lady from Plains*, appeared in print. It received high praise from critics. The *Washington Post* called it "interesting throughout," and the *Christian Science Monitor* referred to it as "a primer for future first ladies who can look to her as an example of grace in the glare of a ruthless spotlight." The book also brought out Mrs. Carter's competitive side. She liked to joke with her husband—who took the "ribbing good-naturedly"—that whereas his memoirs had reached the number-two spot on the *New York Times* best-seller list—behind one of Jane Fonda's workout books—for eleven weeks, hers had held on to the number-one spot for eighteen. Although *Keeping Faith* sold more copies than *First Lady from Plains*, "reprint sales have still not been counted," Mrs. Carter claimed, "and I'm going to beat him yet."[27]

With the house in order, her memoirs completed, and the family finances in good shape, Rosalynn could devote her attention to the projects that had been on her agenda since her days in the Georgia governor's mansion. Mental health remained the centerpiece. Within months of leaving the White House, Carter had begun criticizing the Reagan administration for reversing a number of his presidential initiatives, including those on human rights and the curtailment of arms sales, and Mrs. Carter joined him, attacking the White House's cuts in mental health funding. "*Anybody* would be better than what we have now," she declared in 1984.[28] About one in five adults and one in eight children suffered from mental or emotional problems, yet many of them—including the overwhelming majority of children—failed to receive "appropriate mental health care," she stated. Although there were private organizations that offered assistance, she believed that it was important for the states and the federal government to increase expenditures on community health centers. She also urged both the federal government and private insurance companies to provide parity in health care for people with mental disabilities. "If insurance companies paid for mental illnesses," she declared, "it would be okay to have them."[29] Mrs. Carter resented the stigma that still surrounded mental illness, and the media, she argued, only made matters worse. Journalists gave little attention to the issue, making it difficult to educate the public on the subject; when reporters did cover stories about mental health, they almost always portrayed the mentally ill as violent, even though most were not. The consequences of this public misunderstanding and lack of insurance coverage could be severe in terms of both human suffering and financial hardship, and Mrs. Carter continued to work for positive change.

Besides continuing their own personal agendas, the Carters also kept abreast of politics. Not surprisingly, they supported the Democratic candidate in the 1984 presidential election: Walter Mondale. Reports that Mondale wanted to distance himself from his former boss brought out Mrs. Carter's protective instincts. "The Mondales asked us to campaign for them," she commented. "But Jimmy told Fritz he had to be his own person and win independently."[30] Carter had decided to keep a low profile, believing that doing so would be in Mondale's best interest. Mondale, in turn, chose to downplay his link to Carter, who many considered a weak, even inept, president. Accordingly, Mondale's speeches emphasized his disagreements with his ex-boss during his years as vice president. Democratic Party officials also tried to minimize the ties between their candidate and Carter; they only reluctantly invited him to the party's convention and made sure to schedule his speech for the first day so that it would receive little television coverage. It is unlikely, however, that the Democrats could have done anything to defeat the highly popular Reagan, who went on to win by a landslide, capturing all but the District of Columbia and Mondale's home state of Minnesota.

After the Reagan-Bush years, Bill Clinton's election in 1992 — and particularly his decision to appoint his wife, Hillary, as head of a task force to reform the nation's health care system — gave Mrs.

Carter hope that her goal of parity for mental health care would become a reality. Instead, the Clinton health care reform initiative only continued a long-standing bitterness between the Clintons and the Carters that dated back to Carter's presidency. In 1980, when Cuban president Fidel Castro opened up the port of Mariel to any of his people who wanted to leave the country, Carter offered asylum to those Cubans who wanted to come to the United States. Cubans living in Florida sent hundreds of boats to Mariel, bringing back tens of thousands of people. Because there was no way to document or house so many individuals, the administration decided to set up tent cities, and 18,000 of the new arrivals were sent to Arkansas, where Governor Bill Clinton was seeking reelection. The people of Arkansas were not pleased when it turned out that many of these Cubans had mental disabilities or were criminals; they were even less pleased to learn that President Carter planned to send even more to their state. Thus, when Arkansans went to the polls, they voted Clinton out of office. Carter "screwed me," Clinton later commented. Although Clinton returned to the governorship in 1982, he never forgave Carter for ruining his bid for reelection in 1980.[31]

Matters did not improve following the 1992 election. During a formal affair held prior to Clinton's inauguration, the Carters arrived to find that no seats had been set aside for them. According to one report, Jimmy and Rosalynn "did a slow burn as actors delivered tributes to former presidents, including Reagan, without even acknowledging Carter."[32] Not long afterward, Carter upset the new president when he criticized the Clintons' decision not to send their daughter, Chelsea, to a public school, as he and Rosalynn had done with Amy.

The Clinton health care reform package only served to continue this acrimonious relationship. Although the Clinton administration agreed in principle with Mrs. Carter's call for parity in insurance coverage for mental and physical illnesses, it worried about the financial costs of implementing such parity immediately. Instead, it presented to Congress a plan that would limit mental health care to a total of sixty days of hospital treatment and thirty sessions of outpatient therapy, with the patient having to pay for half those sessions; additional provisions would be phased in over a period of years. An angry Mrs. Carter attacked the plan, saying not only that it lacked parity but also that poorer individuals could not afford the copayment for therapy (although experts argued that, under the plan, impoverished individuals would pay nothing).

Determined to achieve parity in mental health coverage, Mrs. Carter teamed up with an unlikely ally: Betty Ford. The former political rivals had developed a friendship starting in 1981, when they and their husbands, along with former president Richard Nixon, traveled to Egypt for the funeral of Anwar Sadat, who had been assassinated by Muslim extremists opposed to his signing of the Camp David accords with Israel. There was still some enmity between the Carters and Fords as a result of the 1976 election, so Nixon acted as intermediary between them on the flight to Egypt. Nixon did not join the entourage on the return trip to the United States, giving the Fords and Carters more time to talk about issues ranging from politics to skiing and future plans. Afterward, Mrs. Carter commented that "Ford could not have been nicer."[33] The camaraderie between the two former first ladies grew even stronger in 1984, when they shared a stage at a conference put together by Mrs. Ford on the role of the first lady.

During their conversations, Betty Ford and Rosalynn Carter realized that they had a common interest in personal well-being. As first lady, Mrs. Ford had suffered from alcoholism and drug abuse; it was only after her family's intervention that she checked into a rehabilitation clinic in 1978. Cured and inspired, Mrs. Ford opened the Betty Ford Center at Eisenhower Medical Center in Rancho Mirage, California, four years later. Both Mrs. Ford and Mrs. Carter realized the close links among alcoholism, drug abuse, and mental health, thus prompting them to team up in support of mental health legislation. Their alliance would also, they hoped, give bipartisan backing to the cause of parity in insurance coverage.

In March 1994 Mrs. Carter and Mrs. Ford appeared before the Senate Labor and Human Resources Committee. The general public, they testified, favored parity in insurance coverage for mental illness and substance abuse problems. Furthermore, companies such as Digital and Federal Express, which provided full coverage for these illnesses, found that they saved money: employees who received treatment missed far fewer days of work than those who received no treatment. Aiding those with mental illness or substance abuse problems also reduced the number of people who ended up in jail and the number of children placed in foster homes.

The media were criticized for giving little coverage to the Ford-Carter testimony, but one must question whether more extensive publicity would have had any impact. The fact that first lady Hillary Clinton headed the commission on health care reform led to widespread criticism that she had crossed the line of propriety. This echoed the charges leveled at Rosalynn Carter when the public had learned that she was sitting in on cabinet meetings, and it reflected the public's continuing ambivalence regarding the proper role of the first lady. Also detrimental to the Clinton health care proposal were reports that both Bill and Hillary Clinton were involved in scandals, which had an overall negative impact on public support for the administration, and charges from conservatives that the health care program would prove too costly. Republicans' victory in the 1994 congressional election put the last nail in the coffin of the Clinton health care reform initiative.

Yet the 1994 election did not mean the end to all health care reform. In 1996, through the work of Senators Pete Domenici (R-New Mexico) and Paul Wellstone (D-Minnesota), Congress passed the Mental Health Parity Act, which President Clinton signed into law the following year. Although this no doubt pleased Mrs. Carter, it did not do all that she wanted. On paper, the law stated that the dollar limits on insurance coverage offered by employers to those with mental disabilities had to be the same as those that applied to individuals with physical disorders. Businesses, however, found ways around the law, such as placing caps on the amount of time an employee could receive inpatient care.

To this day, Mrs. Carter continues to speak out on the subject of mental health. She rejects the idea that mental illness played any part in the shootings at Columbine High School in Colorado in 1999 or similar incidents. "There's a difference between mental illness and disease with life," she commented to the *Boston Herald*. "The way children live and grow up determines if they are going to be children with behavior problems or be well-adjusted."[34] She believes that the trauma following the terrorist attack on the World Trade Center in September 2001 helped focus attention on mental illness and led to greater compassion for those with mental disorders. But, she adds, the stigma that the mentally disabled are violent has continued, and there remains a lack of parity in insurance coverage. In 2002 she joined the European Union and the American Bar Association in a successful fight to get the state of Georgia to grant clemency to Alexander Williams, who had been sentenced to death for the rape and murder of a sixteen-year-old girl in 1986, but whose lawyer had failed to tell the jury about his client's history of schizophrenia. Later that year, she called for a moratorium on the execution of mentally ill prisoners. Finally, she is a strong supporter of the Mental Health Equitable Treatment Act. First proposed by Wellstone and Domenici in 2001, it is designed to close the loopholes of the Mental Health Parity Act.

The former first lady has also sought to draw attention to the issue of mental health through her work with a variety of institutions and organizations. Chief among them is the Carter Center. Since 1985, that institution has hosted symposia on mental health, with each gathering focusing on a particular aspect of the subject. It also offers fellowships to journalists to do work on mental health. (The former president joked, "I think she loves the fellows more than she loves me!")[35] In addition, Mrs. Carter is chair of the World Federation's International Committee of Women Leaders for Mental Health.

Mrs. Carter can point to some positive changes in terms of Americans' feelings about the mentally ill. Although some stigma remains, pointed out Dr. Thomas Bornemann, head of the Mental Health Program at the Carter Center, "attitudes are changing . . . particularly among young people." Additionally, a growing number of firms have realized that providing parity in coverage can save them money in the long run. But, he added, there remain the problems of educating the public at large and convincing Congress to pass legislation, such as the Wellstone Act. Those in the mental health field "don't do a great job in marketing ourselves," commented Bornemann. Meanwhile, there is no indication that lawmakers have any intention of addressing the issue of parity in coverage anytime soon, which means that it will be up to the states and local communities to address that subject.[36]

An outgrowth of Mrs. Carter's work on mental health is her interest in the subject of caregiving, which encompasses another group of individuals that has long been part of her agenda: the elderly. As a child, she had watched her father die at home. Her mother-in-law, Lillian, who passed away in 1983, had lived alone in Plains and had depended on Jimmy. Although Rosalynn's mother was more independent minded, working well into her eighties and driving a car, she also suffered from a number of physical maladies, including congestive heart failure. The former first lady had siblings in Plains to help take care of Allie, but she still felt guilty that her work with the Carter Center required her to travel so often. Thus, through her own personal experiences and the knowledge gained through her work with the Carter Center, Mrs. Carter realized the importance of addressing the needs of those who provide care to their loved ones. This concern for the mental well-being of caregivers caught the attention of Georgia's state university system, which asked Mrs. Carter to act as director of an institute, separate from the Carter Center, focused on caregiving. The result was the Rosalynn Carter Institute for Caregiving (RCI), which opened in 1987 at the former first lady's alma mater, Georgia Southwestern State University. Working with professional organizations and individuals, the RCI promotes programs to assist caregivers to meet the challenges of their tasks and to educate the public on the needs of caregivers; it also hosts symposia on caregiving.

Along the same lines, Rosalynn Carter, with Susan Golant, has written two books on the subject of caregiving. The first, *Helping Yourself Help Others: A Book for Caregivers*, published in 1994, focuses on caregiving in general. Between 80 and 90 percent of those who need care receive it at home from family or friends, they note. In many cases, theses caregivers find themselves facing financial burdens, and they often suffer from burnout, caused by the stress of attending to their loved ones. The authors provide suggestions for handling these situations, guidelines for when to consider institutionalizing a loved one, a list of organizations that caregivers can turn to for support, and a bibliography of other helpful resources. Four years later, Carter and Golant focused specifically on those with mental disabilities in *Helping Someone with Mental Illness*. Both books were well received, and critics credited the authors with doing much to help caregivers cope.

Mrs. Carter's interest in caregiving likely explained her willingness to become honorary chair of Last Acts. Formed by the American

Hospital Association and more than seventy other organizations, the purpose of Last Acts—which closed its doors in 2005—was to provide both professionals and the public with better information on the care of the dying and to alter Americans' feelings about death. It also made her a strong opponent of assisted suicide. In March 1999, a few days after Dr. Jack Kevorkian was charged with homicide for helping several individuals end their lives, the first lady explained that there were alternatives to assisted suicide. For instance, living wills allow those with terminal illnesses to appoint someone to make medical decisions for them and to specify the type of care they would like to receive. In addition, she noted, hospitals had to make a more concerted effort to control patients' pain. It was vital, she concluded, to give more emphasis to "palliative care, so that at the end of life, we can have choices that are far more attractive than assisted suicide."[37]

The subjects of mental health and elder care were tied to another part of Mrs. Carter's agenda: volunteerism. She noted that, given the opportunity, many individuals continued to work well into their golden years, including her own mother. Others who were forced to retire often felt that life had lost its meaning. To this latter group, the former first lady suggested that they donate their time to help others. "Volunteering is the best way we know to invigorate a life," she told a group of senior citizens in 1988.[38]

Mrs. Carter had been an active volunteer as first lady, and she continued to give her time to various organizations after she left the White House. She even had a hand in creating an international exchange program. During Carter's governorship, he and Rosalynn had established an exchange program between Georgia and Brazil, and Mrs. Carter had made it clear during the 1976 campaign that she wanted to broaden that initiative to all Americans. Thus was born Friendship Force, a nonprofit organization established by the Carters and headquartered in Atlanta. Mrs. Carter was its honorary chair until 2002, when she resigned to protest the organization's fiscal conservatism and its unwillingness to expand its operations. Designed to promote international cultural understanding, the program is open to any adult American. Participants, who pay their own way, travel to foreign countries and live with host families; upon their return to the United States, these "ambassadors," as they are called, reciprocate, welcoming their host families to the United States. By 2006, nearly half a million individuals had taken part in Friendship Force exchanges. Some 350 Friendship Force Clubs, which now exist in more than 50 nations and almost every U.S. state, aid the organization in promoting these exchanges.

But the volunteer organization to which both Rosalynn and Jimmy Carter have devoted their greatest attention is Habitat for Humanity, the brainchild of Millard and Linda Fuller. Born in 1935 in Alabama, Millard Fuller attended Auburn University and, by the mid-1960s, had made millions through a mail-order catalog business. Around the same time, Linda, whom Millard had married in the late 1950s, announced that she wanted a divorce because her husband cared more about money and his job than he did about their relationship. He convinced her to stay with him by promising to give his wealth to charity and live a simpler life. Essentially reborn into the Christian ethic of giving of oneself to help those in need, Millard, Linda, and their children traveled in 1965 to Koinonia Farm, an interracial Christian commune established more than twenty years earlier just outside Plains, Georgia. There they met the commune's founder, theologian Clarence Jordan (and the uncle of Carter aide Hamilton Jordan). Jordan's sermons and his willingness to fight racial injustice inspired the Fullers. A year later, they traveled to Africa, where they met a group of Christian missionaries who wanted to take a business that made blocks for homes and turn it into a nonprofit organization that constructed houses for the poor.

In the meantime, Jordan, who believed that real estate agents and landlords took advantage of the poor, had proposed a new organization, which he called the Fund for Humanity. Essentially, individuals and companies would provide donations and no-interest loans to be used to build housing for low-income families. The Fund for Humanity would make no profit from the homes; the families that received the houses would pay back only the cost, at no interest. When Jordan died unexpectedly in October 1969, the Fullers took over this operation. Motivated both by Jordan and by the missionaries they had met in Africa, and with support from an Indianapolis church, Millard and Linda returned to Africa in 1973 and helped build more than 100 homes in Zaire. In 1976 they returned to the United States and announced the formation of a new organization that would build low-cost housing for families around the world. They called it Habitat for Humanity.

The Carters first became aware of Habitat for Humanity in 1978, when two of their friends announced that they were going to Africa to construct homes for the poor. But it was not until 1984 that Jimmy Carter took part in his first home-building project in Americus, Georgia. He was impressed with the organization, and Rosalynn became hooked later that year when she joined her husband on a project in New York City. Both of them found that Habitat's policy of giving to those in need with no expectation of any material benefit in return conformed with their own Christian values. Since then, both have been actively involved in raising funds for the organization. They also spend a week each year, usually in the summer, on the Jimmy Carter Work Project (JCWP), where they join numerous volunteers and build anywhere from several dozen to hundreds of homes. The first JCWP was a building renovation in New York City; JCWPs have also taken place in Baltimore, Chicago, Charlotte, Los Angeles, Miami, Milwaukee, and San Diego, as well as in Hungary, Mexico, South Africa, and South Korea. During the projects, the Carters insist on being treated like everyone else, which may mean sleeping in a tent, a college dormitory, or even a tepee.

On her first Habitat trip to New York, Mrs. Carter was nervous. Before she and her husband left Plains, she made it clear that "I would do anything but hammer. I didn't think I could use a hammer and I didn't want to use a hammer." But by the end of the trip, she was driving in nails with the best of them and had overseen the laying of floors in two apartments. Carter was impressed with how quickly his wife learned carpentry, and their subsequent construction work together only brought them closer. As he would comment a few years later, "My wife has never been more beautiful than when her face was covered with black smut from scraping burned ceiling joists, and streaked with sweat from carrying sheets of plywood from the street level up to the floor where we were working, cutting subflooring with a power saw, and nailing it down with just a few hard hammer blows."[39]

The final part of Mrs. Carter's continuing agenda has been childhood immunization. During her tenure as first lady, her campaign with Betty Bumpers to ensure that children were vaccinated against preventable diseases led to widespread immunization and to a decline in such illnesses as tetanus and measles. By the early 1990s, however, reports showed that some diseases, among them measles and rubella, were making a comeback. Mrs. Carter and Mrs. Bumpers therefore teamed up again, establishing a program called "Every Child by Two." The purpose of this initiative was to vaccinate all children younger than two years against preventable diseases. It was also vital, Mrs. Carter argued, for insurance companies to do more to cover immunizations and for local groups to give more attention to the vaccination of children. Mrs. Carter and Mrs. Bumpers also championed President Bill Clinton's nomination of Joycelyn Elders as surgeon general; as Arkansas state health director, Elders had worked to increase the number of children receiving vaccinations. Although Elders's nomination was confirmed by the Senate, she was forced to resign in 1994 after suggesting that teaching children about masturbation in schools would reduce pregnancies and sexually transmitted diseases. Finally, Mrs. Carter promoted Georgia's Partners in Health mobile van, which, through public and private funds, provided health care, including immunizations, to impoverished and "hard-to-reach" individuals in the state.[40]

Although Mrs. Carter spent a good deal of time on her own agenda, she also devoted considerable attention to the Carter Center. Actually, for a time, the term "Carter Center" was a misnomer, for rather than having a single, permanent home, it had offices in three different locations in Atlanta. This made coordination difficult, especially as the institution's responsibilities grew. Originally conceived to focus on conflict resolution, by 1986, it was also giving attention to mental health and the combating of malnutrition and disease. All these commitments became too much for the Carters to handle alone, so they gradually hired a top-notch staff of experts to help with each initiative.

In the meantime, Jimmy and Rosalynn Carter raised funds so that they could provide their institution with a permanent home. In 1986, after securing $28 million from private donors, the Carter Presidential Center opened. Consisting of a series of modern, round structures located near downtown Atlanta, the center has two parts. One is the Jimmy Carter Library and Museum. Funded by private donations and staffed by the National Archives and Records

Administration, it houses records and memorabilia from the Carters' years in the White House, as well as manuscript collections from a number of Carter administration officials. The other is the privately endowed Carter Center.

The most important of the Carter Center's initiatives remains conflict resolution. This involves not only resolving disputes between factions or nations at war or on the brink of war but also monitoring elections to ensure that they are conducted fairly so that all parties will agree to abide by the results. The part of the world that has received the greatest attention from Carter has been the Middle East. His failure to achieve a comprehensive peace settlement during his presidency has not deterred him from continuing that effort. In 1983, 1987, 1990, and 1993, Mrs. Carter joined her husband on trips to the region, where he held talks with the leaders of Egypt, Israel, Jordan, Saudi Arabia, Syria, Lebanon, and the Palestine Liberation Organization. In 1996 and 2006 they led Carter Center teams that monitored elections among the Palestinians. Peace in the Middle East was also a key reason for Carter's decision to travel to the Soviet Union in 1987 and hold talks with Premier Mikhail Gorbachev. Reminiscent of her days as first lady, Mrs. Carter insisted on attending her husband's meeting with the Soviet leader, where she not only sat in on the discussion but also acted as note taker.

Latin America has been another area of interest for the Carters. In 1986 they went to Nicaragua, accompanied by Robert Pastor, a member of the National Security Council during the Carter administration. There, they attempted (but ultimately failed) to mediate an end to the ongoing war between that country's leftist Sandinista government and the contras, a group of anti-Sandinista revolutionaries that had received military and financial support from both Argentina and the Reagan administration. Four years later, the Carters returned to Nicaragua, where they observed the election in which the Sandinistas lost to the National Opposition Union's candidate, Violeta Chamorro. In 1989 and 1993 Jimmy and Rosalynn also led Carter Center teams to monitor balloting in Panama, as well as in Haiti in 1990.

The year 1994 proved especially busy for the Carters' peacekeeping efforts, starting with a trip to North Korea in June. Relations between the United States and North Korea had worsened because

Jimmy and Rosalynn Carter monitoring the presidential election in Liberia, October 2005. Courtesy of Deborah Hakes, the Carter Center.

of reports that the government in Pyongyang was seeking to develop nuclear weapons. With the reluctant support of President Clinton (whose relationship with Carter continued to be tense), the Carters traveled to North Korea and held talks with President Kim Il Sung. Afterward, the former president announced an agreement under which North Korea would give up its nuclear ambitions in return for nuclear reactors supplied by the United States. While in North Korea, Mrs. Carter had suggested that her husband make sure to speak with Kim's wife, Kim Song-ae, and she believed that this proved to be key in convincing the North Korean leader to reach an agreement.[41]

In September 1994 the former president traveled to Haiti. In that country's first-ever democratic election, held in 1991, Haitian voters had chosen Jean-Bertrand Aristide as president. Not long afterward, the Haitian military overthrew Aristide and installed a junta led by President Raoul Cédras. An angry Clinton administration was considering the use of military force to restore Aristide to power, but Carter convinced the U.S. president to let him go to Haiti. He was joined by retired general Colin Powell, whose Caribbean American background and military training could be useful in convincing Cédras and his fellow junta members to step down. Although Mrs.

Carter did not travel with her husband this time, she kept in touch with him from Plains. Recalling how helpful Mrs. Kim had been in North Korea, she suggested that Carter talk with Cédras's wife to enlist her aid in convincing her husband to cede power to Aristide. The former president did so, and although he later wrote that he believed the talk with Mrs. Cédras had some impact,[42] Powell's warning of impending U.S. military action no doubt had significantly more. Shortly thereafter, the military government stepped down, restoring Aristide to the presidency.

At the end of the year, the Carters were headed to Europe to try to end the war that pitted Slavic, Christian Serbs against Bosnian Muslims. The conflict had begun in the early 1990s when Serbia encouraged Serbs living in neighboring countries, including Bosnia-Herzegovina, to rise up; Serbia then sent military forces into Bosnia. By 1994, tens of thousands of Bosnians had been massacred. In an effort to stop the bloodshed, aircraft from the North Atlantic Treaty Organization (NATO) bombed Serbian military positions, but the fighting persisted. In 1994 Radovan Karazdic, a high-level Serbian nationalist who had been involved in the Muslim genocide, invited Carter to Bosnia to meet him at his headquarters, about twenty miles from the city of Sarajevo. In December, again with the reluctant support of the Clinton White House, Jimmy and Rosalynn Carter headed to Bosnia. Although the ex-president arranged a cease-fire, it did not last. Only after additional attacks by NATO forces on Serbian positions was a peace agreement reached; afterward, a NATO-led multinational force was dispatched to Bosnia to maintain peace.

In 2002 Carter, with his wife at his side, became the first American president to travel to Cuba since that nation's communist leader, Fidel Castro, seized power in 1959. Following Castro's assumption of control, the United States had imposed an economic embargo on Cuba. Although, as president, Carter had considered normalizing relations with Castro's government, he had not done so because of both strong congressional opposition and anger over Cuban military support for communists in Africa. Still, Carter did not approve of the sanctions and used the trip to symbolize his opposition. The junket also gave him a chance to express his desire to see democracy take hold on the communist-controlled island, which he did by meeting with Cuban dissidents and giving a televised speech to the people of Cuba on the merits of democratic government.

Although the Carters generally saw eye to eye on these missions, they had their periodic disagreements. One of the more serious ones took place on the way back to Atlanta following their 1986 trip to Central America. While in Nicaragua, the former president had learned that some of the contra leaders were prepared to give up U.S. aid to their movement if the Sandinistas would agree to negotiations, and he conveyed this offer to the Sandinista government. But he also believed that if talks between the two sides stood any chance of success, they would need a mediator appointed by the United Nations. Carter therefore informed his wife that he intended to ask UN Secretary-General Javier Pérez de Cuéllar to assign him as the intermediary. She opposed the idea, believing that both the contras and the Sandinistas needed more time to consider the proposal. Their quarrel continued even after they got off the plane, with Carter telling his wife, "But Rosie, it is my duty to keep at it until peace is achieved."[43] She succeeded, however, in restraining her husband's ambitions.

Although Mrs. Carter considered it her right to criticize her husband, she continued to take offense at others who did so. In 1994, for example, the *New Republic* lambasted Carter for meeting with Karazdic, charging that doing so had undermined the very cause of peace for which he stood: "He provides tyrants with the thing that tyranny cannot provide, which is legitimacy." An infuriated former first lady responded that the magazine's "vituperative attack" was uncalled for. "We have attempted to find peaceful alternatives to armed combat," she wrote, even when that has meant meeting with individuals "who have been condemned by our people and the international community. . . . Atrocities are dramatically reduced in a peaceful environment." When Carter criticized President George W. Bush's proposal to wage war against Iraq because of alleged ties between that nation and the terrorist attacks of 11 September 2001, he came under assault from Bush's supporters. Mrs. Carter again stepped in. "What are you going to do, go in and bomb the place and get rid of [Iraqi president] Saddam [Hussein], and have the tribal people run the country?" she asked. "We need to look at the consequences."[44]

Conflict resolution tied in with another of Mr. Carter's initiatives: combating malnutrition and disease. Besides coinciding with the ex-president's Christian ethic of helping the needy and his long-standing belief in human rights, eradicating starvation and preventable disease would lead to fewer quarrels over sources of food and clean water that might escalate into war. Africa became the prime focus of this effort. None of his presidential predecessors had given as much attention to that continent as he had, and Carter remained interested in African affairs after leaving the White House. Thus, in 1985 he founded Global 2000, Inc., whose purpose was to fight malnourishment in Africa. But Carter did not realize just how bad the situation was until he traveled there in 1986 with Norman Borlaug, an agronomist and Nobel Prize winner who had joined the Carter Center. In addition to the primitive state of agriculture on the continent, the former president witnessed the widespread existence of curable diseases, most notably dracunculiasis and onchocerciasis.

Dracunculiasis is a disease caused by the guinea worm. This parasite, which is about two to three feet long and the width of a spaghetti noodle, lays its larvae in water holes, where they are ingested by copepods, or water fleas. It is not uncommon for these water holes to be used by humans for drinking water. If ingested, human stomach acid destroys the flea but not the guinea worm larva, which makes its way through the small intestine. After reaching full size, it pushes its way through the skin, causing severe pain and blisters. Onchocerciasis, or river blindness, is also caused by a parasitic worm, though one smaller than the guinea worm. Blackflies, which breed in rivers, transmit the parasite through their bite; the worm then grows in its human host. Whereas the male worm grows to only an inch or less, the female can reach a length up to two feet, causing protrusions in the skin that resemble leprosy. The female also produces millions of microscopic larvae that make their way through the body; if they reach the eyes, they can cause blindness. Although these diseases affect people outside of Africa, they are most prevalent on that continent. When Mrs. Carter joined her husband on trips to Africa to monitor efforts to stamp out these diseases, she saw the toll they took on people. During one trip to Nigeria, she met a group of individuals suffering from dracunculiasis. "All had worms emerging from their bodies," she wrote in her diary. "It is hard just to look at them, sick and suffering so much." She recalled "one little boy with two worms coming out between his knuckles. His hand was swollen as though it would burst, and he kept lifting it to me, as though I could make the hurting go away."[45]

The Carters have had a significant amount of success in eradicating these diseases. Through discussions with experts, they learned that by digging deeper wells, treating well water with a parasite-killing chemical, and, most simply, covering water supplies with filters, the guinea worm can be controlled. By 2004, cases of dracunculiasis had been reduced by over 99 percent worldwide. The Carter Center took the lead in supplying the drug Mectizan to treat river blindness, and by 2004, the number of cases had decreased dramatically in some parts of the world. In addition, in 2001 the Carter Center began a campaign to eliminate trachoma, a contagious disease that, if untreated, can also cause blindness. Today, the Carter Center helps some 10 million people each year affected by these and other diseases.

Not all the Carters' time is spent on business, however; they also find time for pleasure. While working on their memoirs, they found that they needed someplace to go for peace and quiet. With the help of two friends, Betty and John Pope, they constructed a log cabin next to a stream in northern Georgia. Carter built the furniture for the cabin, and this home away from home provides them with a retreat where they can relax. Retaining their interest in health, they continue to jog, ride bicycles, play tennis, and fly-fish, which Carter taught his wife to do during their years in the White House. They also learned to ski and have become avid bird-watchers. In 1984 they climbed partway up Mount Everest; four years later they ascended Mount Kilimanjaro, followed by Mount Fuji when Carter was seventy years old. Other trips have taken them to China, Spain, and game parks in Africa.

Through their travels, their work, and their active lifestyle, the Carters seem to have found the key to living a healthy, happy life. However, they also took note of those who did not—in particular, members of Jimmy Carter's family: his brother, Billy, had suffered from alcoholism; his father had died of pancreatic cancer; in 1983 that same disease took both his younger sister, Ruth, and then his mother, Lillian. Carter's father, mother, and sister had all smoked. Seeing so many people close to him suffer and die, in 1984 Carter convinced Dr. William Foege, who had headed the Centers for Disease Control during Carter's presidency, to convene a meeting for the Carter Center on preventive health measures. The resulting recommendations, which included not smoking and avoiding a dependence on alcohol, were not surprising. But the combination of those conclusions, the deaths in Carter's family, his work with Habitat for Humanity and other volunteer organizations, and the news in 1985 that Hamilton Jordan, Carter's chief of staff, had been diagnosed with cancer (which he survived) convinced the former president and first lady to write a book together on how to live a long, happy life.

Carter later commented that this book was "the worst thing we ever tried to do together." It led to some serious arguments between them. "I accused him of destroying my memories," recounted Mrs. Carter. The quarrels only got worse when they exchanged what they had put down on paper. According to Carter, his wife viewed his work as a "rough draft" and felt free to mark it up. But if he attempted to do the same with what she had written, she would get angry, acting as though her words had "come from God on Mount Sinai and nobody could modify a word of it." Recalled the ex-president, he and his wife "exchanged increasingly unpleasant comments through our word processors." Mrs. Carter wondered whether the book would end with "a sensational final chapter in which we announce the end of our 40-odd year marriage."[46] Their publisher saved both the book and the Carters' marriage by suggesting that they place an initial next to those events on which they disagreed. They followed his advice, and in 1987, *Everything to Gain: Making the Most of the Rest of Your Life* appeared in print. The book begins with the 1980 election and the uncertainty they felt once they acknowledged that they would not be returning to the White House. The remainder of the book uses both personal anecdotes and the stories of other Americans to explain how the Carters, and others, have found health and happiness. The book received mixed reviews. Letty Pogrebin in the *New York Times* called it "an inspiring account of the creation of a meaningful life." The *Wall Street Journal*'s David

Brooks was less kind. Referring to the work as an example of "the Carters' pallid egomania," he asked whether there was "some punishment a just society can wreak on this sanctimonious duo."[47]

Having lived through the misery of writing a book together, the Carters vowed never to do so again, and they have not. But that did not end the quarrels. On cold winter nights, for instance, they would argue over the temperature of their electric blanket. Carter had been away on a trip, and he felt that he would be returning to a "marriage ... on the verge of destruction." When he got home, however, Rosalynn met him at the front door and announced, "I think our marriage is saved. I just discovered that our dual blanket controls have been on the wrong sides of the bed, and each of us was changing the temperature on the other's side."[48]

The Carters have worked through other difficult issues in their marriage. Having served in the military, Carter has always been picky about punctuality. One year, however, he realized that the date was 18 August—his wife's birthday—and he had failed to buy her a present. To make up for his oversight, he wrote her a note: "Rosalynn, I promise you that for the rest of our marriage, I will never make an unfavorable remark about tardiness." He then signed it and presented it to her. "So far," he later wrote, "I've pretty well kept my promise, and she still agrees that it was the best birthday present I ever gave her."[49] On another occasion, following a squabble, Carter went to his woodshop, took a piece of walnut and carved on it, "Each evening, forever, this is good for an apology—or forgiveness—as you desire," and gave it to Rosalynn. "Although it has sometimes been difficult," he commented, "so far I have been able to honor my promise."[50]

Finding ways to resolve their disputes has allowed the Carters to maintain a strong marriage to this day. She is shier than he is; he gets up much earlier than she does. Although no longer so intent on punctuality, he still likes to live on a schedule. She does not. Nevertheless, their partnership remains strong. They have learned that if they have a disagreement and talking about it does not work, it is best to allow things to cool down before discussing the issue again, or perhaps to write down their thoughts about the problem and share it with the other. They divide their responsibilities at home; she takes care of the finances, just as she did when they worked at the warehouse. In July 2006 they celebrated their sixtieth wedding anniversary. Of former first couples, only George and Barbara Bush have been married longer.

Carter lost his last two siblings, Billy and Gloria, in 1988 and 1990, respectively. Like his parents and Ruth, both died of cancer. In 2000 Rosalynn's mother, Allie, passed away, followed in 2003 by both of her brothers, Murray and Jerry. On a happier note, the Carters have welcomed new family members. They have eleven grandchildren, and in September 2006 they welcomed their first great-grandchild, Henry Louis. Each year, the Carters and their children and grandchildren take a family vacation, with the destination being a group decision. When not traveling with the family or on business, the Carters divide their time between their home in Plains and an apartment at the Carter Center.

With so many responsibilities, the Carters decided to give up their cochairmanship of the Carter Center in 2005 so that they would have more time to devote to their other interests. They still play an active role in the center, however. They are also in the process of opening a Carter Centre in London, which they hope will bring additional support to the causes they support worldwide.

All this work has brought the Carters numerous awards, including Jimmy Carter's Nobel Peace Prize, which he won in 2002. Rosalynn Carter has received a variety of accolades, particularly for her work in mental health, including the American Society of Journalists and Authors Award for *Helping Someone with Mental Illness,* the National Mental Health Association's Volunteer of the Decade Award, and the American Mental Health Fund's Outstanding National Leadership Public Service Award.

Rosalynn Carter still believes that her husband should have been reelected, but she has overcome the bitterness of his defeat. Both of them have discovered fulfilling lives outside of the White House. Although they spend time with the family and sometimes travel for enjoyment, they devote most of their lives to continuing the agendas they began while in the White House or even earlier, in the governor's mansion in Georgia. Some goals remain elusive, such as peace in the Middle East. There is still strong opposition in the

United States to passage of an equal rights amendment, and Congress has yet to guarantee parity in insurance coverage for those with mental disabilities. But the Carters clearly have no intention of giving up the fight for the things they believe in, and they continue to engage in that fight as partners. And they know that when they are gone, the pursuit of their agendas will continue through the Carter Center.

CONCLUSION

AMBIVALENCE SURROUNDING THE OFFICE

In his study of the office of first lady, political scientist Robert Watson contends that first ladies have eleven different duties, including "wife and mother," hostess, "symbol of the American woman," manager of the presidential mansion, "champion of social causes," foreign emissary, and partner to the president.[1] How many of these roles the first lady assumes is up to her and her husband, as is how she goes about assuming them.

These questions of which roles to adopt and how to do so may seem trivial, but they have a real impact on the way the American public views the first lady. Following the 1992 presidential election, the *Wall Street Journal* asked Americans what role they thought incoming first lady Hillary Clinton should play in her husband's administration. Seven out of ten Americans favored her adopting a traditional role in the White House, and six out of ten opposed the idea of her serving in any official capacity. Yet more than 60 percent believed that she had the "knowledge and personal characteristics" to act as one of the president's advisers.[2] These numbers demonstrate that Americans continue to feel ambivalent about the role of the first lady. They do not mind if she advises her husband, as long as she does not seem to assume a status equal to that of an elected or appointed member of the administration, such as the vice president or a member of the cabinet. At that point, the president's wife can expect to come under fire from both the public and the media.

Historically, first ladies who adopted nontraditional roles have faced the greatest scrutiny and criticism. Edith Bolling Wilson was vilified after largely assuming her husband's duties following his debilitating stroke in 1919. Eleanor Roosevelt raised eyebrows by advancing her own agenda, including housing for low-income families, African American rights, and continuation of her husband's New Deal programs during World War II. Controversy also swirled around Betty Ford, who supported the equal rights amendment (ERA) and the right to abortion and commented that premarital sex could reduce the divorce rate; Nancy Reagan, who had undue influence over her husband's schedule and played a role in the sacking of his chief of staff, Donald Regan; and Hillary Clinton, who deprecated housewives and, in the eyes of some, overstepped her position when she headed her husband's health care reform commission.

Conversely, first ladies who adopted more traditional roles that included hosting events, being a wife and mother, and supporting social causes have received praise from their contemporaries. Bess Truman, Mamie Eisenhower, Jacqueline Kennedy, and Barbara Bush all left the White House as popular first ladies. Mrs. Clinton saw her approval rating climb after she changed her hairstyle and began focusing on more "appropriate" issues, such as helping the poor. She even received accolades for standing behind her husband after he was accused of having an affair with White House intern Monica Lewinsky (or at least until the public learned that he had lied about his relationship with Lewinsky). Laura Bush, who has assumed a traditional, low-profile role, had an 82 percent approval rating in the spring of 2006, about 50 points higher than that of her husband.

Margaret Truman, the daughter of Harry and Bess Truman, has suggested another reason for the often low approval ratings of activist first ladies such as Rosalynn Carter. Because what she does receives more public notice than the activities of a more traditional first lady, the activist first lady becomes linked to "all the imbroglios, scandals, and problems of her husband's administration." Thus, when his approval rating drops, it takes hers down as well.[3]

Evidence from the Carter years supports this theory. After the 1976 election, Jimmy Carter had an approval rating of 75 percent; a week before the 1980 election, it had fallen to 44 percent, with 46 percent of Americans viewing him unfavorably. Although Rosalynn Carter's unfavorable rating never came close to his, Americans' approval of her fell from 68 percent in 1977 to 46 percent in late 1980. Even today, the two of them share an interesting dichotomy. In a 2000 survey of seventy-eight presidential scholars, Carter was ranked as the tenth worst president in U.S. history. Yet the same study found that he was also among the ten most underrated chief executives. Likewise, participants in a poll taken in May 2006 by Quinnipiac University ranked Carter among the top five best *and* worst presidents. A 1993 study conducted by the Siena Research Institute ranked Mrs. Carter as the fifth most popular first lady, while the 1996–1997 Watson presidential poll placed her twentieth. The questions the pollsters ask are important, of course, but these numbers suggest that Carter's post–White House efforts to create a better world has led many Americans to see him in a more favorable light. At the same time, many are unwilling to forgive him for what he did, or failed to do, as president. The same appears to be true for Rosalynn Carter. She has received accolades for her work since leaving Washington, yet she is still identified with her husband's policies as president and her own activism as first lady, which some felt went too far.

Activist first ladies whose husbands become unpopular do not necessarily suffer politically themselves, however. In fact, it is possible for the president's wife to receive laurels for her activism if she can walk the fine line between activism and traditionalism. Betty Ford is a case in point. Mrs. Ford entered the White House at a time of change for women. Starting in the 1960s, the nation witnessed a burgeoning feminist movement that emphasized women's equality. Women sought not only the right to make their own choices but also the right to the same opportunities and income as men. This change had implications for the role of the first lady. If she was equal to her husband, should she then seek the same level of input and influence as those around him who had received their posts via election or appointment? If she adopted such a role, would she not anger traditionalists, who would rebuke her and, potentially, her husband? If she did not adopt such a role, would she upset activists, particularly feminists, who looked to her for leadership because of her proximity to the president?

Mrs. Ford recognized this difficulty. "One day, I'd be greeting women stockbrokers in the Map Room," she wrote in her memoirs, "congratulating them for having got out of their kitchens and into the stock market. The next day, in the same room, I'd be greeting a Homemakers Seminar, and congratulating housewives for having stayed in their kitchens."[4] Praise for housewives risked the wrath of feminists, and praise for female stockbrokers risked upsetting traditionalists. Mrs. Ford seemed to be especially good at finding a middle ground that would anger neither. Though supportive of the ERA, a woman's right to an abortion, and women who worked outside the home, she also supported women who chose to be homemakers. Some criticized Mrs. Ford's desire for power in the White House, but others noted that she always emphasized her husband and family in her public statements. Because she was neither too much of an activist nor too much of a traditionalist, Betty Ford left the White House with a popularity rating more than 20 points higher than that of her husband.

Betty Ford was part of a trend toward activism that had reappeared with Lady Bird Johnson's assumption of the post of first lady in 1963. Since 1945, when Eleanor Roosevelt left the White House, first ladies had assumed much more traditional roles, but Mrs. Johnson, an avid conservationist, campaigned aggressively in support of environmental legislation. Rosalynn Carter thus continued the transition from traditionalism to activism that had begun with Mrs. Johnson. But what made Mrs. Carter unlike any other first lady (with the exception of Edith Wilson) was that her statements and actions seemed designed to give her status equal to that of a cabinet member or even the vice president. Ironically, she drew fire not only from traditionalists but also from feminists.

Mrs. Carter promoted an agenda of initiatives that, with the exception of the ERA, traditionalists could support because of their emphasis on social welfare: mental health, aid for the elderly, and volunteerism. Historically, women's most important role was taking care of the family, and traditionalists saw Mrs. Carter as taking the concept of maternal care and expanding it to include the entire country. But Mrs. Carter had no intention of being a traditional first lady. She stated repeatedly that if given the choice between entertaining guests and sitting in on a cabinet meeting, she preferred the latter. She is the only first lady who went abroad as her husband's representative to discuss substantive matters with foreign officials and only the second up to that point to testify before Congress. Both she and her husband acknowledged that she acted as his sounding board, and she campaigned aggressively for him, first for governor and then for president.

Rosalynn Carter clearly had influence in the Oval Office. She had an impact on her husband's decisions to increase funding for her mental health initiative, to supply helicopters to Colombia for drug interdiction, to use Billy Carter's ties to Libya to try to free the American hostages in Iran, to fund relief for the Cambodian refugees, and to conclude the Camp David accords as quickly as possible. She read drafts of his speeches and commented on their content and tone. And her desire to see Joseph Califano replaced reinforced the president's decision to ask for his resignation as secretary of the Department of Health, Education, and Welfare. There were numerous times, however, when the first lady's suggestions were rejected by the president. He refused to sell Israeli Kfir aircraft to Ecuador, to wait until his second term to turn the Panama Canal over to Panama, to take a tougher stance toward the Soviet brigade in Cuba, to turn up the thermostats in the White House, to give Rosalynn more staff, and not to hire Bella Abzug (although he later fired her). Thus, although the president listened to his wife, he made the final decisions, and not always the ones that she favored.

Some of Mrs. Carter's contemporaries argued that she was no different from any wife who supported her husband, provided an ear for his concerns, and made suggestions about how he might handle particular situations. Though not stated explicitly, it is likely that some of her supporters believed that, given the drive for women's equality at the time, there was nothing wrong with a first lady who desired a greater role in her husband's administration than had been the case in the past. Traditionalists, however, did not approve of the idea of an individual who had not been elected or received congressional endorsement exercising so much power. That the media referred to her as "Mrs. President" or the "co-president" fed the belief that Mrs. Carter had assumed duties that were highly inappropriate for her office.

One might have thought that a first lady as active and seemingly influential as Mrs. Carter would have received a strong endorsement from feminists. Yet the opposite occurred. Feminists saw Rosalynn Carter not as one of them but as a woman who had no thoughts separate from her husband's and who seemed more concerned with his welfare than with that of women in general. Margaret Truman noted that the lack of support from feminists was particularly damaging, for it denied Mrs. Carter "a network of powerful women ready to defend, support, and promote her."[5] Although the president's own policies had the most impact on feminists' unwillingness to support him in his reelection bid in 1980, it is safe to say that many women's rights advocates felt that their interests had been ignored by the first lady as well.

Mrs. Carter did not like the criticism she received from either traditionalists or activists, but she had no intention of changing her ways. The shy, insecure child had become an outspoken, strong woman and a full-fledged partner to her husband. This transformation was the result of her life experience, of being placed in situations in which she had no choice but to take on greater responsibilities to ensure her family's welfare, whether as the oldest sibling in a single-parent household or as a young mother whose husband was often away at sea. Throughout the Carters' marriage, their partnership continued to mature, so that by the time Jimmy ran for president, they were all but equal partners, and Rosalynn's actions as first lady were simply a continuation of that relationship.

To many, Mrs. Carter seemed to lack a clear image. Many journalists compared her with Eleanor Roosevelt; others called her the "steel magnolia." Mrs. Carter was respected, and her determination to succeed, her volunteerism and desire to help the less fortunate, and even her southern hospitality drew acclaim. But few people loved her. Among the public and the press, Mrs. Carter neither found love nor, in light of who she was, did she have any desire to.

History is proving to be kinder to Mrs. Carter, and it is likely that her reputation will continue to grow, thanks to both the boundaries she broke as first lady and her work since leaving the White House. There is a lesson here: a first lady who assumes a traditional role might be popular among her contemporaries, but one who breaks new ground will be remembered forever.

NOTES

ABBREVIATIONS USED IN NOTES

FLO   First Lady's Office
FLPO   First Lady's Press Office
FLSF   First Lady's Staff File
FLSO   First Lady's Social Office
JCL   Jimmy Carter Library, Atlanta, Georgia
MHP   Mental Health Project
PO   Projects Office
PPPUS   *Public Papers of the Presidents of the United States*
RSO   Records of the Speechwriter's Office
SF   Subject File
WHCF   White House Central File

PREFACE

1. Melinda Beck et al., "Mrs. President," *Newsweek*, 6 August 1979, 22.

2. "Tie for No. 1 in the Most-Admired-Women List," *New York Times*, 25 December 1980, 47.

3. Those biographies are few in number. See Howard Norton, *Rosalynn* (Plainfield, N.J.: Logos International, 1977), and Dawn Simmons, *Rosalynn Carter: Her Life Story* (New York: Frederick Fell, 1979). Although it is more a story of the 1976 presidential campaign in Florida than a true biography, see also Edna Langford and Linda Maddox, *Rosalynn: Friend and First Lady* (Old Tappan, N.J.: Fleming H. Revell, 1980).

CHAPTER 1: THE MAKING OF A FIRST LADY

1. Allie Smith, interview by Marie B. Allen, 10 November 1978, transcript, Carter/Smith Family Oral History Project, JCL.

2. "Meet Rosalynn Carter," *Family Circle*, October 1976, 4.

3. Rosalynn Carter, *First Lady from Plains* (Boston: Houghton Mifflin, 1984), 12; Doris Betts, "The First 'Good Ole Girl,'" *Life*, March 1980, 128; President and Mrs. Carter, interview by the author, 15 June 2006, Carter Center, Atlanta.

4. Allethea Wall, interview by David Alsobrook, 21 October 1978, transcript, Carter/Smith Family Oral History Project, JCL.

5. Carter, *First Lady from Plains,* 13.

6. Ibid., 13–14; Jimmy and Rosalynn Carter, interview by Ed Bearss, 11 May 1988, transcript, National Park Service Plains Project Oral Histories, JCL.

7. Carter, *First Lady from Plains,* 15, 16.

8. Author's interview with President and Mrs. Carter, 15 June 2006.

9. Carter, *First Lady from Plains,* 17–18.

10. Ibid., 20.

11. Ibid., 22; author's interview with President and Mrs. Carter, 15 June 2006.

12. Jimmy Carter, *Sharing Good Times* (New York: Simon and Schuster, 2004), 15–16; author's interview with President and Mrs. Carter, 15 June 2006.

13. Jimmy Carter, *The Virtues of Aging* (New York: Library of Contemporary Thought, 1998), 35–36.

14. Carter, *First Lady from Plains,* 23.

15. Jerrold Smith, interview by David Alsobrook, 23 June 1979, transcript, Carter/Smith Family Oral History Project, and Allie Smith, interview by Ed Bearss, 19 December 1985, transcript, National Park Service Plains Project Oral Histories, JCL; Hugh Carter and Frances Spatz Leighton, *Cousin Beedie and Cousin Hot: My Life with the Carter Family of Plains, Georgia* (Englewood Cliffs, N.J.: Prentice-Hall, 1978), 68.

16. Carter, *First Lady from Plains,* 26–27.

17. Ibid., 27.

18. Jim Auchmutey, "Over 60 Years of Highs and Lows, Carters Find Happiness as Equals," *Atlanta Journal-Constitution,* 6 July 2006, 1A.

19. Ibid.

20. Carter, *Virtues of Aging,* 91.

21. Kandy Stroud, "Rosalynn's Agenda in the White House," *New York Times Magazine,* 20 March 1977, 58.

22. Carter, *Sharing Good Times,* 42; Carter, *First Lady from Plains,* 47.

23. Carter, *First Lady from Plains,* 49–50.

24. Jimmy Carter and Rosalynn Carter, *Everything to Gain: Making the Most of the Rest of Your Life* (Fayetteville: University of Arkansas Press, 1995), 50–51.

25. Stroud, "Rosalynn's Agenda," 58.

26. Mrs. Jimmy Carter, interview by Joyce Gallagher, 21 December 1974, transcript, Miscellaneous Interviews, JCL.

27. Quoted in Ralph G. Martin, "Rosalynn," *Ladies' Home Journal,* March 1979, 168.

28. Interview with Jimmy and Rosalynn Carter, 11 May 1988.

29. Martin, "Rosalynn," 168.

30. Carter, *First Lady from Plains*, 87.

31. Ibid., 76–77, 83.

32. Ibid., 85–86.

33. Ibid., 69; Rosalynn Carter, with Susan K. Golant, *Helping Yourself Help Others: A Book for Caregivers* (New York: Times Books, 1994), 25.

34. Carter, *First Lady from Plains*, 91–92.

35. Ibid., 95–96.

36. Ibid., 99–100.

37. Interview with Rosalynn Carter, 21 December 1974.

38. Jimmy Carter, *Why Not the Best?* (New York: Bantam, 1976), 168.

39. Carter, *Sharing Good Times*, 49–50; Auchmutey, "Over 60 Years."

40. Carter and Leighton, *Cousin Beedie and Cousin Hot*, 187; Deborah Weil, "Rosalynn Carter," *Atlanta Journal and Constitution*, 11 July 1976, 10G.

41. For examples of Mrs. Carter's schedule, see the Records of the 1976 Campaign Committee to Elect Jimmy Carter, JCL.

42. Author's interview with President and Mrs. Carter, 15 June 2006.

43. Carter and Leighton, *Cousin Beedie and Cousin Hot*, 189–190.

44. Greg Schneiders, telephone interview by the author, 26 January 2006.

45. Ibid.

46. Martin Schram, *Running for President, 1976: The Carter Campaign* (New York: Stein and Day, 1977), 24.

47. Mary Hoyt, interview by the author, 19 August 2005, Washington, D.C.

48. Joyce Leviton, "Jimmy Carter Already Has a 'Running' Mate—His Tireless Wife, Rosalynn," *People*, 13 March 1976, 10; Margaret Truman, *First Ladies* (New York: Fawcett, 1995), 146; Myra McPherson, "White House Confidential," *Washington Post*, 14 December 1978, C1.

49. Marie Ridder, "Jimmy Carter's 'Best Friend,'" *St. Louis Globe-Democrat*, 14 July 1976, 10A.

50. Carter and Leighton, *Cousin Beedie and Cousin Hot*, 158.

51. Mary Finch Hoyt, *East Wing, a Memoir: Politics, the Press, and a First Lady* (Philadelphia: Xlibris, 2001), 115; Kandy Stroud, "She Is Hounded on the Campaign Trail," *Washington Star*, 22 September 1976, FLSF, FLPO, Box 53, JCL.

52. Gail Sheehy, "Ladies and Gentlemen, The Second President—Sister Rosalynn," *New York*, 22 November 1976, 52.

53. Kati Marton, *Hidden Power: Presidential Marriages that Shaped Our History* (New York: Anchor, 2001), 223; "1976: A National Stage for Carter,"

http://theunionleader.com/articles_showa.html?article=14568 (accessed 30 March 2006).

54. Jimmy Carter, *Keeping Faith: Memoirs of a President* (Fayetteville: University of Arkansas Press, 1995), 20.

CHAPTER 2: CREATING A "CARING SOCIETY"

1. For more on Mrs. Ford's activism, see John Robert Greene, *Betty Ford: Candor and Courage in the White House* (Lawrence: University Press of Kansas, 2004).

2. Rosalynn Carter, "Toward a More Caring Society," *MH,* Summer–Fall 1977, 5.

3. "Time to Review Mental Health Rosalynn Says," *Chicago Tribune,* 30 September 1976, FLSF, FLPO, Box 54, JCL; Paul Healy, "Not Really Mrs. President— But . . . ," *New York Daily News,* 7 September 1977, 45.

4. Bourne to Carter, 6 December 1976, Carter, Rosalynn, 12/6/76–7/11/78, Box 28, Records of the Office of Peter Bourne, JCL.

5. MaryAnne Borrelli, "The First Lady as Formal Adviser to the President: When East (Wing) Meets West (Wing)," *Women & Politics* 24, no. 1 (2002): 28–29; Huron to First Lady, 17 February 1977, President's Commission on Mental Health—Memorandums, 1/77–6/78, Box 8, FLO, PO, MHP, JCL.

6. Marlene Cimons, "Mrs. Carter Begins Study of Mentally Ill," *Los Angeles Times,* 21 April 1977, pt. IV, 1.

7. For examples, see WHCF, FLSO, SF, Box 10, JCL; and Mikulski to Carter, 18 February 1977, FG 287 Federal Government Organizations/President's Commission on Mental Health, 4/1/77–4/30/77, Box 10, WHCF, FLSO, SF, JCL.

8. Peter Bourne, *Jimmy Carter: A Comprehensive Biography from Plains to Postpresidency* (New York: Lisa Drew, 1997), 378–379.

9. "Commissioners-Designate of President's Commission on Mental Health, March 29, 1977," President's Commission on Mental Health—Meeting, 4/19/77, Box 8, FLO, PO, MHP, JCL.

10. Rosalynn Carter, *First Lady from Plains* (Boston: Houghton Mifflin, 1984), 259; "Statement by Rosalynn Carter, Honorary Chairperson, the President's Commission on Mental Health, before the Senate Subcommittee on Health and Scientific Research, February 7, 1979," Hearings on Mental Health, 7 February 1979, Box 8, FLSF, FLPO, JCL; "Testimony Makes Rosalynn Wince," *Atlanta Constitution,* 26 May 1977, 1D.

11. PAIA Bulletin 92, "Highlights from the Report of the President's Commission on Mental Health," 27 April 1978, President's Commission on Mental

Health—Implementation, 4/78–11/78, Box 7, FLO, PO, MHP, JCL. See also "Mental Illness in America," undated (circa spring 1978), Mental Health Commission [2], Box 51, FLSF, FLPO, JCL.

12. "Inside the White House (cont'd): Jimmy Sleeps Well, Amy's Mad at Mom & Rosalynn Is Content," *People,* 7 January 1980, 72.

13. "Discussant: Kathryn E. Cade," in *The Presidency and Domestic Policies of Jimmy Carter,* ed. Herbert D. Rosenbaum and Alexej Ugrinsky (Westport, Conn.: Greenwood, 1994), 532; *PPPUS,* 1978, II:792.

14. "Highlights from the Report."

15. Carter, *First Lady from Plains,* 263.

16. Kathy to RSC, 14 November 1978, Mental Health Memorandums, 2/14/77–9/30/80, Box 2, FLO, PO, MHP, JCL.

17. Carter, *First Lady from Plains,* 263.

18. "Statement by Rosalynn Carter."

19. Bryant to Carter, 29 March 1979, President's Commission on Mental Health—Implementation, 1/79–6/80, Box 7, FLO, PO, MHP, JCL.

20. "The President's Partner," *Newsweek,* 5 November 1979, 39; President and Mrs. Carter, interview by the author, 15 June 2006, Carter Center, Atlanta.

21. Joseph A. Califano Jr., *Inside: A Public and Private Life* (New York: Public Affairs, 2004), 361–362, 369; Joseph A. Califano Jr., telephone interview by the author, 6 December 2006.

22. "Panelists' Responses," in Rosenbaum and Ugrinsky, *The Presidency and Domestic Policies of Jimmy Carter,* 544.

23. Ibid., 544–545.

24. Donnie Radcliffe, "Service Stripes," *Washington Post,* 11 June 1980, D1.

25. Carter, *First Lady from Plains,* 265.

26. For more on this issue, see John A. Talbott, "Deinstitutionalization: Avoiding the Disasters of the Past," *Psychiatric Services* 55 (October 2004): 1112–1115; E. Fuller Torrey, "PORT: Updated Treatment Recommendations," *Schizophrenic Bulletin* 30 (2004): 617–618; Philip S. Wang, Olga Demler, and Ronald C. Kellser, "Adequacy of Treatment for Serious Mental Illness in the United States," *American Journal of Public Health* 92 (January 2002): 92–98; Philip S. Wang et al., "Twelve-Month Use of Mental Health Services in the United States," *Archives of General Psychiatry* 62 (June 2005): 629–640.

27. Carter, *First Lady from Plains,* 267.

28. John Osborne, "Rosalynn at Work," *New Republic,* 26 August and 2 September 1978, 12; Rhonda Amon, "Rosalynn Carter: Jimmy's Doing Great Things," *Newsday,* 3 December 1978, Carter, Rosalynn [3], Box 40, FLSF, FLPO, JCL.

29. "Mrs. Carter's Interest in the Cities," *Washington Post,* 10 February 1978, A14.

30. Marjorie Hunter, "Mrs. Carter Sees Political Friends," *New York Times,* 22 March 1979, B12.

31. Carter, *First Lady from Plains,* 271–272; Paulette Douthitt, "At Home with Mrs. Rosalynn Carter," *Albany Herald,* 12 September 1976, 1C.

32. Amon, "Rosalynn Carter: Jimmy's Doing Great Things"; Sally Quinn, "Have You Heard What They're Not Saying about Rosalynn?" *Washington Post,* 25 June 1978, K1.

33. "Women and America: Rosalynn Carter Challenges Communicators," Women and Minorities—Women and America: Rosalynn Carter Challenges Communicators, Box 92, Records of the Office of the Assistant to the President for Women's Affairs, JCL.

34. Carter, *First Lady from Plains,* 271.

35. Kathy Cade, interview by Emily Soapes, 7 January 1981, audio recording, Exit Interview Project, JCL; Quinn, "Have You Heard What They're Not Saying about Rosalynn?"

36. Marguerite Sullivan, "Rosalynn Doesn't Worry about Image," *San Diego Union,* 11 February 1979, D1.

37. "The Distaff Staff," *Women's Wear Daily,* 21 March 1978, 27.

38. For more on the organization and influence of the anti-ERA movement, see Jane J. Mansbridge, *Why We Lost the ERA* (Chicago: University of Chicago Press, 1986); Mary Frances Berry, *Why ERA Failed: Politics, Women's Rights, and the Amending Process of the Constitution* (Bloomington: Indiana University Press, 1986); Donald G. Mathews and Jane Sherron de Hart, *Sex, Gender, and the Politics of ERA: A State and the Nation* (New York: Oxford University Press, 1990); Myra Marx Ferree and Beth B. Hess, *Controversy and Coalition: The New Feminist Movement across Three Decades of Change,* rev. ed. (New York: Twayne, 1994); and Susan M. Hartmann, *From Margin to Mainstream: American Women and Politics since 1960* (Philadelphia: Temple University Press, 1989).

39. Mary Hoyt, interview by the author, 19 August 2005, Washington, D.C.

CHAPTER 3: THE FIRST LADY GOES ABROAD

1. Rosalynn Carter, *First Lady from Plains* (Boston: Houghton Mifflin, 1984), 177; Susanna McBee, "Mrs. Carter's Trip Carefully Crafted to Make Policy Points," *Washington Post,* 29 May 1977, A6; James Nelson Goodsell, "Some Latins Cool to Mrs. Carter's Visit," *Christian Science Monitor,* 7 June 1977, 9.

{ *Notes to Pages 64–73* }

2. For notes from these briefings, see Foreign Trips, Background Material, 1977–1980, Box 24, FLSF, FLPO, JCL.

3. Robert Pastor, telephone interview by the author, 20 September 2005.

4. Levinson to Mrs. Carter, 16 May 1977, Foreign Trips, Background Material, 1977–1980, Box 24, FLSF, FLPO, JCL.

5. Carter, *First Lady from Plains,* 183–184.

6. Terence Todman, telephone interview by the author, 24 January 2006.

7. Author's telephone interview with Pastor.

8. Carter, *First Lady from Plains,* 185.

9. Ibid., 186.

10. Ibid.

11. Susanna McBee, "Ecuadorans Shout 'Bloody Rosalynn,'" *Washington Post,* 3 June 1977, A1.

12. Carter, *First Lady from Plains,* 188–189.

13. Author's telephone interview with Pastor; Carter, *First Lady from Plains,* 192.

14. "Notes from Meeting with President Morales Bermudez," 3 June 1977, Peru, June 3, 1977, Box 24, FLSF, FLPO, JCL; Carter, *First Lady from Plains,* 192–193.

15. Susanna McBee, "'Very Difficult Problems' Separate U.S., Cuba, Mrs. Carter Says," *Washington Post,* 1 June 1977, A12; Susanna McBee, "Neither Rain nor Altitude Represses First Lady on Tour," *Washington Post,* 5 June 1977, A19.

16. Author's telephone interview with Todman.

17. Laura Foreman, "Mrs. Carter Is Given a Low-Key Welcome in Brazil," *New York Times,* 7 June 1977, 5; Burton I. Kaufman and Scott Kaufman, *The Presidency of James Earl Carter Jr.,* 2nd ed. (Lawrence: University Press of Kansas, 2006), 59–60.

18. Copman to Secretary of State, 5 June 1977, Peru, June 3, 1977, Box 24, FLSF, FLPO, JCL.

19. Carter, *First Lady from Plains,* 195; Susanna McBee, "First Lady Stresses Journey Was Her Show," *Washington Post,* 14 June 1977, A11.

20. Carter, *First Lady from Plains,* 195–196.

21. Laura Foreman, "Mrs. Carter Told by 2 Americans of Brazil Ordeal," *New York Times,* 9 June 1977, A1.

22. Memorandum of Conversation, 9 June 1977, Colombia, June 9, 1977, Box 25, FLSF, FLPO, JCL.

23. Carter, *First Lady from Plains,* 199.

24. Mary Finch Hoyt, *East Wing, a Memoir: Politics, the Press, and a First Lady* (Philadelphia: Xlibris, 2001), 151.

25. David Vidal, "Ambassador Rosalynn Carter," *New York Times,* 14 June 1977, 18.

26. Faye Lind Jensen, "An Awesome Responsibility: Rosalynn Carter as First Lady," *Presidential Studies Quarterly* 20, no. 4 (Fall 1990): 770; Hoyt to RSC, 15 September 1977, Hoyt Chron: July–September 1977, Box 28, FLSF, FLPO, JCL.

27. Betty Boyd Caroli, *First Ladies,* expanded ed. (New York: Oxford University Press, 1995), 267; Margaret Truman, *First Ladies: An Intimate Group Portrait of White House Wives* (New York: Fawcett, 1995), 148; Kati Marton, *Hidden Power: Presidential Marriages that Shaped Our History* (New York: Anchor, 2002), 230–231.

28. Georgie Anne Geyer, "Feminism v. Diplomacy," *Washington Post,* 13 January 1978, A13.

29. Hoyt to Bush, 6 February 1978, Hoyt Chron: January–July 1978, Box 29, FLSF, FLPO, JCL; Hoyt, *East Wing,* 161–162.

30. Carter, *First Lady from Plains,* 155–156.

31. "Mrs. Carter to Attend Funeral of Pope Paul," *New York Times,* 9 August 1978, A12.

32. Carter, *First Lady from Plains,* 226.

33. "The President's Partner," *Newsweek,* 5 November 1979, 40; President and Mrs. Carter, interview by the author, 15 June 2006, Carter Center, Atlanta; Zbigniew Brzezinski, with Madeleine K. Albright, Leslie G. Denend, and William Odom, interview by Inis Claude et al., 18 February 1982, transcript, Miller Center, University of Virginia.

34. Kathy Cade, interview by Emily Soapes, 7 January 1981, audio recording, Exit Interview Project, JCL.

35. Carter, *First Lady from Plains,* 279.

36. Ibid., 281.

37. Owen to Carter, 8 February 1980, CO 155 Thailand, 1/21/77–1/20/81, Box 7, and Kathy to RSC, 30 May 1980, CO 81 Khmer, Republic of Cambodia, 2/20/80–1/20/81, Box 5, WHCF, FLSO, SF, JCL.

38. Carter, *First Lady from Plains,* 294.

39. Zbigniew Brzezinski, *Power and Principle: Memoirs of the National Security Adviser, 1977–1981* (New York: Farrar, Straus, Giroux, 1983), 481.

40. Carter, *First Lady from Plains,* 306.

41. Ibid., 309.

42. Kaufman and Kaufman, *Presidency of James Earl Carter,* 169, 228.

CHAPTER 4: HOSTESS AND HOME LIFE

1. "Responsibilities of the Social Office," Hoyt to East Wing Press Staff, undated (circa 13 February 1977), Hoyt Chron: January–March 1977, Box 28, FLSF, FLPO, JCL.

2. Rosalynn Carter, *First Lady from Plains* (Boston: Houghton Mifflin, 1984), 210.

3. Ibid., 211.

4. Ibid., 212.

5. Hoyt to East Wing Staff, 10 March 1977, Hoyt Chron: January–March 1977, Box 28, FLSF, FLPO, JCL.

6. *Living White House,* rev. ed. (Washington, D.C.: White House Historical Association, 1978), 18.

7. Carter, *First Lady from Plains,* 213.

8. Sally Quinn, "Have You Heard What They're Not Saying about Rosalynn?" *Washington Post,* 25 June 1978, K1; Martin Tolchin, "Rosalynn Carter: An Adviser in Her Own Right," *New York Times,* 30 May 1978, B1; Mary Finch Hoyt, *East Wing, a Memoir: Politics, the Press, and a First Lady* (Philadelphia: Xlibris, 2001), 166; Faith Collins, telephone interview by the author, 8 September 2006; Greg Schneiders, telephone interview by the author, 26 January 2006.

9. Hoyt, *East Wing,* 190; Mary Hoyt, interview by the author, 19 August 2005, Washington, D.C.

10. Paula Watson-Irwin, interview by David Ausserbach, 17 October 1979, audio recording, Exit Interview Project, JCL.

11. Carter, *First Lady from Plains,* 215; Hoyt to Van Horn, Box 29, FLSF, FLPO, JCL.

12. Carter, *First Lady from Plains,* 218.

13. Author's interview with Hoyt; *Living White House,* 103.

14. Donnie Radcliffe, "White House Hearts and Followers," *Washington Post,* 14 February 1980, C6.

15. Warren Brown, "Writers Throw First Lady a Curve in Pitch for Carter," *Washington Post,* 23 July 1979, A3.

16. *Living White House,* 127.

17. "Discussant: Gretchen Poston," in *The Presidency and Domestic Policies of Jimmy Carter,* ed. Herbert D. Rosenbaum and Alexej Ugrinsky (Westport, Conn.: Greenwood, 1994), 535.

18. "Crisis or Calm, White House Parties Roll On," *U.S. News & World Report,* 12 March 1979, 41; "Mrs. Carter Knows She Lives 'in Eye of History,'" *Baltimore Sun,* 5 August 1979, Carter, Rosalynn [5], Box 41, FLSF, FLPO, JCL.

19. *Living White House,* 67; Carl Sferrazza Anthony, *First Ladies: The Saga of the Presidents' Wives and Their Power, 1961–1990* (New York: William Morrow, 1991), 280.

20. Joy Billington, "Rosalynn Carter—Two Years Later," *Washington Star,* 7 February 1979, F1.

21. Elisabeth Bumiller, Donnie Radliffe, and Joseph McLellan, "Kennedy Center Honors: The Movers Meet the Shakers," *Washington Post,* 3 December 1979, B1.

22. Author's telephone interview with Schneiders; Kenneth W. Thompson, ed., *The Carter Presidency: Fourteen Intimate Perspectives of Jimmy Carter* (Lanham, Md.: University Press of America, 1990), 229; Thomas O'Neill with William Novak, *Man of the House: The Life and Political Memoirs of Speaker Tip O'Neill* (New York: Random House, 1987), 297.

23. Landrum R. Bolling, "Rosalynn Carter: The President's Partner," *Saturday Evening Post,* March 1980, 88; Judy Pace, "Mrs. Carter Says Busing Not Answer," *Shreveport Times,* 29 September 1980, 1A; author's telephone interview with Schneiders.

24. Author's interview with Hoyt; "Discussant: Gretchen Poston," in Rosenbaum and Ugrinsky, *Presidency and Domestic Policies of Jimmy Carter,* 535–537.

25. Sarah Booth Conroy, "The Case of the Crystal Chandelier: Rosalynn Says No," *Washington Post,* 4 June 1977, C1.

26. Carter, *First Lady from Plains,* 205–206.

27. Betty Glad, *Jimmy Carter: In Search of the Great White House* (New York: Norton, 1980), 72–73; Kandy Stroud, "Rosalynn's Agenda in the White House," *New York Times Magazine,* 20 March 1977, 20.

28. Hamilton Jordan, *Crisis: The Last Year of the Carter Presidency* (New York: G. P. Putnam's Sons, 1982), 70–71.

29. Ralph G. Martin, "Rosalynn," *Ladies' Home Journal,* March 1979, 99; Anthony, *First Ladies,* 275–276.

30. "Inside the White House (cont'd): Jimmy Sleeps Well, Amy's Mad at Mom & Rosalynn Is Content," *People,* 7 January 1980, 72.

31. Claire Safran, "The Women in Jimmy Carter's Life," *Redbook,* October 1976, 93.

32. Vicki Pearlman, "Rosalynn: A Portrait of the First Lady," *Atlanta Journal,* 31 October 1978, 1A; "A Candid Conversation with the First Lady," *New York Daily News,* 6 September 1977, 37; "Mrs. Carter Says She Tells the President 'What I Think,'" *New York Times,* 10 March 1977, 18.

33. Author's telephone interview with Schneiders; author's interview with Hoyt.

34. Mrs. Carter quoted in Gil Troy, *Mr. and Mrs. President: From the Trumans to the Clintons* (Lawrence: University Press of Kansas, 2000), 263; author's interview with Hoyt.

35. Jody Powell, *The Other Side of the Story* (New York: William Morrow, 1984), 122–123.

36. Author's telephone interview with Schneiders.

37. Kandy Stroud, "The Steel Magnolia," *Cosmopolitan,* October 1979, 333; B. Drummond Ayres Jr., "The Importance of Being Rosalynn," *New York Times Magazine,* 3 June 1979, 49; Anthony, *First Ladies,* 297.

CHAPTER 5: THE FIRST LADY AND THE MEDIA

1. "Betty vs. Rosalynn: Life on the Campaign Trail," *U.S. News & World Report,* 18 October 1976, 22.

2. Gail Sheehy, "Ladies and Gentleman, The Second President—Sister Rosalynn," *New York Times,* 22 November 1976, 50.

3. Mary Hoyt, interview by the author, 19 August 2005, Washington, D.C.

4. Howard Norton, *Rosalynn: A Portrait* (Plainfield, N.J.: Logos International, 1977), 99–100; Nina S. Hyde, "Fashion Notes," *Washington Post,* 4 June 1978, M13.

5. Nina S. Hyde, "Rosalynn Carter's Fashion," *Washington Post,* 30 January 1977, H1.

6. Mary Hoyt, e-mail correspondence with the author, 18 March 2006.

7. Kandy Stroud, *How Jimmy Won: The Victory Campaign from Plains to the White House* (New York: William Morrow, 1977), 322–323; author's interview with Hoyt.

8. Author's interview with Hoyt.

9. Barbara C. Burrell, "The Office of the First Lady and Public Policymaking," in *The Other Elites: Women, Politics, and Power in the Executive Branch,* ed. MaryAnne Borrelli and Janet M. Martin (Boulder, Colo.: Lynne Rienner, 1997), 174; Kathy B. Smith, "The First Lady Represents America: Rosalynn Carter in South America," *Presidential Studies Quarterly* 27, no. 3 (Summer 1997): 546.

10. "'I've Never Won an Argument with Her,'" *Time,* 31 July 1978, 12.

11. Sally Quinn, "Have You Heard What They're Not Saying about Rosalynn?" *Washington Post,* 25 June 1978, K1; Kandy Stroud, "The Steel Magnolia," *Cosmopolitan,* October 1979, 334.

12. Stroud, "Steel Magnolia," 334.

13. Faith Collins, telephone interview by the author, 8 September 2006; author's interview with Hoyt.

14. Vicki Pearlman, "Rosalynn: A Personal Portrait," *Atlanta Journal,* 29 October 1978, 1A.

15. William V. Shannon, "The Other Carter in the Running," *New York Times,* 15 September 1976, 45.

16. Myra McPherson, "First Families: In the National Eye," *Washington Post,* 20 January 1977, JEC15; Linda Charlton, "Mrs. Carter's Model Is Very Much Her Own: Mrs. F.D.R.," *New York Times,* 5 June 1977, sec. 4, 4.

17. "Some Surprises as First Lady Sets a Style of Her Own," *U.S. News & World Report,* 14 November 1977, 40.

18. Rosalynn Carter, *First Lady from Plains* (Boston: Houghton Mifflin, 1984), 286.

19. Kenneth W. Thompson, ed., *The Carter Presidency: Fourteen Intimate Perspectives of Jimmy Carter* (Lanham, Md.: University Press of America, 1990), 229–230.

20. "Rosalynn, Cool the Big Talk," *Cleveland Press,* 20 November 1976, A5; "Rosalynn Carter Elected," *New York Times,* 15 June 1977, A20.

21. John Osborne, "Rosalynn," *New Republic,* 19 August 1978, 9.

22. Carter, *First Lady from Plains,* 164–165.

23. Burton I. Kaufman and Scott Kaufman, *The Presidency of James Earl Carter Jr.,* 2nd ed. (Lawrence: University Press of Kansas, 2006), 35–36; David S. Broder, "Human Rights: Jingoists Snap to Attention," *Los Angeles Times,* 30 June 1977, pt. 2, 7.

24. Kaufman and Kaufman, *Presidency of James Earl Carter,* 39.

25. Vera Glaser, "Is Rosalynn Ignoring the Political Facts of Life?" *Detroit Free Press,* 17 March 1978, 1C.

26. Greg Schneiders, telephone interview by the author, 26 January 2006; Zbigniew Brzezinski, *Power and Principle: Memoirs of the National Security Adviser, 1977–1981* (New York: Farrar, Straus, Giroux, 1983), 67.

27. See, for instance, Meg Greenfield, "Mrs. President," *Newsweek,* 20 June 1977; Pearlman, "Rosalynn"; "Second Most Powerful Person," *Time,* 7 May 1979, 22; Godfrey Sperling Jr., "New Ladder of Command at White House," *Christian Science Monitor,* 25 July 1979, 4; Myra MacPherson, "Is Rosalynn Carter Really Running the Country?" *McCall's,* March 1980.

28. PPPUS, *Jimmy Carter,* 1978, II:1412–1413; "Mrs. President," *Newsweek,* 6 August 1979, 22.

29. "Rosalynn's Role," *Christian Science Monitor,* 31 July 1979, 24; Joan Beck, "Who Runs the White House, Staff or Distaff?" *Chicago Tribune,* 3 August 1979;

"Who Elected Rosalynn?" *Manchester Union Leader,* 19 December 1979, Carter, Rosalynn [6], Box 41, FLSF, FLPO, JCL.

30. Richard Cohen, "Rosalynn Carter's Role: Resolving the Mystery," *Washington Post,* 31 July 1979, C1; "Rosalynn Carter and Her Role," *Washington Star,* 16 October 1979, Carter, Rosalynn [5], Box 41 FLSF, FLPO; Carl Rowan, "President Should Consult Rosalynn," *Washington Star,* 3 August 1979, Carter, Rosalynn [6], Box 41, FLSF, FLPO, JCL.

31. "Being First Lady Isn't What It Used to Be," *U.S. News & World Report,* 13 March 1978, 75; "Rosalynn—Spearhead of Carter Campaign," *U.S. News & World Report,* 5 November 1979, 39; Glaser, "Is Rosalynn Ignoring the Political Facts of Life?"

32. MaryAnne Borrelli, "The First Lady as Formal Advisor to the President: Where (East) Wing Meets West (Wing)," *Women & Politics* 24, no. 1 (2002): 26.

CHAPTER 6: THE UNFINISHED AGENDA

1. See Douglas Brinkley, *The Unfinished Presidency* (New York: Penguin, 1998).

2. "Rosalynn—Spearhead of the Carter Campaign," *U.S. News & World Report,* 5 November 1979, 39.

3. Myra MacPherson, "Is Rosalynn Carter Really Running the Country?" *McCall's,* March 1980, 174.

4. T. R. Reid, "Kennedy Winds Up Debating Rosalynn Carter, from Afar," *Washington Post,* 2 February 1980, A4.

5. "Mrs. Carter's Remarks at the B'nai B'rith Women's International Biennial Convention," 12 March 1980, RSO, SF, JCL.

6. Rosalynn Carter, *First Lady from Plains* (Boston: Houghton Mifflin, 1984), 305.

7. Kati Marton, *Hidden Power: Presidential Marriages that Shaped Our History* (New York: Anchor, 2001), 241.

8. Carter, *First Lady from Plains,* 315; Burton I. Kaufman and Scott Kaufman, *The Presidency of James Earl Carter Jr.,* 2nd ed. (Lawrence: University Press of Kansas, 2006), 233.

9. Mark Penders, "Rosalynn Lauds Husband for Handling of Hostages," *New Haven Register,* 14 September 1980, Box 46, FLSF, FLPO, JCL.

10. Shelley Rolfe, "GOP Blasts at Carter Turned Aside by Wife," *Richmond Times-Dispatch,* 26 September 1980; "Campaign Notes," *Washington Post,* 20 September 1980, A4; Carl Freund, "First Lady Needles Reagan on Visit to FW," *Dallas Morning News,* 30 September 1980, 12A.

11. "Campaign Notes."

12. B. Drummond Ayres Jr., "Barbs and Gossamer Line First Lady's Political Trail," *New York Times,* 12 October 1980, 34; "If Carter Gets Re-elected, Give Credit to First Lady," *Allentown (Pa.) Morning Call,* 10 October 1980, Box 46, FLSF, FLPO, JCL.

13. Quoted in Sandra L. Quinn-Musgrave and Sanford Kanter, *America's Royalty: All the President's Children,* rev. and expanded ed. (Westport, Conn.: Greenwood, 1995), 225.

14. Donnie Radcliffe, "Tears and Pride of the Steel Magnolia: Rosalynn Carter on the Aftermath," *Washington Post,* 19 November 1980, E1; "Rosalynn Carter's Interview with AP, UPI, NYT, Washington Post, Washington Star, LA Times and Women's Wear Daily—11/18/80," Box 12, FLSF, FLPO, JCL.

15. Carter, *First Lady from Plains,* 324.

16. Ibid., 323.

17. Ibid., 325.

18. Carl Sferrazza Anthony, *First Ladies: The Saga of the Presidents' Wives and Their Power, 1961–1990* (New York: William Morrow, 1991), 318; "Mrs. Reagan Said to Drop a Gentle Hint," *New York Times,* 13 December 1980, 12; James G. Benze Jr., *Nancy Reagan: On the White House Stage* (Lawrence: University Press of Kansas, 2005), 37.

19. Carter, *First Lady from Plains,* 331.

20. Jimmy Carter and Rosalynn Carter, *Everything to Gain: Making the Most of the Rest of Your Life* (Fayetteville: University of Arkansas Press, 1995), 17.

21. Ibid., 24; Brinkley, *Unfinished Presidency,* 76.

22. Carter and Carter, *Everything to Gain,* 13.

23. Jimmy Carter, *The Virtues of Aging* (New York: Ballantine, 1998), 40.

24. Carter and Carter, *Everything to Gain,* 21.

25. Ibid., 20.

26. Ibid., 16.

27. Ibid., 24; Jonathan Yardley, "Review of *First Lady from Plains,*" *Washington Post Book World,* 1 April 1984, 3; Lucille S. DeView, "Rosalynn Carter's Graceful, Candid Memoir Is Anything But Dull," *Christian Science Monitor,* 10 May 1984, 22.

28. Andrea Chambers, "Former First Lady Rosalynn Carter Is the Second Big-Time Author from Plains," *People,* 30 April 1984, 81.

29. Beverly B. Long, "A Conversation with Rosalynn Carter," *American Psychologist,* July 1986, 833; Rosalynn Carter, "How We Make Mental Illness Worse," *USA Today,* 12 November 1992, 13A; Dr. Thomas Bornemann, interview by the author, 16 June 2006, Carter Center, Atlanta.

30. "Life after the White House: How First Families Adjust," *U.S. News & World Report*, 25 June 1984, 39–40.

31. Brinkley, *Unfinished Presidency*, 355.

32. Susan Page, "At Odds: Effort Underway to Smooth the Ruffled Feathers," *USA Today*, 27 February 1997, 1A.

33. Donnie Radcliffe, "Conversations with First Ladies Betty Ford and Rosalynn Carter on China, ERA and More," *Washington Post*, 15 October 1981, B1.

34. Dana Bisbee, "Ex–First Lady Insists Mental Illness Not to Blame in Rash of School Shootings," *Boston Herald*, 26 May 1999, 066.

35. Tom Davis, "Rosalynn Carter Works for Change Any Way She Can," *Bergen County (N.J.) Record*, 12 October 2004, F1.

36. Author's interview with Bornemann.

37. Rosalynn Carter, "We Need to Confront Fears about Life's End," *USA Today*, 28 March 1999, 17A.

38. Gayle Turim, "Changes," *AIMplus*, January–February 1989, 20.

39. Carter and Carter, *Everything to Gain*, 85; "The Carters Pitch In," *American Health*, March 1988, 58.

40. Bill Torpy, "Rosalynn Carter Visits Gainesville for Health Program," *Atlanta Journal-Constitution*, 28 July 1995, 6B.

41. Brinkley, *Unfinished Presidency*, 424.

42. Jimmy Carter, *Living Faith* (New York: Three Rivers, 2001), 149–151.

43. Quoted in Brinkley, *Unfinished Presidency*, 205–206.

44. "Merry Christmas, Mr. Karadzič," *New Republic*, 9 and 15 January 1995, 7; "Leave My Husband Alone," *New Republic*, 30 January 1995, 4; Michele Watson, "Rosalynn Carter at Peace with Her Work and Herself," *Chicago Tribune*, 6 November 2002, sec. 8, 1.

45. Brinkley, *Unfinished Presidency*, 460.

46. "On the Road with the Carters," *Time*, 15 June 1987, 79; Carter, *Living Faith*, 73; Paul F. Boller, *Presidential Wives: An Anecdotal History*, 2nd ed. (New York: Oxford University Press, 1998), 448.

47. Letty Cottin Pogrebin, "Tough Act to Follow," *New York Times Book Review*, 31 May 1987, 16; David Brooks, "Bookshorts: Numbing, Chilling, Thrilling," *Wall Street Journal*, 23 September 1987, 28.

48. Don Richardson, ed., *Conversations with Carter* (Boulder, Colo.: Lynne Rienner, 1998), 306; Carter, *Living Faith*, 74.

49. Carter, *Living Faith*, 76.

50. Carter, *Virtues of Aging*, 41.

CONCLUSION: AMBIVALENCE SURROUNDING THE OFFICE

1. Robert P. Watson, *The Presidents' Wives: Reassessing the Office of First Lady* (Boulder, Colo.: Lynne Rienner, 2000), 72.

2. Barbara C. Burrell, "The Office of First Lady and Public Policymaking," in *The Other Elites: Women, Politics, and Power in the Executive Branch,* ed. MaryAnne Borrelli and Janet M. Martin (Boulder, Colo.: Lynne Rienner, 1997), 181–182.

3. Margaret Truman, *First Ladies: An Intimate Group Portrait of White House Wives* (New York: Fawcett, 1995), 152.

4. John Pope, "Betty (Elizabeth Anne Bloomer) Ford," in *American First Ladies: Their Lives and Their Legacy,* ed. Lewis Gould (New York: Garland, 1996), 549.

5. Truman, *First Ladies,* 154.

BIBLIOGRAPHIC ESSAY

To conduct research on Rosalynn Carter, the best place to start is the Jimmy Carter Library in Atlanta, Georgia. Although there are still hundreds of thousands of documents yet to be declassified, and many of the papers of the First Lady's Office remain closed, a wealth of information is available. In the First Lady's Office, researchers should examine the papers of the Projects Office, the First Lady's Press Office, and the First Lady's Social Office. Some of the West Wing papers, most notably the White House Central File and the Records of the Speechwriter's Office, are of interest as well.

There are only three biographies of Rosalynn Carter. Howard Norton's *Rosalynn: A Portrait* (Plainfield, N.J.: Logos International, 1977) is a journalist's account of her life; as such, it is more narrative than analytical. Obviously, Norton's book does not delve into her role as first lady; nor does Dawn Langley Simmons's *Rosalynn Carter: Her Life Story* (New York: Frederick Fell, 1979). The third is Mrs. Carter's *First Lady from Plains* (Boston: Houghton Mifflin, 1984), a candid autobiography about growing up in Plains, the partnership that developed between the future first couple, and Mrs. Carter's feelings about, if not her role in making, administration policy.

Several books by Jimmy Carter also have a lot to say about life in Plains and his relationship with Rosalynn before and while they lived in the nation's capital. These include Carter's campaign autobiography, *Why Not the Best?* (Nashville, Tenn.: Broadmann Press, 1975), and his presidential memoirs, *Keeping Faith: Memoirs of a President* (Fayetteville: University of Arkansas Press, 1995). *Sharing Good Times* (New York: Simon and Schuster, 2004) is more anecdotal in nature.

A number of biographies of Jimmy Carter address Rosalynn's influence in his life. Although written nearly thirty years ago, Betty Glad's critical *Jimmy Carter: In Search of the Great White House* (New York: Norton, 1980) remains an important and useful work. In

Jimmy Carter: American Moralist (Athens: University of Georgia Press, 1996), Kenneth Morris depicts a president influenced by a fragmented family and by religious devotion and a former first lady who shared her husband's desire to do good after they left the White House. Peter Bourne, a friend and adviser to both Carters, addresses the president's strengths and flaws, as well as Rosalynn's ability to influence her husband's decision making, in *Jimmy Carter: A Comprehensive Biography from Plains to Postpresidency* (New York: Lisa Drew, 1996). Although largely anecdotal, scholars should also read *Cousin Beedie and Cousin Hot: My Life with the Carter Family of Plains, Georgia* (Englewood Cliffs, N.J.: Prentice-Hall, 1978), by the president's cousin Hugh Carter and Frances Spatz Leighton.

There are numerous books on the lives of American first ladies, many of which devote a chapter to Mrs. Carter. A good place to start is the highly readable essays in Lewis L. Gould, ed., *American First Ladies* (New York: Garland, 1996). Other useful works are Carl Sferrazza Anthony, *First Ladies: The Saga of the Presidents' Wives and Their Power, 1961–1990* (New York: William Morrow, 1991); Betty Boyd Caroli, *First Ladies,* expanded ed. (New York: Oxford University Press, 1995); Gil Troy, *Mr. and Mrs. President: From the Trumans to the Clintons* (Lawrence: University Press of Kansas, 2000); Robert P. Watson, *The Presidents' Wives: Reassessing the Office of First Lady* (Boulder, Colo.: Lynne Rienner, 2000); Kati Marton, *Hidden Power: Presidential Marriages that Shaped Our History* (New York: Anchor, 2001); John B. Roberts II, *Rating the First Ladies: The Women Who Influenced the Presidency* (New York: Citadel Press, 2003); and Margaret Truman, *First Ladies: An Intimate Group Portrait of White House Wives* (New York: Fawcett, 1995). For less detailed or more anecdotal studies, see Paul F. Boller, *Presidential Wives: An Anecdotal History,* 2nd ed. (New York: Oxford University Press, 1998); Peter Hay, *All the Presidents' Ladies: Anecdotes of the Women behind the Men in the White House* (New York: Viking, 1988); Bill Adler, *America's First Ladies: Their Uncommon Wisdom, from Martha Washington to Barbara Bush* (Lanham, Md.: Taylor Trade Publishing, 2002); Cormac O'Brien, *Secret Lives of the First Ladies: What Your Teachers Never Told You about the Women of the White House* (Philadelphia: Quirk Books, 2005); and Elizabeth Simpson Smith, *Five First Ladies: A Look into the Lives of Nancy*

Reagan, Rosalynn Carter, Betty Ford, Pat Nixon, and Lady Bird Johnson* (New York: Walker, 1986).

For studies on Mrs. Carter's predecessor, Betty Ford, see Ford's autobiography, written with Chris Chase, *The Times of My Life* (New York: Harper, 1978), as well as Jeffrey S. Ashley, *Betty Ford: A Symbol of Strength* (New York: Nova History Publications, 2004), and John Robert Greene, *Betty Ford: Candor and Courage in the White House* (Lawrence: University Press of Kansas, 2004).

For studies of Jimmy Carter's 1976 campaign, including Rosalynn's speechmaking and impact on campaign strategy, see Martin Schram, *Running for President, 1976: The Carter Campaign* (New York: Stein and Day, 1977); Jules Witcover, *Marathon: The Pursuit of the Presidency, 1972-1976* (New York: Viking, 1977); and Kandy Stroud, *How Jimmy Won: The Victory Campaign from Plains to the White House* (New York: William Morrow, 1977). The future president often acknowledged his wife's contribution to the campaign in his speeches, collected in *The Presidential Campaign 1976*, 3 vols. (Washington, D.C.: Government Printing Office, 1978). Although her book covers more than just the campaign, Edna Langford, whose daughter married the Carters' son Jack, devotes much of her attention to that effort in Edna Langford and Linda Maddox, *Rosalynn: Friend and First Lady* (Old Tappan, N.J.: Fleming H. Revell, 1980).

As first lady, Mrs. Carter assumed a variety of roles, including hostess, presidential adviser and surrogate, and policy maker. Faye Lind Jensen, "An Awesome Responsibility: Rosalynn Carter as First Lady," *Presidential Studies Quarterly* 20, no. 4 (Fall 1990): 769-775, provides a general assessment of these functions. MaryAnne Borrelli, "The First Lady as Formal Advisor to the President: When East (Wing) Meets West (Wing)," *Women & Politics* 24, no. 1 (2002): 25-46, demonstrates that although a first lady faces certain legal constraints to her power, she can still play an active advisory role. In her essay "The Office of the First Lady and Public Policymaking," in *The Other Elites: Women, Politics, and Power in the Executive Branch*, ed. MaryAnne Borrelli and Janet M. Martin (Boulder, Colo.: Lynne Rienner, 1997), Barbara C. Burrell examines the issue of a first lady's accountability for the administration activities in which she engages. Don Richardson, ed., *Conversations with Carter* (Boulder, Colo.: Lynne Rienner, 1998), a compilation of interviews of the president before, during, and after his tenure in the White House, suggests the extent of the first lady's influence in the administration, as does Kenneth W. Thompson, ed., *The Carter Presidency: Fourteen Intimate Perspectives of Jimmy Carter* (Lanham, Md.: University Press of America, 1990), which also includes an interview with Mrs. Carter. Of interest as well is Burton I. Kaufman and Scott Kaufman, *The Presidency of James Earl Carter Jr.*, 2nd ed. (Lawrence: University Press of Kansas, 2006). Lewis L. Gould's "Modern First Ladies in Historical Perspective," *Presidential Studies Quarterly* 15, no. 3 (Summer 1985): 532–540, looks at the contributions of Lady Bird Johnson, Betty Ford, and Rosalynn Carter to the office of the first lady.

In 1990 Hofstra University hosted a conference on the Carter administration, during which both scholars and former administration officials talked about the president's domestic and foreign policies; there was also discussion of Mrs. Carter and the roles she played. The proceedings of that conference are available in print, edited by Herbert D. Rosenbaum and Alexej Ugrinsky. There are two volumes, but the one of interest to scholars of the first lady is *The Presidency and Domestic Policies of Jimmy Carter* (Westport, Conn.: Greenwood, 1994).

Molly Meijer Wertheimer has written on the speechmaking of modern first ladies; see her *Leading Ladies of the White House: Communication Strategies of Notable Twentieth-Century First Ladies* (Lanham, Md.: Rowman and Littlefield, 2005), and her edited volume, *Inventing a Voice: The Rhetoric of American First Ladies of the Twentieth Century* (Lanham, Md.: Rowman and Littlefield, 2004).

Mrs. Carter's domestic agenda requires further attention from scholars. There are no studies of her immunization campaign, her support for volunteerism, or her attempt to improve care for the elderly. Gerald Grob's "Public Policy and Mental Illness: Jimmy Carter's Presidential Commission on Mental Health," *Milbank Quarterly*, 2005, is an excellent study of her mental health initiative. On mental health, scholars should also consult Helen Chilton Kiefer, ed., *Sourcebook on Mental Health*, 1st edition (Chicago: Marquis Academic Media, 1979), which includes excerpts from the 1978 report of the Commission on Mental Health, as well as articles on other aspects of mental health. Bruce Dohrenwend et al., eds., *Mental Illness in the United States: Epidemiological Estimates* (New York:

Praeger, 1980), is based on the report of the commission's Panel on Nature and Scope of the Problems.

Mrs. Carter resented Joseph Califano's lack of interest in her mental health project and supported her husband's decision to replace him as secretary of the Department of Health, Education, and Welfare (HEW). In his memoirs, *Governing America: An Insider's Report from the White House and Cabinet* (New York: Simon and Schuster, 1981), Califano mentions the first lady only in passing, focusing his criticisms on the president. The more recent *Inside: A Public and Private Life* (New York: Public Affairs, 2004) does not mention Rosalynn Carter at all, and its tone toward the president is less vitriolic; however, the HEW secretary's resentment at being forced out of office is still apparent.

Scholars have devoted extensive attention to efforts to ratify the equal rights amendment (ERA), although these works tend to ignore the role played by Mrs. Carter. On this score, see Jane J. Mansbridge, *Why We Lost the ERA* (Chicago: University of Chicago Press, 1986); Mary Frances Berry, *Why ERA Failed: Politics, Women's Rights, and the Amending Process of the Constitution* (Bloomington: Indiana University Press, 1986); and Donald G. Mathews and Jane Sherron de Hart, *Sex, Gender, and the Politics of ERA: A State and the Nation* (New York: Oxford University Press, 1990).

The Carter White House issued reports on its support of women's interests, and these were compiled in Barbara Haugen, ed., *Women, a Documentary of Progress during the Administration of Jimmy Carter, 1977 to 1981* (Washington, D.C.: Executive Office of the President, 1981). For more on the feminist movement of the 1960s and 1970s and the Carter administration's relationship with women's rights activists, see Myra Marx Ferree and Beth B. Hess, *Controversy and Coalition: The New Feminist Movement across Three Decades of Change*, rev. ed. (New York: Twayne, 1994); Susan M. Hartmann, *From Margin to Mainstream: American Women and Politics since 1960* (Philadelphia: Temple University Press, 1989); Winifred D. Wandersee, *On the Move: American Women in the 1970s* (Boston: Twayne, 1988); Flora Davis, *Moving the Mountain: The Women's Movement in America since 1960* (New York: Simon and Schuster, 1991); Janet M. Martin, *The Presidency and Women: Promise, Performance, and Illusion* (College Station: Texas A&M University Press,

2003); and Bella Abzug and Mim Kelber, *Gender Gap: Bella Abzug's Guide to Political Power for American Women* (Boston: Houghton Mifflin, 1984).

The only secondary source that focuses strictly on Mrs. Carter's foreign policy activities is Kathy B. Smith's "The First Lady Represents America: Rosalynn Carter in South America," *Presidential Studies Quarterly* 27, no. 3 (Summer 1997): 540–548. However, it appeared before any of the East Wing papers had become available at the Carter Library, and Smith conducted no interviews with those who actually went on that trip. David Harris's *The Crisis: The President, the Prophet, and the Shah—1979 and the Coming of Militant Islam* (New York: Little, Brown, 2004) omits important parts of the U.S. response to the Iranian revolution and the hostage crisis, such as President Carter's decision to send General Robert Huyser to Iran. However, this book is both well researched and well written, and it includes some information relevant to Mrs. Carter's role in foreign policy making.

More material on Rosalynn Carter's diplomatic activities can be found in the memoirs written by some Carter administration officials, but interestingly, Secretary of State Cyrus Vance is not among them. In *Hard Choices: Critical Years in America's Foreign Policy* (New York: Simon and Schuster, 1983), the former secretary of state barely mentions the first lady, which may be a reflection of his relationship with her. The Carters were much closer to national security adviser Zbigniew Brzezinski, who competed with Vance for influence in the White House. Indeed, in *Power and Principle: Memoirs of the National Security Adviser, 1977–1981* (New York: Farrar, Straus, Giroux, 1983), Brzezinski has much more to say about Mrs. Carter's role in foreign policy making and is clearly deferential toward her. Scholars should also look at *Crisis: The Last Year of the Carter Presidency* (New York: Putnam, 1982), by former chief of staff Hamilton Jordan. Though much of this work is about the effort to free the hostages in Iran, Jordan also addresses Rosalynn Carter's influence in the White House.

There is no work solely on Mrs. Carter's role as hostess. Though anecdotal, a good place to start is *The Living White House,* rev. ed. (Washington, D.C.: White House Historical Association, 1978). Also of interest is Lucy Moorhead's *Entertaining in Washington* (New York: Putnam's Sons, 1978).

There are several books devoted to the families and, specifically, the children of presidents, and they all provide short biographies of the Carter children: Barbara Kellerman, *All the President's Kin*, reprint ed. (New York: New York University Press, 1984); Sandra L. Quinn-Musgrave and Sanford Kanter, *America's Royalty: All the President's Children*, rev. and expanded ed. (Westport, Conn.: Greenwood, 1995); Doug Wead, *All the Presidents' Children: Triumph and Tragedy in the Lives of America's First Families* (New York: Atria, 2003); and Bonnie Angelo, *First Families: The Impact of the White House on Their Lives* (New York: HarperCollins, 2005).

Much more scholarship is needed on relations between the press and the first lady and first family. *East Wing, a Memoir: Politics, the Press, and a First Lady* (Philadelphia: Xlibris, 2001), by the first lady's press secretary and East Wing coordinator, Mary Finch Hoyt, has much to say about Rosalynn Carter's personality, relations between the White House and feminists, and the first family, particularly Amy Carter. The president's press secretary, Jody Powell, also comments extensively on White House–media relations and the first family in *The Other Side of the Story* (New York: William Morrow, 1984). In "Magazine Coverage of First Ladies from Hoover to Clinton: From Election through the First One Hundred Days of Office," *American Journalism* 14, no. 3-4 (Summer–Fall 1997): 495-519, Liz Watts concludes that a first lady can expect more positive treatment from the press if she adopts the traditional role of hostess or social advocate than if she attempts to become a political activist.

Relations between the executive and legislative branches were tense during Carter's presidency. Numerous studies of the Carter administration, such as that of Kaufman and Kaufman, examine this subject. Also useful is Thomas O'Neill, with William Novak, *Man of the House: The Life and Political Memoirs of Speaker Tip O'Neill* (New York: Random House, 1987).

For the 1980 election and the relationship between Rosalynn Carter and Nancy Reagan, see Mrs. Reagan's memoirs, written with William Novak, *My Turn: The Memoirs of Nancy Reagan* (New York: Random House, 1989); James G. Benze Jr., *Nancy Reagan: On the White House Stage* (Lawrence: University Press of Kansas, 2005); and Anne Edwards, *The Reagans: Portrait of a Marriage* (New York: St. Martin's, 2003).

The best work on the Carters' post–White House activities is Douglas Brinkley's *The Unfinished Presidency* (New York: Penguin, 1998). The Carters themselves have written about their lives since leaving Washington. In *Everything to Gain: Making the Most of the Rest of Your Life,* (Fayetteville: University of Arkansas Press, 1995), Jimmy and Rosalynn Carter share how they adjusted to living in Plains again and use personal accounts to suggest how people can lead fulfilling lives in their later years. Jimmy Carter's *The Virtues of Aging* (New York: Ballantine, 1998) also discusses how people can enjoy retirement. The impact of faith on his life, including his postpresidential career, is the subject of *Living Faith* (New York: Three Rivers Press, 2001). In his recent and controversial book *Palestine: Peace Not Apartheid* (New York: Simon and Schuster, 2006), the former president describes how he and his wife have sought to resolve the Israeli-Palestinian conflict. Rosalynn Carter has continued her interest in caring for the elderly and the mentally ill and, with Susan K. Golant, has written books on both topics: *Helping Yourself Help Others: A Book for Caregivers* (New York: Three Rivers Press, 1995) and *Helping Someone with Mental Illness: A Compassionate Guide for Family, Friends, and Caregivers* (New York: Three Rivers Press, 1999).

INDEX

Abortion, 28, 56, 171
Abourezk, James, 128
Abzug, Bella, 56, 125, 172
Adams, Abigail, 110
Aduldet, Phumiphol, 84
Age Discrimination in Employment Act (1967/1978), 50
Allen, Priscilla, 41
American Convention on Human Rights (1969), 71
American Legion, 60
Anderson, Ann, 59
Anderson, John, 138
Aristide, Jean-Bertrand, 159
Ayres, B. Drummond, 140

Baltimore Sun, 104
Baryshnikov, Mikhail, 98
Bayh, Birch, 55
Beck, Joan, 130
Begin, Aliza, 81 (photo)
Begin, Menachem, 79–80, 81 (photo), 143, 144
Benefield, Carol, 96
Birch Society, 60
Blumenthal, Michael, 85
Borlaug, Norman, 162
Bornemann, Thomas, 152
Boston Herald, 151
Bourne, Peter, 24, 38–39, 41, 44–45, 48
Brezhnev, Leonid, 80
Brinkley, Douglas, 133
Brokaw, Tom, 103
Brooks, David, 164–65
Brown, Jerry, 136–37

Brown, Harold, 87
Brown v. Board of Education (1954), 12
Brubeck, Dave, 100
Bryant, Thomas, 38, 39, 40, 41, 45–47
Brzezinski, Muska, 82
Brzezinski, Zbigniew, 64, 75–76, 78, 81–82, 87, 88, 89, 98, 127, 130
Bumpers, Betty, 54, 156–57
Bumpers, Dale, 54
Bush, Barbara, 166, 169
Bush, George H. W., 148, 166
Bush, George W., 161, 169
Bush, Laura, 169
Bush, Rhonda, 77
Byrd, Robert, 110

Caddell, Pat, 74, 142
Cade, Kathy, 36, 37 (photo), 44, 45–46, 48, 55, 83, 85, 96
Califano, Joseph, 45, 47, 107, 125, 172
Califano, Mark, 47
Callaghan, James, 101
Capuano, Thomas, 72
Carter, Amy, 17, 18, 19, 21, 23, 25, 27, 78, 97, 101, 103, 112–14 (photo on 113), 131, 141, 144, 149
Carter, Annette, 20, 101, 108, 109 (photo), 114, 115
Carter, Billy, 11, 16, 88–89, 115, 126, 163, 166, 172
Carter, Caron, 20, 101, 115, 127, 128 (photo)
Carter, Earl, 6, 8, 11, 14, 20, 163
Carter, Gloria, 15, 166
Carter, Henry Louis, 166

{ 199 }

Carter, Hugh, 8, 30
Carter, James Earl III ("Chip"), 10, 13, 14, 16, 20, 21, 31, 101, 114, 15, 127, 128 (photo), 134
Carter, James Earl IV, 101, 128 (photo)
Carter, Jason, 101, 102 (photo), 114
Carter, Jeff, 11, 13, 14, 16, 20, 21, 31, 101, 109 (photo), 114, 115
Carter, Jimmy
  and affection for RC, 7–8, 33, 111–12, 156
  and African-Americans, 12–13, 14, 28, 103
  awards received by, 166
  and Carter Center, 145, 157–64, 166
  childhood, 4
  desire for privacy, 107, 114–15
  domestic policies as president, 35–36, 45, 47, 49, 125, 127, 133, 135, 137, 139
  and election of 1962, 14–15
  and election of 1966, 16–17
  and election of 1970, 17, 21
  and election of 1976, 23–33, 55, 92, 94, 99, 101, 115, 173
  and election of 1980, 133–42
  and election of 1984, 148
  and Equal Rights Amendment, 22, 57, 58
  and exercise, 14, 110–11, 144, 163
  and feminism, 56–57, 58, 173
  financial well-being of, 12, 13, 144
  fiscal conservatism of, 20–21, 26, 35–36, 40, 44, 45, 46, 51, 53, 105, 106, 111, 112, 120, 133
  foreign policies as president, 49, 62–63, 67, 68, 70–71, 72, 75–83, 85–86, 87, 88–89, 95, 126, 127, 128, 133–43, 149, 160, 172
  as Georgia governor, 18, 19, 20–21, 22–23
  as Georgia state senator, 15, 16
  as host in White House, 94, 95, 98–101, 106
  as introvert, 18, 106, 107, 115
  love of music, 14, 99
  marital difficulties, 11–12, 164–65
  marriage to RC, 8–9
  memoirs, 145, 146, 163
  and mental health, 21–22, 37, 38, 39, 40, 44, 46, 152
  as micromanager, 127, 129
  naval career of, 6–11, 18
  partnership with RC, ix, 1, 13, 15, 16, 25, 28, 33, 111, 124, 129–30, 165–66, 173
  personality of, 14, 18, 73–74
  photos, 32, 65, 81, 113, 159
  post–White House life, 133, 144–67
  and press, 103, 115, 138, 161
  and public opinion polls, 129, 131, 134, 138, 139, 140, 170
  relationship with children, 14, 166
  and religion, 16–17, 156
  and self-improvement, 14, 111
  travel to Africa, 162–63
  travel to Europe, 75–76, 78, 158, 160, 161, 163
  trips to Latin America, 158, 159–60, 160–61
  trips to Middle East and Asia, 76–77, 86–87, 158–59, 160, 163
  and volunteerism, 155, 156, 164
Carter, John William ("Jack"), 10, 12–21, 31, 101, 102 (photo), 114
Carter, Judy, 18, 20, 101, 102 (photo), 114, 146, 147
Carter, Lillian, 6, 8, 9 (photo), 11–12, 16, 17–18, 24–25, 29–30, 50, 134, 153, 164
Carter, Rosalynn
  and abortion, 28, 56
  as activist first lady, ix–x, 35, 107–8, 116, 132, 169, 171–74
  as adviser to JC, 27–28, 30, 31, 47, 56, 61, 77, 79, 80, 82, 87, 88–89, 103, 123–24, 125–26, 136, 159–60, 161, 172
  affection for JC, 5, 7, 33, 111–12

{ *Index* }

and African-Americans, 12–13, 28, 103–4, 108
and alcohol, 5, 19, 105, 121
and art, 22
awards, 48–49, 166
and Carter Center, x, 145, 152, 153, 157–61, 163, 166
childhood, 1–5, 6 (photo), 173
and childhood immunization, 35, 54, 122, 156–57
compared to Eleanor Roosevelt, 29, 123–25, 126, 173
daily schedule, 110–11, 112
death of father, 4, 88
desire for privacy, 91, 107, 114–16, 127
and the elderly, 19, 35, 49–50, 117, 122, 152–54, 171
and election of 1962, 15
and election of 1966, 16
and election of 1970, 17, 21
and election of 1976, 24–33, 36–37, 55, 115, 117–18, 119, 123, 154, 173
and election of 1980, 89, 103, 134–43
and election of 1984, 148
and Equal Rights Amendment, 22–23, 35, 54–58, 60, 104, 108, 122, 129
and the environment, 22
and exercise, 14, 110–11, 144, 163
and feminism, x, 28–29, 56–58, 76–77, 90, 105, 173
financial well-being of, 2, 4–5, 12–13, 144
as first lady of Georgia, 17–23
fiscal conservatism of, 19–20, 26, 44, 51, 53, 105–6, 112, 118–20
hatred of failure, 15, 125, 142
health of, 115, 146
as hostess in the White House, 50, 78, 91, 92–101, 103–8, 116, 117, 143, 172
image of, 29, 35, 57–58, 122–25, 126, 173
independence of, 3, 9–10, 11, 16, 21, 33, 35
influence of, ix, 40, 46–48, 57–58, 74, 88–90, 97, 103, 124–26, 130–31, 132, 172
as introvert, 106, 107, 115
love of music, 14, 99
marital difficulties, 11–12, 164–65
marriage to JC, 1, 8–9
memoirs, 145–47, 163
and mental health, x, 19, 21–23, 35–49, 53–54, 57, 59, 104, 108, 117, 121–22, 126, 131, 147–53, 166–67, 171–72
as navy wife, 9–11, 18
partnership with JC, ix, 1, 13, 15, 16, 25, 28, 33, 35, 111, 124, 129–30, 165–66, 173
personality of, 1, 5, 13, 15, 17, 18, 33
photos, 32, 43, 52, 65, 81, 84, 113, 141, 159
political astuteness of, 21, 27, 33, 35, 49, 51, 60, 118
portrayed as "steel magnolia," 29, 116, 126, 173
post–White House life, 133, 144–67
and press, 29–30, 31, 32, 51, 58–59, 68, 70, 71, 74, 76–77, 78–79, 97, 98, 103, 104–5, 112, 114, 115–16, 117–32, 138, 140, 147, 148, 161, 173
and prison reform, 23
protectiveness of JC, 15, 30, 126–27, 129, 148, 161
public ambivalence toward, ix–x, 74–75, 76, 78–79, 90, 121, 130–32, 151, 168–74
and public opinion polls, ix, 74, 131, 170
relationship with children, 13–14, 15–16, 33, 91, 112–16, 117, 127, 166
relationship with Lillian Carter, 8, 11–12, 16, 17–18, 25, 29–30
relationship with White House West Wing staff, 45–47, 82, 96–97, 117, 125, 172
religion and, 3, 5, 18, 111, 156
as representative for JC, ix, 52, 61–79, 82–85, 106, 121, 172

Carter, Rosalynn *(continued)*
   and self-improvement, 14, 111
   as speaker, 17, 23–24, 29
   and staff, 36, 59–60, 92–94, 97–98, 110, 117
   testifies before Congress, ix, 46
   travel to Africa, 162–63
   travel to Asia and Middle East, 76, 80, 82–85, 86, 90, 121–22, 158–59, 163, 172
   trips to Europe, 75–76, 89, 158, 160, 163
   trips to Latin America, 61–77, 86, 90, 117, 120–21, 122, 127, 158, 160–61, 172
   and volunteerism, 35, 50–54, 57, 122, 154–55, 156, 171, 173
   wardrobe of, 117, 118–20
   and White House decor, 91, 108–10
Carter, Ruth, 2, 5, 6, 7, 53, 164, 166
Carter, Sybil, 16
Carter Center, 145, 152, 157–64, 166, 167
Castro, Fidel, 64, 66, 149, 160
Ceaușescu, Nicolae, 97
Cédras, Raoul, 159
CERCLA (Comprehensive Environmental Response, Compensation, and Liability Act, Superfund) (1980), 48
Chamorro, Violetta, 158
Charlie Daniels Band, 98
Charlton, Linda, 124
Chase, Chevy, 112
Chicago Tribune, 121, 130
Christian Science Monitor, 130, 147
Church, Frank, 81
Cities in Schools project, 53, 114
Cleveland Press, 126
Cliburn, Van, 19
Clinton, Bill, 132, 148–49, 151, 157, 159, 160
Clinton, Chelsea, 149
Clinton, Hillary, 148–49, 151, 168, 169

Cohen, Richard, 130–31
Coleman, Julia, 4
Collins, Faith, 97, 123
Communities in Schools project, 53
Community Mental Health Centers Act (1963), 44
Comprehensive Environmental Response, Compensation, and Liability Act (CERCLA, Superfund) (1980), 48
Conger, Clement, 110
Contras, 158, 161
Correo (Peru), 70
Costello, Paul, 137
Crimmins, John H., 71
Cronica, La (Peru), 70
Cronkite, Walter, 103
Cruikshank, Nelson, 50

Daily News (Jamaica), 70
DC General Hospital, 51
Denver, John, 98
Desai, Morarji, 76
D'Estaing, Giscard, 144
Detroit Free Press, 129
Dobelle, Edith ("Kit"), 64, 80, 94, 97–98
Dobelle, Evan, 94
Dolvin, Emily ("Sissy"), 19
Domenici, Pete, 151, 152

Eisenhower, Mamie, 169
Eizenstat, Stuart, 47
Elders, Joycelyn, 157
Equal Rights Amendment, 22–23, 35, 54–58, 60, 104, 108, 122, 129, 167, 169, 171
Estado, O (Brazil), 71
Every Child by Two vaccination program, 157
Everything to Gain: Making the Most of the Rest of Your Life (JC and RC), 164–65
Excelsior (Costa Rica), 70

Fascell, Dante, 63
Feminine Mystique, The (Friedan), 54
Feminism, ix, 24, 28–29, 54–58, 76–77, 90, 105, 170–71, 173
Fenderson, Jane, 83, 93–94, 96
First Lady from Plains (RC), 47
Fitzpatrick, Mary, 23
Florida Almanac of the Democratic Party, 25
Floyd, Annie, 12–13
Foege, William, 164
Folha de Sao Paulo (Brazil), 71
Ford, Betty, 22, 29, 34, 35, 57, 59, 92, 117, 131, 150–51, 169, 170–71
Ford, Gerald, 22, 30, 31–32, 54, 68, 92, 95, 150
Franklin, Benjamin, 110
Friedan, Betty, 54
Friendship Force international exchange program, 154–55
Fukuda, Takeo, 144
Fuller, Linda, 155–56
Fuller, Millard, 155–56
Fund for Humanity, 155

Gardner, John, 38, 40
Geisel, Ernesto, 70–71
Georgia Southwestern State College/University, 5, 153
Georgia State College for Women, 8
Getz, Stan, 99
Geyer, Georgie Anne, 76–77
Gillespie, Dizzy, 99
Glaser, Vera, 129, 131
Global 2000, Inc., 162
Golant, Susan, 153
Gorbachev, Mikhail, 158
Gottlieb, Ruth, 19
Gottlieb, Roland, 19
Gracious Entertaining, 19
Green Door program for the mentally ill, 53–54
Greenfield, Meg, 121, 130
Guarnieri String Quartet, 98

Habitat for Humanity, 155–56, 164
Harnett, William Michael, 110
Harris, La Donna, 41
Hatfield, Paul, 78
Hayes, Helen, 103
Hayes, Lucy, 105
Helping Someone with Mental Illness: A Compassionate Guide for Family, Friends, and Caregivers (RC and Golant), 153, 166
Helping Yourself Help Others: A Book for Caregivers (RC and Golant), 153
Hesburgh, Theodore, 85
Hoover, Herbert, 135
Hoover, Lou Henry, 34
Horowitz, Vladimir, 99
Houderi, Ali, 89
Hoyt, Mary, 29, 31, 36, 59, 60, 64, 66, 73, 77, 80, 83, 92–98, 101, 107, 113, 114, 118, 120, 123, 124 (photo), 126, 127, 135
Hoyt, Steve, 98
Hurst, Joe, 15
Hussein, King, 96
Hussein, Saddam, 161

Jackson, Andrew, 110
Jackson, Sir Robert, 85
Jay, Peter, 101
Jimmy Carter Work Project, 156
John Paul II (pope), 99
Johnson, Lady Bird, ix, 22, 34, 35, 57, 61, 124–25, 171
Johnson, Lyndon, 38, 108
Jordan, Clarence, 53, 155
Jordan, Hamilton, 24, 36, 53, 87–88, 97, 98, 126, 155, 164

K-1 (submarine), 11
Karazdic, Radovan, 160
Keeping Faith: Memoirs of a President (JC), 146, 147
Kennard, Byron, 105

Kennedy, Edward, 46, 47, 103, 133–34, 136–38
Kennedy, Jacqueline, 32, 34–35, 59, 105, 124, 169
Kennedy, John F., 34, 99, 105
Kennedy, Rosemary, 6
Kevorkian, Jack, 154
Khmer Rouge, 82–83
Khomeini, Ruhollah, 86, 87
Kim Il Sung, 159
Kim Song-ae, 159, 160
Kirbo, Charles, 15, 30
Kissinger, Henry, 62, 77
Klemesrud, Judy, 29
Kostelanetz, André, 98
Kriangsak, Chamanand, 83, 84

Lance, Bert, 45, 111, 127, 129
Langford, Edna, 18, 20, 25–26, 145
Last Acts, 153–54
Levinson, Jerome, 64
Lewinsky, Monica, 169
Lewis, John, 99
López Michelson, Alfonso, 72–73
López Portillo, Carmen, 75, 94–95, 96, 105
López Portillo, José, 62, 94–95, 105
Love, Ruth, 40

MacArthur, Thelma, 3
MacBean, Madeline, 19, 20 (photo), 64, 66, 71, 96, 135
MacPherson, Myra, 135
Manchester Union Leader, 32, 130
Manley, Norman, 64–66
Marker, Gail, 53
McCall's, 130
McClellan, Diana, 114
McGovern, George, 36
McIntyre, James, 46
McPeake, Ellen, 53
Mental Health Equitable Treatment Act (Wellstone Act), 152

Mental Health Parity Act (1996), 151
Mental Health Systems Act (1980), 47, 48, 57
Mikulski, Barbara, 39
Milliken, Bill, 53
Mondale, Joan, 31, 59, 93, 138
Mondale, Walter, 30–31, 58, 78, 94, 99, 138, 148
Morales Bermúdez, Francisco, 69–70
Morris, Edmund, 145
Morrison, Richard D., 41
Mudd, Roger, 134
Mulligan, Gerry, 99
Muskie, Edmund, 30, 36, 93, 120
Muskie, Jane, 36, 120

Nación, La (Costa Rica), 70
National Cambodia Crisis Committee (NCCC), 85
National Organization for Women (NOW), 76, 77
NATO (North Atlantic Treaty Organization), 160
Navy Wife, The, 9
NBC Nightly News, 121
NCCC (National Cambodia Crisis Committee), 85
Nelson, Willie, 99
New Republic, 127, 161
Newsweek, 120, 121, 130
New York Times, 29, 64, 71, 120–21, 123, 124, 126, 131, 140, 147, 164
Nixon, Pat, 34, 35, 57, 61
Nixon, Richard, 28, 92, 140, 150
North Atlantic Treaty Organization (NATO), 160
NOW (National Organization for Women), 76, 77
Nuclear Nonproliferation Treaty (1968), 71

Oduber, Daniel, 67
Older Americans Act (1965/1978), 50

O'Neill, Thomas ("Tip"), 107
OPEC (Organization of Petroleum Exporting Countries), 68, 73
Organization of Petroleum Exporting Countries (OPEC), 68, 73
Osborne, John, 127

Pahlavi, Mohammad Reza, 86–87
Palestine Liberation Organization (PLO), 158
Pastor, Robert, 64, 66–67, 69, 70, 71, 158
Paul, Alice, 54
Paul IV (pope), 78
People, 29
Pepper, Claude, 50
Pérez, Andrés, 73
Pérez de Cuéllar, Javier, 161
Perlman, Itzhak, 98
Playboy, 31, 118
PLO (Palestine Liberation Organization), 158
Pomfret (submarine), 10
Pope, Betty, 163
Pope, John, 163
Postal Revenue and Federal Salary Act (1967), 39
Poston, Gretchen, 80, 92–93 (photo), 94, 96, 99, 104, 108
Pot, Pol, 83
Powell, Colin, 159–60
Powell, Jody, 80, 97, 114, 115, 126
Pregnancy Discrimination Act (1978), 58
Price, Leontyne, 100
Project Propinquity, 53

Quinn, Sally, 59, 97, 122

Rafshoon, Eden, 109
Rafshoon, Gerald, 32, 109, 125
Ray, Robert D., 85
Reagan, Nancy, 143, 169

Reagan, Ronald, 49, 89, 137–42, 143, 147, 148, 149, 158
Regan, Donald, 169
Reynolds, Frank, 103
Rhodes, James, 97
Richmond Times-Dispatch, 121
Rickover, Hyman, 11
Ridder, Marie, 30
Roe v. Wade (1973), 56
Roosevelt, Eleanor, ix, 29, 34, 46, 61, 123, 124–25, 126, 169, 171, 173
Roosevelt, Franklin, 20
Roosevelt, Quentin, 112
Roosevelt, Theodore, 112
Rosalynn Carter Institute for Caregiving, 153
Rosalynn Plan, 51–52
Rosebaugh, Lawrence, 72
Rostropovich, Msitslav, 100
Rowan, Carl, 131
Rural Health Clinics Act (1977), 50

Sadat, Anwar, 79–80, 81 (photo), 126, 144, 150
SALT (Strategic Arms Limitation Treaty), 62, 80–82
Sandinistas, 158, 161
Saturday Evening Post, 107
Saturday Night Fever, 114
Saturday Night Live, 111–12
Schlafly, Phyllis, 55, 56, 60
Schmidt, Hannelore, 96
Schmidt, Helmut, 95, 96
Schneiders, Greg, 27, 97, 107, 113, 115, 130
Sea Wolf (submarine), 11
Segovia, Andrés, 100
Serkin, Rudolf, 96
Shannon, William, 123
Sheehy, Gail, 118
Shreveport Times, 107
Shriver, Sargent, 82
Sills, Beverly, 98

Silveira, Antonio Azeredo de, 71
Slater, Gerald, 99
Smith, Allethea, 2
Smith, Allie, 1–3, 4–5, 8, 11, 17, 25, 49, 153, 154, 166
Smith, Edgar, 1–3, 4–5, 6, 8, 88, 153
Smith, Jerry, 2, 3, 166
Smith, John, 1
Smith, Murray, 2, 166
Staggers, Harley, 48
Starr, Richard, 73
Staubach, Roger, 141
Steinem, Gloria, 22, 57
Stern, Isaac, 98, 100, 106
St. Louis Globe-Democrat, 30
STOP ERA, 55
Strategic Arms Limitation Treaty (SALT), 62, 80–82
Strauss, Robert, 125
Stroud, Kandy, 120, 122
Superfund (Comprehensive Environmental Response, Compensation, and Liability Act, CERCLA) (1980), 48

Talmadge, Herman, 12
Taylor, Billy, 100
Teresa, Mother, ix, 131
Thomas, Helen, 123
Thornton, Lee, 115–16
Time, 121
Todman, Terence, 64, 66–67, 70, 71
Torrijos, Omar, 77
Townsend, Wayne, 55
Travolta, John, 114
Treaty of Tlatelolco (1967), 71
Trudeau, Margaret, 118
Trudeau, Pierre, 118
Truman, Bess, 169
Truman, Harry, 169

Truman, Margaret, 169, 173

Ullman, Al, 127
U.S. News and World Report, 104, 117, 131

Vance, Cyrus, 64, 74, 81–82, 87, 88, 127, 137
Vance, Gay, 64
Verrett, Shirley, 98
Vesco, Robert, 67–68
Vilas, Franklin, 40

Waldheim, Kurt, 85
Wallace, George, 26
Wall Street Journal, 164
Walters, Barbara, 115
Washington, George, 132
Washington Post, 47, 51, 63, 70, 120–21, 123, 130, 147
Washington Star, 114, 131
Watson, Robert, 168
Watts, Glenn, 41
Waxman, Henry, 47
Weddington, Sarah, 58, 126
Wellstone, Paul, 151, 152
Wellstone Act (Mental Health Equitable Treatment Act), 152
Wexler, Anne, 125
White Citizens Councils, 12
Wiedrich, Bob, 121
Williams, Alexander, 152
Wilson, Edith Bolling, ix, 34, 123, 169, 171
Wilson, Woodrow, 123
Women's Wear Daily, 119–20
Wyoming (battleship), 9
Wyszynski, Stefan, 75–76

Zorinsky, Edward, 78

www.ingramcontent.com/pod-product-compliance
Lightning Source LLC
Chambersburg PA
CBHW072333310125
21253CB00004BA/260